401(k)s For Du...

Cheat Sheet

Building Your Retirement Nest Egg

- Save in a tax-deferred retirement account as soon as you can, to get more bang for your investment buck.

- Start by saving just 1 percent of your pay if that's all you can afford.

- Save for retirement even if you think it's too late. It's never too late.

- Save at least the amount your employer matches, otherwise you're throwing money away.

- Aim to put away 10 percent of your income for retirement each year; increase your savings rate each time you get a raise.

- Aim to build a nest egg that's at least 10 times your annual pay when you retire.

- Take any company stock your employer gives you, but don't invest your own money in it. Remember Enron.

- Roll your retirement money directly into a new tax-deferred account when you change jobs. Don't cash it out.

- Don't take a hardship withdrawal or loan unless absolutely necessary.

Investing

- Come up with a plan. Know what you're doing and why: Don't invest blindly, hoping that it'll all come out well in the end.

- Establish realistic expectations, and then pick funds that have the potential to meet your goals. Learn from others, but build the portfolio that's right for you.

- Remember that higher risk doesn't guarantee a higher return.

- Avoid funds that have dramatic up-and-down swings, particularly if you're nearing retirement.

- Invest in a mix of asset types, because no one knows which investments will be hot at any point in time.

- Find a professional to help you choose the best investments.

For Dummies: Bestselling Book Series for Beginners

401(k)s For Dummies®

Taking Money out Early

- Calculate how much tax you'll owe on a hardship withdrawal *before* you withdraw the money. You'll owe income tax, plus, likely, a 10 percent early withdrawal penalty if you're under 59½. Your employer withholds some taxes, but you need to make up the rest.

- Remember that a $10,000 withdrawal at age 35 will result in a loss of more than $210,000 by age 65, assuming a 9 percent investment return.

- If you borrow from your 401(k), try to continue making new contributions while repaying the loan.

- Don't take a loan if you're likely to leave your employer before repaying it. Any unpaid loan balance will likely be taxable when you leave.

Managing Your Nest Egg When You Retire

- Develop a strategy to deal with the taxman, because you will have to pay taxes when you take money out of the plan.

- Consider keeping at least one-third of your money in stocks during your retirement years. Converting everything into fixed-income investments leaves your money vulnerable to inflation.

- Don't ignore inflation. What costs $10,000 the first year you retire will cost $20,328 in your 25th year of retirement, assuming a modest 3 percent inflation rate.

- Establish realistic investment return expectations (such as no more than 6 to 8 percent) during your retirement years. Don't be lured into high-octane stocks that may fizzle.

- Plan to withdraw no more than 6 to 7 percent of your retirement account each year to reduce the potential of running out of money.

Copyright © 2002 Wiley Publishing, Inc. All rights reserved.

Item 5468-9.

For more information about Wiley Publishing, call 1-800-762-2974.

For Dummies: Bestselling Book Series for Beginners

401(k)s

FOR

DUMMIES®

by Ted Benna and
Brenda Watson Newmann

Wiley Publishing, Inc.

401(k)s For Dummies®

Published by
Wiley Publishing, Inc.
111 River Street
Hoboken, NJ 07030
www.wiley.com

Copyright © 2003 by Wiley Publishing, Inc., Indianapolis, Indiana

Published by Wiley Publishing, Inc., Indianapolis, Indiana

Published simultaneously in Canada

For general information on our other products and services or to obtain technical support, please contact our Customer Care Department within the U.S. at 800-762-2974, outside the U.S. at 317-572-3993, or fax 317-572-4002.

Wiley also publishes its books in a variety of electronic formats. Some content that appears in print may not be available in electronic books.

Library of Congress Cataloging-in-Publication Data:

Library of Congress Control Number: 2002110280

ISBN: 07645-5468-9

Manufactured in the United States of America

10 9 8 7 6 5

1B/RV/QS/QU/IN

About the Authors

Ted Benna is commonly referred to as the "father of the 401(k)" because he created and gained IRS approval for the first 401(k) savings plan. Ted is a nationally recognized expert on retirement issues whose articles and comments have appeared in myriad publications. He's received many citations for his accomplishments, including:

- ✔ 2001 National Jefferson Award for Greatest Public Service by a Private Citizen

- ✔ 2001 Impact Player of the Year selected by *Defined Contribution News*

- ✔ One of eight individuals selected by *Money* magazine for its 20th Anniversary Issue Hall of Fame

- ✔ One of four People of the Century selected by *Business Insurance*

Ted has been profiled in *The New York Times, Pensions & Investments, USA Today, Employee Benefit News, Human Resource Executive, Fortune, Plan Sponsor, Kiplinger,* and many other publications. He's authored three other books: *Helping Employees Achieve Retirement Income Security* (Investors Press), *Escaping the Coming Retirement Crisis* (Pinon Press), and *Tips for Successfully Managing Your 401(k)* (401(k) Association).

During his 40-plus-year career, Ted has helped thousands of employers establish, restructure, and administer their retirement programs. He is president and founder of the 401(k) Association, and a special consultant to mPower Advisors and MassMutual Retirement Services.

Brenda Watson Newmann is a writer and editor dedicated to helping ordinary folks understand complicated topics. From 1998 to 2003 she was in charge of editorial content for the mPower Cafe, a leading educational Web site for retirement investors. Under her direction, the site won accolades including *Forbes* magazine's "Best of the Web."

Brenda keeps attuned to the concerns of 401(k) investors through the e-mails she receives regularly from readers. She frequently writes articles on retirement investing, and she's been interviewed by media outlets, such as *USA Today* and *Investor's Business Daily*.

Brenda began her writing career with The Associated Press, and was a foreign correspondent in Germany and Switzerland. She is a graduate of Stanford University and the Johns Hopkins University School of Advanced International Studies.

Dedication

I dedicate this book to Ellie, my first and only wife, who has been my life companion for 40 plus years; our four children, Debbie, Dave, Steve, and Dan; their spouses, Drew, Donna, and Laura; and our grandchildren, Mark, Neil, Matthew, Ryan, Michael, Olivia, Alison, and Christopher. You have all helped to make my life worthwhile.

— Ted Benna

To my husband, Robin, for his unwavering support of my work and his ability to make me laugh, and to Adeline and Dominic for patiently accepting my refrain of "not now, Mommy's busy writing" during this project.

— Brenda Watson Newmann

Authors' Acknowledgments

Our thanks to the many people at Wiley Publishing, Inc. who helped bring this book to fruition. Thanks especially to Acquisitions Editor Pam Mourouzis for getting the project off the ground and to Allyson Grove, our Project Editor, for her fine work orchestrating this book's creation. Thanks also to copyeditor Greg Pearson for making sure we remembered to dot our i's and cross our t's, and to the talented folks in Production for creating this attractive book. Many thanks to everyone else at Wiley Publishing, Inc. who played a role in bringing this book to the reading public.

We're also grateful to our technical reviewers, attorneys Marla Kreindler and Jeffrey Bakker, for lending their expertise to this book and ensuring that we didn't leave out anything important.

Brenda acknowledges her colleagues at mPower who have worked through thick and thin to bring professional investment advice and education to ordinary folks trying to plan for retirement. Finally, she sincerely thanks everyone — family, teachers, co-workers, and friends — who has ever taken the time to explain something unfamiliar to her in layman's terms. That is the spirit in which this book is written.

Publisher's Acknowledgments

We're proud of this book; please send us your comments through our Dummies online registration form located at www.dummies.com/register/.

Some of the people who helped bring this book to market include the following:

Acquisitions, Editorial, and Media Development

Project Editor: Allyson Grove

Acquisitions Editor: Pam Mourouzis

Copy Editor: Greg Pearson

Technical Editors: Marla J. Kreindler, Jeffrey J. Bakker

Editorial Manager: Jennifer Ehrlich

Editorial Assistant: Carol Strickland

Cartoons: Rich Tennant, www.the5thwave.com

Production

Project Coordinator: Dale White

Layout and Graphics: Joyce Haughey, Tiffany Muth, Barry Offringa, Jacque Schneider, Jeremey Unger

Proofreaders/Quality Control: TECHBOOKS, John Bitter

Indexer: TECHBOOKS

Publishing and Editorial for Consumer Dummies

Diane Graves Steele, Vice President and Publisher, Consumer Dummies

Joyce Pepple, Acquisitions Director, Consumer Dummies

Kristin A. Cocks, Product Development Director, Consumer Dummies

Michael Spring, Vice President and Publisher, Travel

Brice Gosnell, Publishing Director, Travel

Suzanne Jannetta, Editorial Director, Travel

Publishing for Technology Dummies

Andy Cummings, Vice President and Publisher, Dummies Technology/General User

Composition Services

Gerry Fahey, Vice President of Production Services

Debbie Stailey, Director of Composition Services

Contents at a Glance

Table of Contents

· ·

Introduction

• •

*B*umper sticker we'd love to see: "I'd Rather Be Managing My 401(k)."

Made you snicker? We agree. Most of us have better things to do with our time than pore over 401(k) statements and investment brochures — and that's precisely why we wrote this book.

Every day, through our work, we hear from people who want to save and invest for a secure retirement but aren't sure how to get started or how to do it the right way. Particularly after the decline of the stock market in the early 2000s, and the Enron fiasco, in which many 401(k) participants lost a good chunk of money, people are anxious to find out what to do with their retirement savings.

This uncertainty among workers isn't surprising, because the concept of retirement has changed dramatically over the last decade or so. Social Security seems less than secure, and it was never meant to cover all your retirement needs, anyway. Most people can't count on receiving a traditional fixed pension from their employer. The burden of retirement planning is falling squarely on your shoulders at a time when you're living longer and need more money to finance retirement.

You probably *wouldn't* rather be managing your 401(k) — you'd rather take in a movie, watch a ball game, or pursue your favorite hobby. But it's hard to enjoy yourself if you're plagued by a nagging worry that you could end up destitute in retirement.

We've got good news for you. Although you *do* have to take responsibility for your own retirement saving, you *don't* have to let retirement planning take over your life. Investing a bit of time now in ways we explain in this book should enable you to eventually sit back and relax.

About This Book

This book explains essential 401(k) rules in easy-to-understand language so that you can manage your retirement accounts in a way that leaves you better off in the long run.

When you hear stories about people losing their entire retirement savings, you can bet that they weren't following accepted investment practices. This book also explains how to manage risk in your investments and minimize the chances of big losses.

We give examples to show why you should start saving for retirement as soon as you can, because the longer your money stays in your 401(k), the bigger your potential nest egg. In fact, if you take only one message away from this book, we hope that it's "Save as much as you can as early as you can, and invest it sensibly."

But, don't let the title fool you. *401(k)s For Dummies* is a useful book even if you have a different type of retirement plan. Sure, we explain the basic rules — and even some obscure ones — of 401(k)s. We include information that's completely up to date, including new rules that went into effect in 2002.

We also look at two 401(k) cousins, the 403(b) and 457 plans, used by teachers, healthcare workers, state and local government officials, and many nonprofit employees. These plans are similar to 401(k)s but not identical. Participants in these plans often complain that they don't have the information resources available that 401(k) participants have. We include a chapter on each plan and also note where 401(k) information in the book is relevant to these plans. We explain rules for IRAs and how to use an IRA rollover to your advantage when you change jobs.

Beyond that, we explain basic principles of long-term investing to help you decide which investment options are right for you. We also give you guidelines to figure out how much you need to save for retirement, and then, after you retire, how to manage withdrawals from your accounts so that your money can last. These are important concepts for 401(k) investors, but they're equally important for everyone else.

Something else you'll find in this book that you probably won't find elsewhere is our section on retirement plans from an employer's point of view, with tips for small-business owners on choosing a plan (including the new one-person 401(k)).

We explain things in a way that's easy to understand; we go into as much detail as necessary for a basic understanding, but no more, and we refer you to additional resources. And heck, Ted Benna created the first 401(k) plan. How much more authoritative can you get?

Conventions Used in This Book

We have to say this loud and clear: Nothing in this book should be taken as tax advice or investment advice for your specific situation. Everyone is unique, and all we can do is explain some of the more important rules and give you guidance to help you make your own decisions. Also, because the rules are so complicated, we explain the general rules but leave some of the more technical exceptions to your own expert advisors. We know that most people want someone to tell them exactly what to do, but our lawyers won't let us do that. You need to consult an investment advisor or tax advisor for advice on your specific situation. But rest assured, reading this book will help you understand the advice that you receive and may save you money by enabling you to have fewer and shorter meetings with your advisors!

Foolish Assumptions

This book is for readers who are either thinking about participating in a 401(k) or other retirement plan, or who already are participating in a retirement plan but have doubts about what they're doing. We assume that you have an idea that it's important to save for retirement, but you're not sure whether you're doing it right, or how to get started.

We try to make things as simple as possible, but we can't avoid throwing in some math. We assume that you understand basic economic principles, such as inflation and earning a return on an investment.

For more information about the general investing concepts we cover, we recommend *Investing For Dummies* and *Mutual Funds For Dummies*, 3rd Edition, both by Eric Tyson (Wiley Publishing, Inc.), as well as other resources listed throughout the book.

How This Book Is Organized

This book is divided into six parts. You can read through from start to finish, or you can use the book as a reference tool and zero in on the different sections that provide the answers to your questions.

Part 1: Getting Started

Should I sign up for my 401(k)? How much can I save in it? What do I have to do to get an employer matching contribution? This part answers these questions and more, explaining the basic features of 401(k) plans and the advantages you get by investing in one.

Part 11: Finding an Investment Strategy That Lets You Sleep at Night

Investing money can be nerve-wracking, especially if you feel like you don't know what you're doing. This part explains how to make investment risk work to your advantage, how much investment return you can expect over the long run, how to understand the different investment options in your 401(k) plan, and how to select a portfolio of investments that's right for your situation. It also includes guidelines for investing in company stock that should help you avoid your own personal Enron.

Part 111: Getting Your Hands on Your Money

Withdrawing money from a 401(k) is not as easy as writing a check or visiting your local bank teller. This part explains the rules for taking money out while you're working (it's not easy!), when you change jobs, and when you retire. It explains how to keep your retirement savings intact with a rollover. It also explains when you *have* to take money out. (It's funny. For decades, it was nearly impossible to get your money out, and then all of a sudden you're required to withdraw it!)

Part 1V: Floor Plans of the Other Types of "4" Plans

Maybe you don't have a 401(k). Or maybe you do, but your *spouse* has one of those other funny-sounding plans that starts with "4" and is offered outside the private sector. This part explains the rules for 403(b) plans (also known as tax-sheltered annuities or TSAs) and 457 "deferred comp" plans — and why these plans exist in the first place.

Part V: From the Employer's Perspective: Finding the Right Plan

Offering a retirement plan isn't a piece of cake for an employer. Strict rules make administering these plans complicated and potentially expensive. This part explains why employers offer retirement benefits and what they have to consider when choosing a plan and a company to administer it. We include a chapter that outlines different types of retirement plans that may make more financial sense for small-business owners than a 401(k).

Part VI: The Part of Tens

This part looks at common participant mistakes and how to avoid them, as well as bad excuses for not participating, and why they're bad. It also includes answers to real questions from individuals and employers about situations — both common and unusual — that can arise in 401(k) plans.

Icons Used in This Book

Throughout this book, you'll find helpful icons that highlight particularly useful information. Here's a quick rundown on what they all mean.

Pay attention to this because it may save you time, money, or aggravation.

Importantissimo. Commit this information to memory.

Ignoring this information may result in painful financial consequences.

You don't have to know this detailed information, but it wouldn't hurt. Skip it if you're in a hurry or not interested. (There aren't many of these.)

This paragraph contains terms that are useful for you to know (although, they may make your eyes glaze over), especially when you deal with folks in your benefits office.

Drink some strong coffee or take a few deep breaths before you read this paragraph, because it contains math.

This information may affect the value of your retirement account (nest egg) over time.

Where to Go from Here

The beauty of *401(k) For Dummies* is that we've organized it so that you can start reading anywhere without risking total confusion. Here are a few suggested starting points, depending on why you picked up the book.

- ✔ If you're just starting your first job with a 401(k), Part I is a very good place to start.

- ✔ If you think that your money isn't invested properly, you don't understand the investments in your plan, or you're scared of investment risk, start with Part II.

- ✔ If you need to take money out of your 401(k) for an emergency, to put a down payment on a home, or to pay for college expenses, or if you're changing jobs or retiring, Part III is the place for you.

- ✔ If you want to feel better about your own situation by reading about other people's problems and dumb mistakes, go directly to Part VI.

- ✔ If you're entirely happy with your 401(k) and the investments in it, give a copy of this book to someone who isn't!

Part I
Getting Started

The 5th Wave   By Rich Tennant

"Oh, her? That's Ms. Lamont, our Plan Administrator.
She's going to help me determine your eligibility in
our 401(k) Plan."

In this part . . .

Saving in a 401(k) is potentially one of the best deals that you'll ever get. 401(k) plans offer significant tax breaks and other advantages, and very few drawbacks. But you have to know what you're doing in order to get the full benefit from your plan. This part explains how 401(k) plans work, how to evaluate the plan your employer offers, and what to do when you sign up for your plan.

Chapter 1

Benefiting from Your 401(k)

· ·

In This Chapter

▶ Understanding how a 401(k) plan works

▶ Getting the most tax savings, extra money, and other advantages

▶ Improving your chances for an ideal retirement

· ·

*N*ot too long ago, many people would ask, "What the heck is a 401(k)?" Today, however, 401(k) is a household word. People discuss their 401(k) investments at social gatherings. These once-obscure plans are in the national media nearly every day.

401(k) plans have helped more than 40 million workers save for retirement. Because Social Security alone won't provide adequate retirement income, and fewer companies offer a traditional pension plan, 401(k)s have become an essential part of the average worker's future plans.

Even young people, for whom retirement would normally be low on the priority list, have jumped on the retirement savings bandwagon. They're the smart ones, because in some respects, *how long* you save is more important than *how much* you save.

Unfortunately, the stock market nosedive and corporate scandals in the early 2000s caused 401(k) plans to come under some fire. Many workers who made bad investment choices saw large drops in the value of their accounts. Some blamed the 401(k) itself, but that's like blaming the messenger who brings you bad news. If you take the time to understand and follow basic investing principles (see Chapters 5 and 6), your 401(k) can grow into a nest egg that can help you retire comfortably.

The beauty of a 401(k) is that it makes saving easy and automatic, and you probably won't even miss the money that you save.

Defining What a 401(k) Does for You

A 401(k) plan lets you put some of your income away *now* to use *later*, presumably when you're retired and not earning a paycheck. This procedure may not appeal to everyone; human nature being what it is, many people would rather spend their money now and worry about later when later comes. That's why the federal government approved tax breaks for 401(k) participants to enjoy now. Uncle Sam knows that your individual savings are going to be an essential part of your retirement, and wants to give you an incentive to participate.

When you sign up for a 401(k) plan, you agree to let your employer deposit some of your paycheck into the plan as a *pre-tax contribution*, instead of paying it to you. Your employer may even throw in some extra money known as a *matching contribution* (see Chapter 2). You don't pay federal income tax on any of this money until you withdraw it.

Of course, there's a catch. Some 401(k) plans may not allow you to withdraw money while you're still working. Even if yours does allow you to withdraw money while working, if you're under 59½ years old, withdrawals can be difficult and costly. Check out Part III for a full explanation of these rules and regulations.

How much your 401(k) will be worth when you retire depends on a number of factors, such as what investments you choose, what return you get on those investments, whether your employer makes a contribution, and whether you withdraw money early. The next few sections take a look at the benefits of participating in a 401(k).

Lowers how much tax you pay

A 401(k) lets you pay less income tax in the following two ways:

- **Lower taxable income:** You don't have to pay federal income tax on the money you contribute pre-tax to your 401(k) plan until you withdraw it from the plan.

- **Tax deferral:** You don't pay tax on your 401(k) investment earnings each year — only when you make withdrawals.

The government provides these big tax breaks in an attempt to avoid having a country full of senior citizens who can't make ends meet. (Nice to know the government's on top of things, huh?)

Lower taxable income

The money that you contribute to a 401(k) reduces your *gross income*, or *taxable income* (your pay before tax and any other deductions). When you have lower taxable income, you pay fewer of the following income or wage taxes:

- **Federal taxes:** These taxes increase as your income increases — for 2002, the rate for most workers is either 15 or 27 percent, and the top tax rate is 38.6 percent.

- **State taxes:** Many states impose their own income or wage taxes, ranging from less than 1 percent to as much as 12 percent in 2002, depending on the state.

- **Local/municipal government taxes:** Many local and municipal governments also have income or wage taxes.

In most states, you aren't required to pay state or local taxes on contributions to your 401(k). However, a few states may require you to list all or part of the money that you contribute to a 401(k) as taxable income on your state tax return. You still get the federal tax break, however. Check with your state and local tax authorities if you're not sure what the rules are where you live.

Taxes that you don't avoid, because everybody has to pay them on gross income (including 401(k) contributions), are Social Security/Medicare (FICA) and unemployment (FUTA).

Here's an example of how you save money when you contribute some of your pay pre-tax to a 401(k). Assume that:

- Your gross pay is $2,000 each pay period.

- You're in the 27 percent federal tax bracket.

- Your state income tax is 2 percent, local income tax is 1 percent, and your FICA/FUTA taxes are 7.65 percent.

- Contributions you make to a 401(k) plan are exempt from state and local tax.

Say you don't contribute to a retirement plan. Look what happens to your income after you pay all those taxes:

Gross pay	$2,000
Federal income tax	−$350
State income tax	−$40
Local wage tax	−$20
FICA/FUTA taxes	−$153
Take-home pay	$1,437

Now assume that you contribute 6 percent, or $120, per paycheck to a 401(k) plan. Your FICA/FUTA taxes will be the same, but the other taxes are lower because they're based on a lower income (your gross income minus your retirement contribution). Here's how it breaks down:

Gross pay	$2,000
Retirement contribution	−$120
Federal income tax	−$329
State income tax	−$38
Local wage tax	−$19
FICA/FUTA taxes	−$153
Take-home pay	$1,341

You invested $120 for your retirement, but your take-home pay is reduced by only $96. For the time being, you're up $24 that would otherwise have gone to the government. You don't have to pay these taxes until you withdraw your money from the plan. As a general rule in this tax bracket, if you contribute $1, your take-home pay is reduced only by about 70 to 80¢.

Here's another way of looking at it. Without a 401(k) plan, taxes eat away the money that you could save. Assume that your employer doesn't offer a 401(k) or other retirement plan, and your total tax rate is 37.65 percent (7.65 percent FICA/FUTA, 27 percent federal income tax, 2 percent state income tax, and 1 percent local wage taxes). After paying these taxes, it takes almost 16 percent of your gross income to have 10 percent left to invest for retirement. The following example shows how this works.

Assume that you earn $50,000 a year, and your goal is to save 10 percent, or $5,000. You would have to earn $8,017 in order to have $5,000 left "after-tax."

Pre-tax earnings required	$8,017
Federal income tax	–$2,164
State/local wage tax	–$240
FICA/FUTA taxes	–$613
Amount left to save	$5,000

Now assume that your employer offers a 401(k) plan, and you can save the $5,000 in your 401(k) account. In this case, the only tax you have to pay at the time you make the contribution is FICA/FUTA. As a result, you need to earn only $5,414 in order to be able to contribute $5,000 to the 401(k) plan.

Pre-tax earnings required	$5,414
Federal income tax	–$0
State/local wage tax	–$0
FICA/FUTA taxes	–414
Amount left to save	$5,000

Without a 401(k) plan, it takes you $8,017 in pre-tax income to save $5,000 after taxes. When you can save pre-tax money in your 401(k), it only takes $5,414 to save the same $5,000. In other words, with a 401(k), it will cost you less of your current earnings to save the same amount. Pretty good deal, don't you think?

Some plans allow you to make *after-tax* contributions. You don't get the initial tax break of lower taxable income, but you do benefit from deferring taxes on your investment earnings.

Tax deferral

In addition to the income tax savings on your contributions, you also save when it comes to paying tax on your investment earnings.

The gains in your 401(k) aren't taxed annually, as they would be in a regular *taxable* bank savings account, a personal mutual fund account, or a brokerage account (which you may use to buy and sell stocks and other investments). With a 401(k), you defer paying taxes on your investment earnings until you withdraw the money.

Figure 1-1 shows how tax-deferred compounding lets your money grow faster than it would in a taxable account. It compares the results of investing $5,000 at a 9 percent return in a tax-deferred account with investing $3,750 in a taxable account ($3,750 = $5,000 less income tax) at a 9 percent return, taxed each year at a 25 percent tax rate.

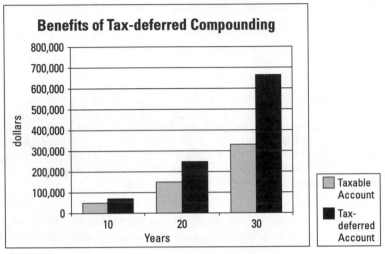

Figure 1-1: Positive impact of tax-deferred compounding.

Gets you something extra from your employer

Whoever said there's no such thing as a free lunch didn't know about *employer matching contributions* — money that your employer will contribute to your 401(k) if you contribute to the plan. (Not all employers make this type of contribution, but many do.)

The most common formula is for the employer to put in 50¢ for every dollar you contribute up to 6 percent of your salary. Because 50¢ is half of one dollar, the most your employer will contribute is half of 6 percent, or 3 percent of your salary. You get this full 3 percent only if you contribute 6 percent of your salary. Chapter 2 gives examples of how this matching contribution works.

The employer matching contribution can be the single most important feature of your 401(k) plan. The more you get from your employer, the less you have to save out of your own paycheck to achieve an adequate level of retirement income. In fact, if your employer offers a matching contribution, make sure that you contribute enough to your plan to get it all. If you don't, this money will be lost to you.

How 401(k) became a household "word"

The 401(k) is named after the section of the IRS "rulebook" (the Internal Revenue Code, or IRC) that governs how it works.

Section 401 applies to many different tax-qualified retirement plans — those with special tax advantages for you and your employer. It begins with paragraph (a) and includes paragraph (k), which was added when Congress enacted the Tax Reform Act of 1978.

Paragraph (k) was one of those special interest paragraphs added to the bill in the 11th hour. Its original objective was to cover a specific type of Section 401 plan that was sponsored by banks for their own employees.

It was only a couple of years later, when Ted was designing a retirement plan for a company, that he realized that paragraph (k) offered additional possibilities. The result was the first 401(k) savings plan with employer matching contributions and employee pre-tax contributions made through payroll deductions. It wasn't universally accepted at first, but after the Treasury Department okayed it in 1981, it began to catch on.

And the rest, as they say, is history.

You may have to stay with your company for a minimum length of time before the employer contributions *vest,* or belong to you, a topic we discuss in more detail in Chapter 2. But if you can meet that requirement, the money's yours, as well as any return it's earned in the meantime.

Saving Without Tears

A big benefit of signing up for your 401(k) plan is that you don't have to think about the fact that you're saving. "Out of sight, out of mind" is what happens to most people — they don't even miss the money, because it's taken out of their paycheck before they have a chance to spend it.

This semi-forced savings is one of the most valuable benefits of 401(k) plans. The payroll deduction has the power to convert spenders into savers. Most people are unable to save over a long period of time if they have to physically write the check or make the deposit each pay period. Saving becomes the last, not the first, priority. Many participants have said that the 401(k) has helped them save thousands of dollars that they otherwise would have spent carelessly.

It's a good idea to increase your 401(k) contributions if you get a raise or a bonus. In fact, do it right away so that you don't get used to spending the extra money.

Taking Your Savings with You When You Change Jobs

When you change jobs, you can take your 401(k) money with you — and keep the tax advantages — by putting it into your new employer's 401(k), 403(b), or 457 plan, or into an IRA (Individual Retirement Account).

Transferring your money to a new employer's plan or an IRA is known as a *rollover* or *trustee-to-trustee transfer.* See Chapter 8 for more on rolling your money into an IRA; see Chapter 10 for details about 403(b)s, and Chapter 11 for information about 457 plans.

Many employers require you to work for a minimum number of years before the employer contributions are yours to keep (known as *vesting*). See Chapter 2 for more details on vesting procedures.

Because your 401(k) is "portable," you can build up a retirement nest egg even if you change jobs fairly frequently. This beats the traditional defined-benefit pension plan (in which you receive a set amount from your employer each month in retirement, if you qualify). With those plans, you can lose *all* retirement benefits if you don't work at the company for the minimum vesting period — this can be at least five years, or even longer at some companies.

Letting the Pros Work for You

Have you ever wished that you could hire a professional money manager to handle your investments? A 401(k) lets you take a step in that direction by offering *mutual funds.*

Mutual funds are investments that let you pool your money with the money of hundreds or thousands of other investors. An investment expert called the *fund manager* decides how to invest all this money, trying to get the best return on your investment based on the fund's *investment objective.* Because the fund manager invests your money along with the money contributed by other investors in the fund, she has more money to invest and can spread it around to different companies or sectors of the economy. This *diversification* helps reduce the amount of risk that you take with your investments. (We explain more about selecting investments, including mutual funds, in Chapter 6.)

What does this mean for you? If you choose your fund carefully, you benefit from a professional money manager who's seeking the best return for the fund's investors, based on the fund's investment objectives.

In most cases, your employer is responsible for choosing the mutual funds (and any other investments) offered by your 401(k) plan. More than 8,000 mutual funds are registered in the United States. If your employer does a good job of narrowing the offering down to a handful, it can save you a lot of time.

Rather than rely on choices made by their employer, however, some investors prefer to choose their own investments, such as individual stocks, mutual funds, or other investments that aren't included in their plans. Some 401(k) plans now offer a *brokerage window* that allows you to choose your own investments. But you generally pay an extra fee if you use this feature. Chapter 6 has more details on brokerage windows.

Buying More When Prices Are Low

When you invest a specified amount at regular intervals, as you do with automatic 401(k) contributions from your paycheck, you are using an investment strategy called *dollar cost averaging.* (You didn't know you were that smart, did you?) This investment strategy may lower the average price that you pay for your investments. How? Because you're spending the same amount each time you invest, you end up buying more shares of your investments when prices are low and fewer shares when prices are high. By averaging high and low prices, you reduce the risk that you will buy more shares when prices are high.

Of course, if stock prices only go up for the entire time you invest, this strategy won't work. But if you contribute to a 401(k) over a long period of time, there will likely be periods when prices go down.

Improving Your Chances of an Ideal Retirement

Investing in a 401(k) gives you a chance at extra savings for your retirement years. The additional savings can mean the difference between merely surviving retirement and actually living it up.

Did you ever stop to think how much money you'll need in retirement to keep up your current lifestyle? Most financial planners suggest that you'll need at least 70 to 80 percent of your pre-retirement income. But many people may need closer to 100 percent, or more.

Some people think that their Social Security benefits alone will be enough to cover their retirement needs. The unfortunate fact is, you shouldn't rely on Social Security to finance your retirement. Financial security during retirement requires income from a variety of sources. Social Security's current problems are serious, but the system was never intended to be the sole source of retirement income for Americans.

Try to estimate how big a retirement account you'll need, and develop a savings plan to try to accumulate that amount. When you retire, you'll have to manage your nest egg so that you don't run out of money before you die. Chapter 4 explains why and how to set up a savings plan for your 401(k) during your working years, and Chapter 9 looks at ways to make this money last after you retire.

Protecting Your Money

Investing money always involves some risks, but money in a 401(k) plan is protected in some ways that money in an ordinary savings account, brokerage account, or IRA isn't.

Meeting minimum standards

401(k) plans are governed by a federal law called *ERISA* — the Employee Retirement Income Security Act. Passed in 1974, ERISA sets minimum standards for retirement plans offered by private-sector companies. (Some nonprofits also follow ERISA rules, but local, state, and federal government retirement plans, as well as church plans, don't have to.)

ERISA requirements include:

- ✔ Providing information to you about plan features on a regular basis, including a *summary plan description* outlining the plan's main rules, when you enroll in the plan and periodically thereafter

- ✔ Defining how long you may be required to work before being able to sign up for the plan or before employer contributions to the plan are yours to keep if you leave your job

- ✔ Detailing requirements for the *plan fiduciary*, essentially including anyone at your company or the plan provider who has control over the investment choices in the plan (A fiduciary who breaks the rules may be sued by participants.)

This last point, *fiduciary responsibility*, is important to understand. Essentially, it means that anyone who has a decision-making role in your 401(k) plan's investments is legally bound to make those decisions in the best interests of the plan participants (you and your co-workers), and *not* in the best interest of the company, the plan provider, or the fiduciary's cousin Joe. For example, the committee in charge of choosing a 401(k) provider shouldn't choose Bank XYZ just because the company president's cousin runs the bank.

But this doesn't necessarily mean that you can sue your employer if your 401(k) doesn't do well. (Keep in mind that lawsuits are often costly and won't endear you to your employer.) If you lose most of your money because you make bad investment decisions or the stock market takes a nosedive, but your employer has followed ERISA rules, your employer is off the hook. Your employer may gain limited protection through something called *404(c)*. Without going into too much detail, Section 404(c) of ERISA requires your employer to provide you with specific information about your plan, including information about the investment options, and to allow you to make changes in your investments frequently enough to respond to ups and downs in the market. In return, *you* assume liability for your investment results.

Plan operation was a critical point in the case of Enron, the Houston-based energy trading company that declared bankruptcy in late 2001. Many employees suffered huge losses in their 401(k)s because they had invested heavily in Enron stock based on the rosy picture that was painted by senior management about the company's fortunes. When that rosy picture turned out to be a fake, employees hollered that they wouldn't have invested so much in Enron stock (one of their 401(k) investment options) if they had known the truth.

Avoiding losses in bankruptcy

Many people wonder whether their 401(k) money is at risk if their employer goes belly-up. The answer is usually no, with a few caveats:

- ✔ If the money is in investments that are tied to your employer, such as company stock, and the employer goes bankrupt, you may lose your money. (This is a compelling argument for you to limit the amount of your 401(k) that you invest in a single stock.)

- ✔ In the case of fraud or wrongdoing by your employer or the trustee of the 401(k) account, your money may be at risk. (The trustee would be personally liable to return your money, but that's no help if he has disappeared.) These situations are rare; what's more, your employer is required to buy a type of insurance — a *fidelity bond* — when it sets up the plan, that may enable you to recoup at least some of your money in the event of dishonesty. (Fidelity bonds generally cover 10 percent of the amount in the entire plan, or $500,000, whichever amount is smaller.)

- ✔ Part of your money may be lost if your employer goes out of business or declares bankruptcy before depositing your contributions into the trust fund that receives the 401(k) money that is deducted from your paycheck.

Federal law says that if you declare personal bankruptcy, your creditors generally can't touch your 401(k). They may be able to get at your other savings, but your 401(k) should be protected. Exceptions include if you owe money to the IRS or if a court has ordered you to give the money to your ex-spouse as part of a divorce settlement. In both of those cases, your 401(k) money is vulnerable.

Watching Out for Potential Pitfalls

The tax advantages you get with a 401(k) have a flip side: rules. Rules about when you can take your money out, and whether you'll have to pay a penalty, and even what you can invest in. All of these are out of your control after you decide to contribute to a 401(k) plan. This section tells you what pitfalls to watch out for.

Withdrawing money while you're working is difficult

It can be difficult, if not downright impossible, to make a withdrawal from your 401(k) while you're working for the company that sponsors the plan.

Many employers permit you to borrow money from your 401(k), but not necessarily for any old reason. Many plans permit *hardship withdrawals,* which are withdrawals from your account to pay expenses when you're in financial difficulty. Your employer may permit withdrawals only for reasons approved by the IRS. (Check out Chapter 7 for a more detailed discussion of loans and hardship withdrawals.)

People often think that they're automatically allowed to withdraw money from a 401(k) for higher education expenses or for buying a home, and that they won't owe an early withdrawal penalty on the amount. This is false. Your plan *may* allow you to make a withdrawal for these reasons, but it doesn't *have* to.

When you leave your employer, either to retire or to change jobs, you generally have a window of opportunity to get your money. In most cases, you can receive payment of your account or transfer the money into an IRA or another employer's retirement plan (see Chapter 8). We highly recommend transferring the money to another plan or IRA, or leaving the money in the plan, to avoid a high tax bill (see the following section).

Taking money out before 59½ costs more

If you do manage to withdraw your money using a hardship withdrawal before you turn 59½, you'll be heavily taxed. Not only will you owe federal and perhaps state and local income tax on the amount withdrawn, you'll also owe a 10 percent federal early withdrawal penalty on the entire amount. Some states may also impose additional early withdrawal penalties of a few percent. All of these combined could mean that you pay more than 50 percent of your withdrawal in taxes and penalties, depending on your tax bracket.

Taking out a loan lets you avoid these penalties; however, other costs are involved. We explain these costs in Chapter 7.

Earning more may mean contributing less

If you earn enough to qualify as a highly compensated employee, your contributions to your 401(k) plan may be limited to only a few percent of your salary. Many 401(k) plans are required to pass *nondiscrimination tests* each year to make sure that highly paid employees as a group aren't contributing a lot more to the plan than their lower-paid colleagues. In requiring these tests, Congress is looking out for the little guy (and gal). Chapter 3 explains how these tests work, and who qualifies as "highly compensated."

Being at the mercy of your plan

A well-administered, well-chosen, flexible 401(k) plan can be a wonderful benefit. A poorly administered plan with bad investment choices and little flexibility can be a nightmare. We've heard stories of companies that don't invest employee contributions on time or that take money from the plan, companies that don't let employees contribute the maximum permitted, or companies where employees pay useless fees for a plan because the managers who set it up were incompetent, uninformed, or even criminals.

In most cases, the tax benefit of a 401(k) is a good enough reason to take advantage of the plan offered by your employer. However, if the investments offered by the plan are truly bad, the fees charged are exorbitant, or the administration of the plan is questionable, you may be better off investing your retirement money elsewhere until you have a better 401(k).

We talk more about understanding your 401(k) plan's features in Chapter 2. We also provide suggestions for how you can try to improve your plan if it falls short.

Telling the Employer's Point of View

For employers, setting up and running a retirement plan is no cake-walk. An employer has to select a plan, decide how to administer it, find a company to provide the investments, comply with paperwork and other regulations, possibly contribute money to employees' accounts, and so on. Small-business owners may find that 401(k)s don't meet their needs. Chapter 12 gives information on retirement plans for small-business owners, and guidelines for choosing one. Chapter 13 provides tips for larger employers on running a 401(k) in the best interests of their participants.

Chapter 2

Understanding the Important Features of Your 401(k)

● ●

In This Chapter

▶ Measuring your employer's contribution

▶ Calculating your contributions and catch-up contributions

▶ Timing when your employer's contribution belongs to you

▶ Finding out when you can start participating

▶ Breaking open your 401(k) piggy bank while you're working

▶ Understanding what investments you can choose

▶ Determining how much you pay in fees

▶ Getting extra help and services

▶ Trying to get your plan changed

● ●

401(k) plans are like snowflakes — each one is unique. Federal laws govern many aspects of 401(k) plans, but employers are allowed to be more *restrictive* with their plan rules (for example, they may limit your contributions to a lower level than what Uncle Sam permits). If you're looking for a standard 401(k) plan, be aware that there's no such animal. Each company creates its own plan, and some are better than others.

If you want to get the most out of your 401(k) plan, you have to understand how it works. This chapter covers questions to ask yourself, your employer, or your plan provider when evaluating a 401(k) plan.

How Much Your Employer Contributes

An employer contribution is the single most important feature of any retirement plan. The more you get from your employer, the less you have to save on your own.

Employers aren't required to offer a retirement plan, nor are they required to contribute to a 401(k) plan. Employers that help you save for retirement demonstrate a commitment to your future.

We don't want to get too technical, but at this point it'll be helpful to explain the two broad categories of retirement plans that employers can choose from:

- *Defined benefit plans* are traditional pension plans in which the amount you receive (the benefit) is "defined" up front based on factors such as your salary in your final year (or years) of your career with the company. Your employer is responsible for making sure that there's enough money in the plan to pay this benefit. Your grandfather probably had this kind of plan, but fewer and fewer of these critters are available today.

- *Defined contribution plans* include 401(k)s and similar plans in which the *contributions* to your account are "defined" by you and your employer. Your eventual benefit depends on how much is contributed and how well your investments do. Many different types of defined contribution (or "DC") plans are available, including the following:

  - 401(k)
  - 403(b) (see Chapter 10)
  - 457 "deferred comp" (see Chapter 11)
  - Defined contribution/money purchase pension
  - Employee stock ownership plan (ESOP)
  - Stock bonus plan
  - Simplified Employee Pension (SEP) (see Chapter 12)
  - Profit-sharing (see Chapter 12)
  - SIMPLE IRA (see Chapter 12)

That's a lot of names; we include them so that you'll know what you have if your employer offers one of them. Your employer may make a contribution to one or more of these types of accounts.

In some cases, you get the employer contribution only if *you* contribute (matching contribution). In others, you get the employer contribution no matter what (non-matching contribution). We explain more about matching and non-matching contributions in just a minute.

Employers can choose their own schedule for depositing contributions into your account. Some may do this every pay period, while others may deposit a year's worth in one shot. The contributions can be deposited at any time until the tax-filing deadline for that year, including extensions (September 15 for an employer with a December 31 fiscal year-end). So the employer contribution for one year may not show up in your account until the following year.

The match game: Employer matching contribution

The key to employer matching contributions is that *you* have to contribute money to the plan in order to get the employer's contribution. If you don't contribute to the plan, you don't get the employer's money.

Employers use different formulas for calculating their match. A common formula is 50¢ on the dollar up to 6 percent of salary. What does that mean? For every dollar you contribute to your 401(k) plan up to 6 percent of your salary, your employer will contribute 50¢.

Here's a concrete example. Say you earn $50,000 a year. Six percent of your salary is $3,000. For every dollar you contribute to your 401(k) plan up to $3,000, your employer will contribute an additional 50¢. If you contribute $3,000, your employer will contribute an additional $1,500. You end up with $4,500 after only contributing $3,000 of your own money. However, if you contribute only $1,000, your employer will contribute an additional $500, and you'll miss out on $1,000 in potential employer contributions.

How much will your employer contribute if you put in $4,000? If you answered $2,000, or 50 percent of your contribution, you're wrong. If you contribute $4,000, your employer will still only contribute an additional $1,500 because the match only applies to $3,000, or 6 percent of your salary. (We admit that was a bit of a trick question, but we just want to keep you on your toes!)

Here's another way of looking at it. Suppose that you earn $50,000, and you want to put aside 10 percent in your 401(k). If your employer contributes up to 3 percent of salary as a match, you need to contribute only 7 percent of your salary to achieve your 10 percent savings goal. There are no taxes on the 3 percent employer contribution until it is withdrawn from the 401(k). Your total savings are as follows:

Employer contribution of 3 percent:	$1,500
Employee contribution of 7 percent:	$3,500
Total contribution:	$5,000

An employer matching contribution gives you an incentive to save, and it can give your savings a powerful boost. It makes sense for you to contribute at least the full amount that your employer will match. Employers may make higher (dollar-for-dollar, for example) or lower (25¢ on the dollar, for example) matching contributions and may match higher or lower percentages of salary. There's no set rule, and some employers are more generous than others. But after an employer sets the formula for the matching contribution, it must meet the commitment until it amends the *plan document* (the official document detailing the plan's rules) with a new formula.

You typically have to work for your employer for a certain period of time before you can leave the company without forfeiting (losing) your employer's contributions. We discuss this rule, known as *vesting*, in the "Vesting: When Your Employer's Contribution Is Yours to Keep" section later in this chapter.

Looking at the whole picture

If you're trying to judge whether your employer (or a prospective employer) offers good retirement benefits, don't make the common mistake of focusing only on the 401(k) and overlooking the many other types of retirement plans and employee benefits. Be sure to look at the total package of compensation, retirement plan contributions, and employee benefits.

For example, if your employer contributes 5 percent of your pay to a cash balance pension plan (a type of defined-benefit plan), it may be better than a 3 percent employer matching contribution in a 401(k) plan. An employer contribution equal to 10 percent of pay in a profit-sharing plan is generally better than a 401(k), even if it includes an employer matching contribution. In fact, if your employer contributes 10 percent or more of pay to a retirement program, you don't need to make any comparisons — it's a great retirement program.

Some employers make what's called a *variable or discretionary matching contribution* — a hybrid of profit-sharing and matching contributions. You have to contribute to your 401(k) to get it, as with an ordinary matching contribution, but the amount of the contribution varies at the discretion of your company. For example, the amount of your matching contribution may depend on the success of your company from one year to the next.

A little something extra: Employer non-matching contribution

Some employers contribute to their employees' 401(k) accounts (or to another plan) whether the employee contributes or not. This is called a *non-matching contribution*. For example, your employer may deposit a profit-sharing contribution into the 401(k) on your behalf, either alone or in addition to a matching contribution. In a good year, for example, your employer may contribute 5 percent of each eligible employee's pay as a profit-sharing contribution, plus a 25 or 50¢ matching contribution. You get the 5 percent no matter what, but you only get the additional matching contribution if you put some of your salary into the plan. In a bad year, the company may only make the matching contribution and forgo the profit-sharing contribution, or it may even forgo both contributions!

A company may also make *a non-matching employer contribution* that's *not* based on its financial results. The employer may contribute a specific percentage of your pay each year — typically between 3 and 5 percent — regardless of whether the company does well. A non-matching employer contribution is frequently used when a company has discontinued a defined-benefit pension plan (described earlier in this section) in favor of a defined-contribution arrangement.

Automatic contributions may also be made in what's called a *Safe Harbor 401(k)*. This type of plan doesn't have to pass certain federal nondiscrimination tests that are part of the law governing 401(k)s (we explain more about these tests in Chapter 12).

How Much You Can Contribute

"How much can I contribute to my 401(k) plan?" seems like a fairly simple question to answer. Not necessarily. There *are* federal limits on contributions, but your plan is allowed to be more restrictive. Also, high-income earners may have their contribution levels capped due to special restrictions required by law. (We explain rules for highly compensated employees in more detail in Chapter 3.)

What Uncle Sam allows (he's extra generous if you're 50 or older)

Table 2-1 shows the maximum pre-tax contributions that you can make under federal law. (*Pre-tax contribution* refers to money taken out of your paycheck before you pay federal income taxes — it reduces your taxable income so that you pay less federal income tax for the year.)

The limits apply only to your pre-tax contributions and do not include contributions from your employer. The same limits apply for 403(b) plans (see Chapter 10) and 457 plans (see Chapter 11). However, with a 457 plan, the employer contribution *does* count toward these limits.

The *regular limit* in the table applies if you're under 50. In the year that you hit the big 5-0 and every year thereafter, you may make an additional pre-tax contribution, known as a *catch-up contribution*, which raises your total possible contribution to the amount listed in the column on the far right. Why the special tax break? We like to think that it's because Uncle Sam is well over 50 himself (look at his white hair, after all). In reality, Congress approved this extra tax break to help workers who may not have contributed much to their own retirement savings early on, particularly women who may have stepped out of the work force to raise children or care for ailing relatives.

There's a catch, though — even though federal law allows this type of contribution, your plan has to change its rules to specifically allow catch-up contributions before you can actually make them. Your plan isn't required to allow these contributions. The law only changed in 2002, and some plans may be slow to adopt this change. Ask your employer or plan provider whether your plan allows catch-up contributions. If it doesn't, keep after your employer or plan provider to amend the plan.

Table 2-1	Annual Contribution Limits		
Year	Regular Limit	Age-50 Catch-up Limit	Maximum Total Limit for 50 and over
2002	$11,000	$1,000	$12,000
2003	$12,000	$2,000	$14,000
2004	$13,000	$3,000	$16,000

Year	Regular Limit	Age-50 Catch-up Limit	Maximum Total Limit for 50 and over
2005	$14,000	$4,000	$18,000
2006 and beyond	$15,000	$5,000	$20,000

A small number of 401(k) plans allow you to make "after-tax" contributions. You can't deduct these contributions from your income tax, but you can benefit from them in another way — the gain on your investment isn't taxed every year. It grows *tax deferred,* and you pay income tax only on the investment gains when you withdraw them. However, you may be able to achieve a better result by investing in a *Roth IRA,* especially if your employer doesn't match after-tax contributions. You also make after-tax contributions to a Roth, but you pay *no* income tax when you withdraw the money at retirement. (Read more about Roth IRAs in Chapter 8.) The limit on after-tax contributions is part of the "percent of pay" limit we explain in the next section.

A few small businesses (under 100 employees) may offer what's known as a SIMPLE 401(k) plan. These plans have fewer administrative requirements for the employer, but the tradeoff is lower contribution limits than those outlined in Table 2-1. With the introduction of Safe Harbor 401(k) plans in the late 1990s, which also have fewer administrative requirements for the employer but allow the higher 401(k) contribution limits presented here, most employers have switched away from the SIMPLE 401(k). By the way, SIMPLE stands for *Savings Incentive Match Plan for Employees.* Another plan, called a SIMPLE IRA, is still used fairly often, particularly by companies with fewer than 10 employees. We explain Safe Harbor 401(k)s and SIMPLE IRAs in Chapter 12. We agree, the existence of so many types of plans is confusing!

Percent-of-pay limit

So far, so good. But you need to be aware of another limit that can cap your contributions. Before the new tax law went into effect in 2002 (EGTRRA — the Economic Growth and Tax Relief Reconciliation Act, not the newest gourmet breakfast item), your contributions (pre-tax and after-tax) combined with your employer's contributions couldn't be more than 25 percent of your pay or more than $35,000, whichever figure was smaller. As a result, employers had to limit the percentage of pay that you could contribute. For example, you may have been limited to a maximum of 20 percent of your pay if your employer contributed 5 percent.

The good news is that, under the new federal tax laws, the combined employee/employer limit is 100 percent of pay with a $40,000 maximum. (Just to complicate matters, the age-50 catch-up contribution can be made in addition to the $40,000 maximum, but not on top of the 100 percent of pay limit.) However, your employer must modify its plan before you can contribute this higher percentage.

In reality, you can't contribute a full 100 percent even if your employer doesn't make a contribution, because you must pay Social Security taxes, and possibly state and local taxes, on your income before making your 401(k) contributions. (Chapter 1 explains these taxes in more detail in the section "Defining What a 401(k) Does for You." You may also have other pre-401(k) pay deductions for medical coverage or contributions to a Section 125 flexible benefits plan.

But, if you can afford to do so, you may be able to contribute quite a chunk of your pay as long as you remain under the limit. If you're a lower-income saver, or if you start a second career after earning a military, police, or other pension, being able to contribute the higher percentage can be a real plus for you. For example, if you retired from the military with a pension that covered most or all of your everyday expenses, but you became bored and decided to go back to work part-time earning $14,000, you could contribute $11,000 of this amount to a 401(k) in 2002 (or possibly $12,000 if you were eligible to make a catch-up contribution).

The only fly in the ointment would be if your employer still has the old limit of 25 percent of pay written into your plan. In that case, you could only contribute $3,500, which is 25 percent of $14,000.

Vesting: When Your Employer's Contribution Is Yours to Keep

When your employer puts money into your 401(k) plan, that money doesn't necessarily belong to you right away. Most companies require that you stay employed with them for a certain amount of time before the contributions *vest,* or are yours to keep if you leave your job. They use this requirement to encourage you to stay on the job.

The employer contributions are generally deposited in the account right away, earning a return on your behalf even before they vest. If you leave your job before the employer contributions vest, you forfeit those contributions plus any earnings on them.

The contributions you make from your salary are always yours to keep, and you can take them with you when you leave. This section refers only to contributions made by your employer.

Your employer can't make you wait forever to vest. There are maximum lengths of time for matching and non-matching contributions. What are they? Keep reading to find out.

Vesting of matching contributions

Employer matching contributions must generally become yours to keep either

- ✔ All at once on a specified date within three years
- ✔ Gradually over six years

The first method is known as *cliff vesting*. With this method, you must go from 0 to 100 percent vested after you have earned three years of service, at the most (the period can be shorter). The second is called *graded vesting*, or *graduated vesting*. With this method, you must go from 0 to 100 percent vested by increases of 20 percent over a period of six years, at the most.

Table 2-2 shows a comparison of the two vesting schedules, looking at the maximum number of years of service that an employer can generally require.

Table 2-2	Longest Allowed 401(k) Matching Contribution Vesting Schedules	
Years of Service	*Cliff*	*Graduated*
Less than 2	0%	0%
2 but less than 3	0%	20%
3 but less than 4	100%	40%
4 but less than 5	100%	60%
5 but less than 6	100%	80%
6 or more	100%	100%

An employer may choose a faster vesting schedule (and may even choose to have your matching contributions 100 percent vested at all times) but probably not a longer one. (Some technical exceptions exist, but they're rare.) According to the Profit-Sharing/401(k) Council of America, a little more than one-third of plans have *immediate vesting* (you don't have to wait at all), and a similar number have graduated vesting. A little more than one-quarter of plans offer cliff vesting.

Vesting of non-matching contributions

All employer contributions that are not matching contributions, such as profit-sharing or automatic contributions, may take longer to vest. The maximum requirement for cliff vesting is five years, and the maximum requirement for graded vesting is seven years.

Why are the rules different for matching and non-matching contributions? You'll have to ask Congress. The new laws Congress passed containing the shorter vesting schedule refer only to employer matching contributions. Non-matching contributions still fall under the old (pre-2002) rules.

Exceptions (You knew this was coming, right?)

A few other situations may cause immediate vesting of matching and non-matching employer contributions, no matter how many years you may have worked at the company. These situations are

- If your employer terminates your 401(k) plan
- If you reach "normal retirement age" (This is defined by the plan, but it is usually age 65.)
- If you die before you leave the company
- If you become disabled, as defined in the plan
- If you're among a "substantial portion" (such as more than 20 percent) of plan participants who are laid off due to the closing of a plant or division, or are otherwise part of a large layoff

To find out which rules apply to you, check your summary plan description.

When You Can Start Participating

Sarah is a top-notch worker who's being wooed by two companies. The job offers are identical in every way except one: Company A will let her start participating in the 401(k) plan right away, while Company L (for "loser") will let her join only after she's worked there for one year. Which employer will nab Sarah? If Sarah is smart, it's Company A.

Why does it matter if she has to wait a year to join? One year is the maximum length of time that an employer can make you wait. Employers that impose this limit usually require you to wait until the next entry date after fulfilling the year of service — for example, the first day of each quarter (such as January 1, April 1, July 1, and October 1).

What does this mean for Sarah? If she were hired on January 12, 2002, she wouldn't be able to start contributing to the plan until April 1, 2003 — Company L's first entry date after completing one year of service if it uses the schedule outlined in the previous paragraph. If she changed jobs more than five times during her working life and had to wait one year each time to join a plan, she could lose out on at least five years of retirement benefits, seriously reducing her long-term savings.

Until the late 1990s, it was common to make new employees wait one year before they could join a 401(k) plan. But plan eligibility periods have been shrinking. New employees are now often eligible to join the plan within 90 days or less. Quarterly entry dates are being replaced by immediate or monthly entry dates. Keep this in mind when you're evaluating a potential employer's 401(k) plan.

Accessing Your 401(k) Plan Money While Working

The tax breaks you get with a 401(k) plan come with a price. It can be very costly to take your money out of the plan before you retire, if you can even do it at all.

Don't wait for an emergency, or any other reason to access your 401(k) money, before checking on the rules of your plan. You may find that you can't make a withdrawal or that you will lose about half the value in taxes and penalties if you do make a withdrawal.

Federal law allows three ways to get money out of your 401(k) while you're working for the employer sponsoring the plan. But keep in mind that your employer isn't *required* to allow these features, so they may not be available in your plan. (We discuss these features in detail in Chapter 7.) The three ways to obtain money from your 401(k) are

- ✔ **Unrestricted access to plan assets after you reach age 59½.** The amount withdrawn becomes part of your taxable income for that year.

- ✔ **Withdrawals for financial hardships as defined by law and IRS regulations.** *Hardship withdrawals*, as they're known, are fully taxable and are usually also subject to an additional 10 percent federal early withdrawal penalty (and possibly additional state and local penalties, as well).

- ✔ **Plan loans.** These are subject to numerous restrictions. (You may get a plan loan to pay for excessive medical expenses, but you shouldn't assume that you'll get one to buy a yacht.)

The first two options listed are known as *in-service withdrawals,* because you make them while you're "in the service of" your employer.

Strangely enough, federal law makes it theoretically easier to withdraw your employer's contributions than your own pre-tax deferrals while you're working. Your employer may allow you to take the employer contributions out for any reason. But most employers place restrictions on withdrawals of their contributions because they want you to use the money for retirement, so you probably won't be able to use those to buy your yacht, either.

Loans and in-service withdrawals are a mixed blessing because, while they give you some flexibility with your money, they'll likely reduce the ultimate value of your retirement nest egg. But being able to withdraw these savings can be an important plan feature if you think that you may need your money before reaching age 59½. This is particularly true for younger employees who have a long way to go until retirement.

What Investments You Can Choose

When it comes to your 401(k) investment choices, you're at the mercy of your employer. Your employer chooses the investment options that will be offered by the plan. Generally, these are mutual funds and, possibly, stock in your employer's company. Some companies offer a *brokerage window*, which lets you invest in individual stocks and bonds in addition to the mutual funds offered by the plan. (Think of it as a "window" to a larger universe of stocks, bonds, and mutual funds.)

Most plans let you decide how to invest your money among the options offered. A very small number of plans do *not* let you choose how the money is invested — the employer decides for you. In this case, the employer has greater fiduciary liability for the account's investment performance.

Many 401(k) plans offer at least ten investment choices. Your plan may have more than this, or not as many. More important than the number, though, is the *quality* and *range* of the investments offered. Although not required, at a minimum your plan should ideally offer

- A large-company stock fund

- A small-company stock fund

- A bond or other fixed-income fund

- A money market (cash) fund

- A mutual fund that invests in international stocks and/or bonds

These different categories, or classes, of investments are called *asset classes*. (We discuss asset classes and investing in more detail in Chapter 6.)

When judging the quality of funds offered in your plan, remember that it's impossible for employers (or anyone else, for that matter) to pick consistently top-performing fund options in each category. What's more, funds that can boast top short-term performance records may not even be the best choices for long-term investors in a 401(k) plan. You need to use appropriate criteria for judging a mutual fund's performance.

How Much You Pay for Plan Expenses

A 401(k) plan provides a service to you, and it's not free. You're charged various fees and expenses for the administration of the plan, your account, and your investments inside the account. These charges aren't unusual, but you want to assess whether you're paying a reasonable amount.

Figuring out whether you're paying a reasonable amount can be harder than it sounds. You won't get a bill that lists exactly how much you're paying in fees. Nor will you necessarily see an entry on your 401(k) statement that reports all fees deducted. Instead, you have to do some detective work to find out what you're paying.

It's worth the effort. In most cases, fees are deducted from your *investment return* — the money being earned by your investments. The higher the fees, the more they'll reduce your eventual balance.

For example: Say you and your spouse each contribute $5,000 a year to 401(k) plans from age 30 to age 65. You both earn an average 8 percent return on your investment (before fees). Your spouse's plan charges 1 percent in fees annually. Your plan charges 2 percent. Do you think this 1 percentage point will make a big difference in the end value of your accounts? You bet it will. Your spouse will have $641,000. Assuming everything else is equal, you'll have $521,000 — around $120,000 less!

There's no "right" amount of fees to pay — although, if you're paying more than 1 percent of your account balance, you're probably paying too much. As with just about everything in investing, you have tradeoffs to consider; if your plan charges relatively high fees but provides many useful services, you may be satisfied.

If you think that your plan fees are too high, you don't necessarily have to abandon your 401(k), especially if your alternative is not saving for retirement at all. At least contribute enough to get the employer matching contribution, and explore other ways to save for retirement, such as an IRA. (Read Chapter 8 for more information about IRAs.)

401(k) fees can be tricky to understand because of the way plans are put together. Generally, you have a fixed administrative cost and variable costs associated with individual investment choices. Many plans are administered by financial companies that combine some or all of these fees and charge all participants' accounts the same percentage fee. (In this case, the higher your account balance, the higher the dollar amount you'll pay.)

Most 401(k) fees are expressed in *basis points*. One hundred basis points equals 1 percent. How much is 150 basis points? If you said 1.5 percent, you're right. Fifty basis points equals 0.5 percent.

There are four common types of services, for which fees may be charged, that you are likely to receive in your 401(k):

✔ Recordkeeping and other administrative functions

✔ Investment management

✔ Benefit transactions

✔ Education and advice

Administrative functions

401(k) plans involve a lot of number crunching and recordkeeping. Someone has to keep track of how much money is in each person's account and where the money is invested. Someone also has to roduce your monthly, quarterly, or annual account statement. The plan needs to carry out federally required testing and reporting. These administrative functions need to be paid for.

Most employers hire an outside firm to handle these administration functions. In many cases, the *plan provider* (the financial company that offers your plan's investments, such as Fidelity or Vanguard) also handles the administration. But your employer may also hire separate companies — one to provide the investments, and the other to handle the administration of the plan.

Administration fees may be as much as $100 a year (or more) per participant. This fee may also be a fixed cost, regardless of how much money is in each participant's account. When it comes to administrative costs, the key question is: Who pays — you or your employer.

The best scenario is that your employer pays, which is usually what happens during the first few years after starting a plan.

Employers commonly shift payment of the administrative fees to you, the participant, as the plan matures. But when they do this, they won't necessarily charge each participant $100. They will likely charge it as a percentage of everyone's account. For example, say your plan has 100 participants. The total administrative fee is $10,000 (100 × $100). If all participant accounts added together are worth $5,000,000, with some people having $200,000 in their accounts and others having $10,000, the plan fee is 0.2 percent of each person's account. (The $10,000 administrative fee is 0.2 percent of $5,000,000.) The people with a $200,000 balance pay $400, while the people with $10,000 balances pay $20.

You may not realize that you're paying administrative fees. The expense may be clearly shown on your statement, or it may be hidden and simply reduce your investment return.

Investment management

The 401(k) plan set up by your employer provides you with choices for how to invest your money. Most 401(k) plans limit these choices to mutual funds. (We talk more about mutual funds and 401(k) investing in Part II.) What's important to know here is that most, if not all, mutual funds charge some kind of investment fee to pay for the expense of managing the fund. These fees range from very low to pretty high, depending on the type of mutual fund. Each mutual fund that you invest in will likely charge this type of fee.

Managers come with a price tag

Generally, a mutual fund with a fund manager who constantly buys and sells stocks to try to improve the fund's return (an *actively managed fund*) will have a higher investment fee than an index fund that doesn't involve a manager who picks the investments. (We explain index funds and other investments in Chapter 6.)

The annual fee for an actively managed stock fund is usually in the 1 to 1.5 percent range, compared to 0.20 to 0.40 percent for an index fund. These fees are usually referred to as the fund's *expense ratio*. The fees may also be expressed as *basis points* (100 to 150 basis points for the managed fund, compared to 20 to 40 basis points for the index fund).

Retail mutual funds (available to the average individual investor) are likely to be more expensive in a 401(k) plan than *institutional* funds (geared toward traditional pension plans or other entities with large amounts to invest). Retail mutual funds are preferred by many participants due to brand-name comfort and because the funds can be readily tracked in the daily papers and other publications. You won't find daily performance results of institutional investment managers in the financial section of your paper, but the lower fees may make them a better deal than the higher-cost retail funds. Some large companies use institutional funds to help keep fees, including administrative and investment costs, low.

Factoring in wrap fees

Sometimes a 401(k) plan provider charges what's known as a *wrap fee*. Small plans with fewer than 100 participants are most often charged this fee, which is likely to be anywhere between 0.5 and 1.5 percent of the total assets in the plan (everybody's accounts combined). The wrap fee is added to the normal fund management fee and the administrative fees.

An insurance company, bank, or brokerage firm may charge this wrap fee if it offers funds managed by a number of different mutual fund companies, including ones the provider owns. For example, the provider may offer the well-known Fidelity Magellan fund but add an additional 100-to-150-basis-point annual fee to the standard fee charged by Fidelity.

The wrap fee explains why the return that you see printed in the newspaper for the funds you invest in may be different from what you see on your 401(k) statement. If the wrap fee is 1.5 percent, for example, your returns will be reduced by 1.5 percent each year, as compared with what's in the newspaper. This may not sound like much, but a 1.5 percent additional wrap fee reduces your 30-year savings by 30 percent!

Getting the 411 on investment fees

Looking at a fund's prospectus will generally help you see what fees are charged. The *prospectus* is a document that tells you things such as what companies the mutual fund invests in, how often the manager buys and sells stocks within the fund, and what the manager is trying to achieve (the fund *objective*). It also tells you the expense ratio. But it doesn't include information about a wrap fee charged by the 401(k) provider. Getting this information is often difficult because providers who charge wrap fees are often reluctant to disclose their fees. A prospectus should be available from your employer, the plan provider, or the fund company that runs the fund (try the company's Web site or request one by phone).

Some mutual funds that aren't sold to the general public aren't required to provide a fund prospectus. Getting straight answers on fees for these funds can be very difficult. Ask the plan provider for fee information, and get your employer involved, too.

The United States Department of Labor Web site (www.dol.gov/pwba/pension.htm) has a free brochure for 401(k) plan participants that explains how plan fees work. (A separate brochure has information for employers.)

You should find out what your plan charges in fees, and then tell your employer if you think it's too high. There may be a good reason for the fees charged by your plan (such as extra services, which we discuss in a minute), or there may not be.

Benefit transactions

If your plan offers special services, such as loans or hardship withdrawals, you'll probably have to pay a fee when you take advantage of them. For example, you may be charged one fee when you take the loan, and a separate annual fee for each year that it takes you to repay it. You may even have to pay a fee for the privilege of taking your money out of the plan when you change jobs or retire. These fees are commonly in the $50 to $100 range.

You usually have to pay these fees yourself, because you trigger the transactions.

Education and advice

It's not enough for your employer to simply offer a 401(k) plan. You need help understanding how to use and manage it. At a minimum, your employer can and should provide additional support that includes

- ✔ A retirement calculator to help you determine how much you'll need when you retire and how much to invest to reach your goals

- ✔ Information about the various types of mutual funds to help you understand your investments

- ✔ Account statements (at least quarterly) and other tools to help you measure your progress

- ✔ On-site educational seminars about investing, goal-setting, and taking advantage of a 401(k)

Additional features, which are being offered by more and more 401(k) plans, can include

- ✔ An 800-number to call for assistance in managing your plan investments

- ✔ Internet access to detailed information about your plan investments (including fee information and historical investment results)

- ✔ The ability to make changes at any time, such as moving money from one investment to another or changing your contribution amount

- ✔ Investment advice and financial planning assistance

All of these support services are designed to help participants understand the plan and manage their investments, and they involve additional expenses that must be paid. The added value you receive from these services may warrant higher fees. Chapter 6 tells you where to find advice, education, and retirement calculators if your employer doesn't offer them.

What — no fees?

Some representatives of financial organizations tell employees who have 401(k) plans that they do not pay any fees. If someone tells you this, don't believe it. No organization that runs a 401(k) plan does so for free. The question is *how* participants pay the fee — not whether they pay one. You don't actually write a check to pay a fee, but the reduction in your investment return is a powerful form of payment.

A move toward lower-cost investment alternatives began a few years ago, and it will continue. Previously, when the stock market was strong throughout the 1990s, participants were indifferent to fees. It was hard to get worked up about an extra 0.5 percent in fees when net investment returns were 15 percent or higher. In a down market, that half a percentage point looks a lot more important.

Trying to Improve Shortcomings in Your Plan

If you don't think your plan is up to snuff, you can try to convince your employer to change it. Don't get your hopes up too high, though. Making a change to a 401(k) plan is complicated for the employer, so there has to be a really good reason for doing so.

For example, many small employers simply can't afford to make a matching contribution. You can petition them until the cows come home, but, for economic reasons, they won't budge.

 For information about what other plans nationwide offer, contact the Profit-Sharing/401(k) Council of America through its Web site (www.psca.org) or by phone at 312-441-8559.

Employers often need to be reminded that the 401(k) helps to attract and retain employees. Armed with information about competitive plans, employers may be able to shape a plan that attracts more top-quality employees. The top three complaints employees have about their 401(k) plans are

- ✔ Poor investment performance

- ✔ Lack of available information (especially about fees)

- ✔ Not enough funds offered, or not the right types of funds

Here's a look at each complaint in more detail, as well as what you may be able to do about them.

Poor investment performance

If you have a caring employer, and if your investments really are performing poorly, you may be able to make a change.

Sometimes participants ask the employer to replace one fund with another that they think is performing better. This change may seem like a no-brainer, but it's not. The employer needs to look not only at the fund's recent performance, but also at long-term returns and other measures. Comparing the fund's performance with that of similar funds is also important. If similar funds are also going through a bad spell, and the fund itself is solid and makes sense as part of the plan, a couple of years of less-than-ideal performance isn't necessarily reason to boot it out of the plan completely.

401(k) plans are governed by a law known as ERISA — the Employee Retirement Income Security Act. ERISA lays out minimum standards for 401(k)s and other types of pension plans. One thing ERISA says is that your employer has a responsibility (known as *fiduciary responsibility*) to make sure that the plan is operated in the best interest of the participants. (Anyone else who exercises control over plan assets or management — which may include the plan trustee or the plan provider — is also considered to have fiduciary responsibility.) This responsibility covers a number of issues, including what mutual funds you can invest in. Your employer must be able to show that it acted responsibly in choosing funds to offer in the plan. Changing funds every few years on a whim would probably not qualify as responsible. ERISA allows plan participants to sue *fiduciaries* (those who have control over the plan assets) for breaching their responsibilities. (We discuss ERISA in more detail in Chapter 1.)

Lack of available information

Timely access to investment information is another big issue. Managing a retirement account in the best of circumstances is hard, but it's almost impossible when important information isn't available.

Employees are often shocked to discover that employers are required (by ERISA) to provide to them only three pieces of information about their 401(k):

 ✔ **A summary plan description (or SPD).** The plan description explains the general terms of the plan — who is eligible and when, the types of contributions permitted, vesting, withdrawal rules, and so on. Although it's useful when you need to know your plan's rules, the information about plan investments is typically limited to generic fund descriptions. Some SPDs don't even give fund descriptions; they say only that participants can split their contributions among various funds selected by the employer.

✔ **A summary annual report (or SAR).** The annual report isn't exactly what you'd call useful up-to-date information. The SAR is pulled from a form that your employer has to file with the Department of Labor within seven months after the plan year ends. But the information on the form is for the previous year, ending December 31 (if the plan year ends on December 31), so the information is dated by the time you receive it. The summary annual report lists general financial results for the year for the entire plan, including total contributions, interest, dividends, realized and unrealized gains, and benefit distributions. None of this information helps you decide how to invest your money.

✔ **An annual statement of their account.** This statement doesn't have to include detailed information on the actual return and expenses for each participant's investments. It may be limited to the beginning balance, contributions, withdrawals, investment gains or losses, and ending balance. Still, a growing number of service providers are reporting a lot more information, including each participant's specific *rate of return* (the percentage by which your own investments grew, or shrank, over the year). These voluntary efforts are to be applauded (and you should point them out to your employer as a good example of what to do — if your plan doesn't offer them yet).

However, notice that none of these documents are required to explain how much you pay in fees.

So, now that we've told you what isn't very useful, here's what *is* useful: services and information that your employer isn't required to provide. These include

✔ Sending statements every quarter (every three months) instead of only once a year

✔ Providing a toll-free number that you can call to ask investment and other plan account questions

✔ Giving you Internet access to plan information

Many employers offer these services. If your employer doesn't offer these services, you should request them.

Investment advice:
More than 5¢, but well worth it

A growing number of employers offer their employees the opportunity to receive investment advice from independent companies such as mPower, Financial Engines, and Morningstar. These online companies recommend how to invest money in your 401(k) plan so that you have a better chance of meeting your retirement goals. You can pay a fee individually to access one of these services over the Internet if your employer doesn't offer one. (We explain more about advice in Chapter 6.)

A number of employers don't yet offer advice services, because they worry that employees who aren't happy with the advice they receive may sue. Although the Department of Labor has ruled that it's okay for employers to make independent advice available to their employees, many companies are still concerned about potential liability exposure. At the time of writing, several members of Congress had proposed laws permitting, even encouraging, employers to provide advice. You can expect to see a lot of movement in this area over the next few years, following the Enron, WorldCom, and similar debacles, and the stock market downturn. We believe that letting employees invest on their own, without advice, creates greater risk than providing good investment advice.

The bottom line is that most participants probably don't get enough information to manage their 401(k)s wisely. What can you do? You can consider signing up for an advice service. Your employer may offer one as a benefit, or you can sign up on your own. (We tell you how in Chapter 6.)

Some funds offered by 401(k) plans are special funds created by the provider, and they aren't available to the general public. In this case, you need to ask the provider or your employer for information about the fund. Written requests are usually the most effective.

Here's a sample letter asking for more information about plan fees:

Dear 401(k) Plan Representative:

Planning for my retirement is a serious matter. I want to do everything I can to be sure that I have an adequate income during my retirement years.

Unfortunately, I haven't been able to make informed investment decisions, because I can't get adequate information about the fees that I pay. I called the service center at the Outback Investment Company, and their representative told me that I don't pay any fees. Perhaps I should consider this wonderful news, but I'm not dumb enough to believe that it's true.

As a result, I'm requesting a written explanation of all the fees that I pay, including the ones deducted from plan assets by the organizations that invest and manage the plan, and that reduce the net investment return I receive.

Sincerely,

401(k) Plan Participant

Not enough funds or not the right funds

You may be convinced that your plan needs to offer more or better mutual funds. In some cases, you may be right; in others, you may not be. In any case, you have a better chance of getting your plan sponsor to listen and take action if you submit detailed written complaints. Generic complaints that simply state that a plan's investment options stink aren't very useful. It's best to explain why, specifically, you're dissatisfied. It may be the fact that a particular type of fund isn't offered, or it may be generally due to high fees or poor performance.

Here's a sample letter that may get the attention of a plan sponsor:

Dear 401(k) Plan Representative:

I take 401(k) investing very seriously, because I want to do everything I can to be sure that I have an adequate income when I retire. As you know, investment return has a major impact on the savings that I, and other participants, will accumulate.

I am very dissatisfied with the return of our large-cap stock fund, the Outback Super Stock Fund. In the past year, the return for this fund was 2.4% less than the S&P 500 index. During the last three years, the fund returned an average of 2.6% less than the S&P. This fund has also ranked in the bottom quartile for three years, and it only has a two-star Morningstar rating.

It would clearly be in the best interest of all participants to replace this fund with a similar fund that has a better track record and rating.

Sincerely,

401(k) Plan Participant

Keeping it all in perspective

401(k) plans today may have problems, but they've come a long way, baby.

In the early days, all administrative activity was paper-based, labor intensive, and slow. Participant accounts were generally updated on specific *valuation dates* (dates when the value of the account was calculated and recorded) only once or twice a year. The really advanced plans updated participant accounts quarterly — four times a year. If you wanted to change your investments or take a distribution (withdrawal), you could do so only on these valuation dates. Because of cumbersome administration, you usually had to wait six to eight weeks *after* the valuation date for the transaction to be completed.

Today, the administration of 401(k)s has moved from cumbersome paper-based processing to electronic processing. Most participants can get information about their accounts and investments all day and every day, from anywhere in the world. You should be able to change investments and make other transactions just as easily.

Participant education didn't even exist in the early days of 401(k) plans. Now, more and more employers offer good education programs, although unfortunately not all of them do. Individuals can also find investment education in special retirement planning sections of many financial Web sites. Some Web sites, such as mPower Cafe (www.mpowercafe.com), are entirely devoted to retirement investment education.

This letter contains specific reasons for the dissatisfaction of the fund. The reasons are supported by Morningstar ratings, an independent source. The letter also properly identifies the type of fund and compares its performance with the *S&P index,* an appropriate benchmark for this type of fund. (Chapter 6 has more information about S&P and other indexes.) Gathering this information may appear to be very difficult, but it isn't. The Morningstar.com Web site (or other similar fund resources we mention in Chapter 6) provides all of this information.

Consider your company culture before you attack the 401(k). You don't want to be labeled a troublemaker if this is how your employer views people who complain. At your company, a casual remark at the water cooler followed up by an e-mail with "just the facts" may be enough to spur someone in a position of authority to consider a change.

If you fail to get the information you need, consider writing to the United States Department of Labor. Explain what efforts you've made to get the information and the responses you received. Letters should be addressed to: The Assistant Secretary of Labor, Pension and Welfare Benefits Administration, 200 Constitution Ave., N.W., Washington, D.C. 20210-1111. You can go to the United States Department of Labor's Pension and Welfare Benefits Administration Web site at `http://askpwba.dol.gov/` and click on Postal Mail/National Office for up-to-date information.

In the end, as you evaluate your 401(k) plan, you're really evaluating the corporate citizenship of your employer. If your employer realizes the importance of having a strong 401(k) plan, that's a good sign.

Chapter 3

Signing Up for Your 401(k)

● ●

In This Chapter

▶ Understanding the rules for participating

▶ Seeing how much you can save if you're highly paid, low-paid, or somewhere in between

▶ Filling out the paperwork

▶ Deciding who gets your money if you die

● ●

*W*e occasionally hear from individuals who are self-employed or whose employers don't offer a retirement plan, who want to know how they can "open a 401(k) account." Unfortunately, it's not that simple. Unlike an IRA that you can open on your own, a 401(k) is only available through your employer.

Companies aren't required to offer 401(k) plans (or any retirement plan, for that matter). The fact that your employer offers a 401(k) doesn't mean that you're automatically eligible to contribute, though. Before joining your employer's 401(k) plan, you must fulfill your employer's eligibility requirements.

After you qualify to join the 401(k), you'll have some decisions to make. How much will you contribute from each paycheck? How will your contributions be invested? Who should inherit the account if you die?

Reading this chapter can help you understand the paperwork you need to fill out when you sign up for your 401(k) plan. It also explains how much you're allowed to contribute, whether you're just signing up or whether you've been participating for years.

Figuring Out Whether You're Eligible

Your employer isn't required to let all employees join the 401(k) plan immediately. What's more, certain groups of employees can be excluded altogether. When interviewing for a job, be sure to ask what the rules are for that company's 401(k) plan.

Sometimes you play a waiting game

As a new hire, you may be able to participate immediately, you may have to wait up to one year before you're eligible to join the plan, or you may never be eligible to participate in the plan. After you meet the requirements, you have to wait until the plan's *next entry date* to actually begin contributing to the account. The entry date is the first date you can actually contribute to the plan after satisfying the eligibility requirements. Some employers have a plan entry date every pay period, while others may have only a few during the year. As a new hire, you're better off with a company that lets you join the plan shortly after you begin your employment. You can find out why in Chapter 2.

If your plan requires you to work for one year before becoming eligible for the 401(k) plan, different definitions of "year" are possible. For example, a year can mean

- 12 months of employment
- At least 1,000 hours of work during the course of 12 months of employment (working 20 hours a week for 50 weeks, for example)

Ask your human resources department for more information.

If you have to work 1,000 hours in one year to become eligible for the plan, you generally don't need to work 1,000 hours in subsequent years to *remain in the plan*. However, the number of hours you work in subsequent years may affect your eligibility to receive employer contributions. It may also affect how soon those contributions *vest*, or become your property. (See Chapter 2 for more on matching contributions and vesting.)

Sometimes you can't join at all

Employers are allowed to exclude certain employees from participating in the 401(k) plan. These employees include

- ✔ **Union employees covered by a collective bargaining agreement.** Federal law prohibits employers from offering *any* retirement or other benefit plan to union members that hasn't been agreed on through collective bargaining. This includes 401(k) plans — even those funded entirely by employee contributions. Labor laws require union employees who want a 401(k) to include it in their contract demands.

  Union managers often prefer traditional defined-benefit pension plans (see Chapter 2), which guarantee benefits at retirement. This is the main reason that 401(k) coverage is lower among union employees. It's also why 401(k) plans for union employees typically don't include an employer matching contribution — the employer is already contributing to the defined-benefit plan.

- ✔ **Nonresident aliens.** Employers are allowed to exclude employees who live outside the United States and aren't U.S. citizens from participating in the plan. However, employees who are residents of the United States (including green card holders) but are not U.S. citizens can't be excluded simply because they're not U.S. citizens.

- ✔ **Leased employees.** Leased employees are people who work for a company temporarily, often placed through an agency.

- ✔ **Specific categories of employees.** Under certain circumstances, an employer may exclude a specific category of employees, such as hourly workers or the employees of a specific business unit, from participating in the 401(k) plan. Generally, an employer can legally exclude a group if it makes up less than 30 percent of all employees. For example, your plan may permit only salaried workers to participate, and exclude hourly wage earners, if the hourly workers account for only 10 percent of the staff. However, even if the 30 percent test isn't satisfied, a variety of other exceptions may apply. Determining the categories of employees that may be excluded can be very complicated.

  Finally, you may be excluded if you're under 21. The exclusion would have to apply to all employees under 21, though; an employer couldn't permit some to participate and not others.

Sometimes you're automatically in

A small number of 401(k) plans use what's called *automatic enrollment*. Eligible employees are automatically signed up for the plan unless they refuse in writing. A percentage of salary is deferred into the plan for automatically enrolled employees, and often is deposited in the most conservative investment option.

If your plan has automatic enrollment, don't be lazy — be sure to come up with an investment plan to diversify your money among different investments. Also, consider contributing more than the amount your employer automatically deducts, which is likely to be too small to build up a sufficient nest egg.

Determining How Much of Your Salary to Put Aside

When you enroll in your 401(k) plan, you'll need to fill out a *salary deferral* agreement. Salary deferral refers to the amount of your pay that you want your employer to put in the 401(k) plan rather than in your paycheck.

The form you have to fill out may require you to select a percentage of salary to defer, or it may ask for a dollar amount. In fact, it may even give you a choice, such as the one shown in Figure 3-1. What's the difference? Take a look:

✔ The percentage of salary is easy because it's the same no matter how many pay periods you have. If you want to contribute 10 percent of your pay, you simply list "10%" on the form.

✔ For a dollar amount, you need to figure out the total amount you want to contribute for the year and then divide it by the number of pay periods. Say you get paid twice a month. If you earn $30,000 and you want to put $3,000 a year into your 401(k), you list $125 a pay period as a dollar amount ($3,000 divided by 24 equals $125). If you're paid once a month, you need to put down $250 a pay period.

If you work irregular hours or earn variable pay such as overtime, bonuses, or commissions, contributing a percentage of pay usually works better. If your gross pay varies from one pay period to another, you may not earn enough in some pay periods to cover the fixed contribution you've chosen.

SECTION I - Salary Deferral Election		

Participant should complete A or B.

A. ☐ **I elect to contribute** the following pay to the Plan each pay period:

☐ _____ **% OR** ☐ $_____

B. ☐ **I elect NOT to contribute** to the Plan.

SECTION II - Salary Deferral Election of Bonuses and Commissions		

I elect ☐ **to apply** ☐ **not to apply** the percentage or fixed dollar amount specified in Section I(A) above to any bonuses and/or commissions I may receive as compensation.

Figure 3-1: Sample 401(k) salary deferral form.

Some employers won't let you include overtime or other forms of non-base pay as compensation for the purposes of contributing to a 401(k). In this case, contributions may be based only on your base pay or something less than your total compensation.

How do you decide what percentage or dollar amount to put aside? To begin with, you need to consider several factors:

- ✔ The government's restrictions

- ✔ Your own plan's restrictions

- ✔ Your budget's limitations

- ✔ The amount you need to get the full employer matching contribution

Also, remember that the most important thing is to start contributing as soon as you're eligible. Even if you only contribute 1 percent of your salary to begin with, it's a start. After you're in the habit of saving, it gets easier and easier. But if you put it off, it only gets harder.

Gauging the limits of the law

The *federal dollar limit for pre-tax salary deferrals* is probably the best-known 401(k) limit (not to mention a mouthful to say!). Despite its scary title, this limit is easy to understand. It's the cap on how much income you can have your employer put into the 401(k) rather than into your paycheck. In 2002, the limit is $11,000, plus an additional $1,000 "catch-up contribution" if you're age 50 or older. Limits rise each year through 2006; see Table 2-1 in Chapter 2 for details.

The tax legislation that created these limits is due to expire at the end of 2010. If Congress doesn't extend the tax legislation, in 2011 we'll revert to the limits that existed in 2001 ($10,500 in pre-tax contributions and no catch-up contributions).

Another federal limit to be aware of is the *percentage-of-pay limit*. This limit applies to all contributions made to your 401(k) by you and your employer, as well as to all contributions to other defined contribution plans, such as profit-sharing plans or 403(b) plans. Beginning in 2002, these contributions can't total more than 100 percent of your pay, or $40,000, whichever is less. The $40,000 limit is expected to rise periodically with inflation.

The 100-percent-of-pay limit includes catch-up contributions, but the $40,000 dollar limit does not. The pre-tax contribution limits discussed in Chapter 2 don't include the catch-up contribution either.

Measuring your plan's maximums

Your 401(k) plan isn't allowed to let you contribute *more* than the federal limits discussed in the previous section, but it can restrict you to *less*.

Old-fashioned limits

Your employer may be behind the times. Previously, through 2001, contributions to your 401(k) by you and your employer were limited to 25 percent of your pay. Because of this rule, many employers limited employee pre-tax contributions to 15 or 20 percent of salary. Beginning in 2002, however, the limit was raised to 100 percent of salary, so employers have no need to cap contributions at 20 percent, although your employer may still do so. Ted suggests that plans raise the limit specified in the plan document to around 80 percent, which gives everyone plenty of flexibility.

"Highly compensated employee" rule

Under federal law, employers must test their plans each year to ensure that no "discrimination" exists in favor of highly paid employees. As an example, the contribution percentages of highly paid employees are added up as one group, and the contribution percentages of lower-paid employees are added up as a second group. The average contribution percentage of the highly paid employees can't be more than 2 percentage points above those of the lower-paid group. For example, if lower-paid employees as a group contribute an average of 4 percent of salary to the 401(k), highly paid employees can only contribute 6 percent. (The formula is actually more complex, but this example gives you the basic idea.)

The *Safe Harbor 401(k)* used by some employers doesn't require the nondiscrimination test. You can read more about Safe Harbor plans in Chapter 12.

Highly compensated employees are often referred to as *HCEs*, while lower-paid workers are referred to as *non-HCEs*. We mention these terms so that you'll be familiar with them should you encounter them. However, we try to spare you from having to wade through too many acronyms in this book.

The key question is: How much do you have to earn to qualify as "highly compensated"? The rules are pretty tricky. If you earn less than $85,000 and you don't own more than 5 percent of your company (and you aren't related to, or married to, anyone who does), you aren't highly compensated. If that's the case for you, feel free to skip this section. Otherwise, keep reading — but do a few jumping jacks first to make sure that you're fully alert.

You're considered highly compensated in a given year if you own more than 5 percent of your company in that year or the previous year. You may also be considered highly compensated in a given year if you earned more than a specified salary in the previous year. Here's a concrete example. You'd be considered an HCE in 2002 if you owned more than 5 percent of your company in either 2001 or 2002. Also, you *may* be considered an HCE in 2002 if your salary in 2001 was more than $85,000. (We say "may" because a possible exception exists for the salary rule. See the "Exception to highly paid dollar limit" sidebar in this chapter for details.) For 2003, the dollar limit goes up. You'll be an HCE in 2003 if you own more than 5 percent of your company in 2002 or 2003, and you *may* be an HCE in 2003 if you earn more than $90,000 in 2002. (Hey, we never said this stuff was easy.)

Exception to highly paid dollar limit

If you earn more than the HCE salary limit, you still may not be considered an HCE even if your company has a lot of highly paid employees. A company is allowed to limit its designated HCEs to only the top 20 percent of employees. So, for example, if 40 percent of employees at your company earned more than the $90,000 dollar limit in 2002, your company could choose to designate only the top-paid 20 percent of non-excludable employees as HCEs who may have their contributions capped or receive refunds in 2003. This flexibility doesn't exist with the ownership rule, though. If you own more than 5 percent of the company in 2002 or 2003, you'll be considered an HCE for 2003.

Calculating an HCE refund

If your plan fails the nondiscrimination test during any year, refunds will probably be made. The system for determining who gets a refund, and how much it is, is somewhat complicated. First the plan has to determine how far the highly compensated employees were over the limit. Say the lower-paid employees in the plan contributed 4 percent on average, and there are three highly compensated employees in the plan. One of the highly compensated employees contributed 8 percent, one contributed 7 percent, and one contributed 6 percent. Their average contribution is 7 percent, which is 1 percent too high. (Because the lower-paid employees contributed 4 percent, the highly compensated employees are limited to 6 percent.)

The HCE who contributed the largest dollar amount (rather than highest percentage of pay) is the first to get a refund. This rule can cause tension among highly compensated employees, because the one who caused the plan to fail by contributing 8 percent isn't the one who has to take a refund.

If you're highly compensated, your contributions will likely be limited to bring your combined contributions down to an acceptable level (in other words, in line with lower-compensated employees).

Say you're highly compensated and you want to contribute 10 percent for a year in which HCE contributions have to be capped at 6 percent. If your plan is on the ball, you'll find out about the problem early and have your contributions capped at 6 percent.

By the way, there's another way your employer can resolve this problem. Your employer can give an extra contribution to some or all of the lower-paid employees to make up for the discrepancy. This contribution is called a *QMAC (qualified matching contribution)* or *QNEC (qualified nonelective contribution)*. If you receive one of these contributions, it must be vested right away. This option is less popular among employers, because it costs them extra and it's complicated. (Go figure, right?)

There's another limit that may come into play (if you're our one reader who earns more than $200,000). You're not allowed to make 401(k) contributions or receive employer contributions based on more than $200,000 in compensation for 2002. So, if you earn $220,000 and contribute 5 percent of salary, your contributions have to stop at $10,000 (5 percent of $200,000) instead of $11,000 (5 percent of $220,000). Any employer match would apply to the $10,000, as well.

Estimating what your budget can afford

Talking about how much you're allowed to put into the plan is fine, but what about how much you can *afford* to put into the plan? If money is tight, you may be tempted to wait and start saving "in a couple of years" when you're earning more or have less debt. The problem with that strategy is that the longer you wait to start saving, the harder it gets psychologically. You get used to spending the money you have. Also, by waiting to participate, you lose a lot of potential savings.

The following example (also illustrated in Figure 3-2) shows how you can cheat yourself big time by waiting just a few years to start saving.

Ken, Rasheed, and Lisa all earn $25,000 a year. They all decide to contribute 5 percent of their salary, or $1,250, to their 401(k) plans, but over different periods of time. Assuming that each has an average *annual return* (how much the money increases in value when it's invested) of 8 percent, look at the surprising results:

- ✔ Ken waits eight years to begin saving. In years 9 through 30, he contributes a total of $27,500 to the plan ($1,250 × 22 years), and his account balance grows to $71,827. (The extra comes from his 8 percent return, which is reinvested in the account each year without being taxed.)

- ✔ Rasheed starts saving right away, but he stops after eight years. He contributes only $10,000 to the plan ($1,250 × 8 years), but because he started earlier, his money has more time to grow through the magic of compounding. He ends up with $74,897 — $3,000 more than Ken after 30 years.

- ✔ Lisa saves for the entire 30 years. She contributes only $10,000 more than Ken, in total (over the eight years when Ken doesn't contribute), but her $37,500 contribution grows to $146,724 — twice that of Ken's, because her money benefited from compounding for a longer period of time.

You can see that it pays to start saving early and to keep saving. In this example, each person is saving a little more than $100 per month. If that seems like too much for you now, consider contributing a smaller amount. Sometimes that's the best way to get started. For example, consider saving $10 per week, or $520 a year. You can save $10 while only reducing your take-home pay by about $8 per week, because you save the $10 before paying taxes, while you get your take-home pay after paying taxes. Just about anyone who's earning more than $20,000 can probably find a way to save $8 a week. If you keep a record of your nonessential spending for just one week, you may find that eliminating one or two things is easy. (In Chapter 4, we suggest ways to "find" money to save if you're on a tight budget.)

Remember that even a small amount of savings makes a big difference over time. That $10 per week invested for 35 years with an 8 percent return will eventually be worth about $90,000! Any employer matching contribution will increase this amount (see the section "Getting the most from your employer matching contribution" later in this chapter for more info). This amount probably won't be enough to live on during all of your retirement years, but it will certainly be a big help.

After you start saving, your goal should be to increase your savings rate each year. Perhaps the easiest way to do this is to save more each time you get a raise. Assume that you start by contributing 1 percent of your pay, and you receive a 4 percent pay increase. Use part of the raise to increase your 401(k) contribution rate to 2 percent. Keep doing this each time you get a raise, until you reach a point where your savings plus any employer contribution is likely to provide an adequate level of retirement income. (We give guidelines in Chapter 4.)

Advantages of Starting to Save Early Through a 401(k) Plan

Year	A) KEN waits 8 years to start saving		B) RASHEED starts saving early, quits after 8 years		C) LISA starts saving early and keeps at it!		What you invest and what you earn
	Annual Investment	Year end value @ 8%	Annual Investment	Year end value @ 8%	Annual Investment	Year end value @ 8%	**A – started late** 22 years @ $1,250
1	$0	$0	$1,250	$1,295	$1,250	$1,295	Total saved $71,827
2	0	0	1,250	2,694	1,250	2,694	Amount invested 27,500
3	0	0	1,250	4,205	1,250	4,205	Investment return 44,327
4	0	0	1,250	5,836	1,250	5,836	
5	0	0	1,250	7,598	1,250	7,598	**B – started early** 8 years @ $1,250
6	0	0	1,250	9,501	1,250	9,501	Total saved $71,827
7	0	0	1,250	11,557	1,250	11,557	Amount invested 27,500
8	0	0	1,250	13,777	1,250	13,777	Investment return 44,327
9	1,250	1,295	0	14,879	1,250	16,174	
10	1,250	2,694	0	16,069	1,250	18,763	**C – started early & continued**
15	1,250	11,557	0	23,611	1,250	35,167	30 years @ $1,250
20	1,250	24,579	0	34,692	1,250	59,271	Total saved $71,827
25	1,250	43,713	0	50,973	1,250	94,687	Amount invested 27,500
30	1,250	71,827	0	74,897	1,250	146,724	Investment return 44,327

The figures indicated reflect employee contributions only. In this example, investment return is calculated at 8%. Your own 401(k) investment return may be higher or lower, depending on the performance of the funds offered and how you invested the money in your account.

Figure 3-2: Payoffs of saving early in a 401(k).

Bonus for low- and moderate-income savers

Congress approved an extra tax break to encourage low- and moderate-income earners to save with 401(k)s and other retirement accounts. This tax credit is available in tax years starting with 2002 and continuing through (including) 2006. You may qualify if you're single and have taxable income of $25,000 or less, or if you're married and have joint taxable income of $50,000 or less. If this applies to you, you can claim a *non-refundable tax credit* for your contributions up to a certain amount. What does that mean? You can subtract a percentage of your contribution to your 401(k) from your tax bill, as well as lower your taxable income, by making the contribution. (Contributions to an IRA, 403(b), or 457 may also qualify for this tax credit.)

Here are the limits for the tax credit.

If you're single and have an adjusted gross income (AGI) of ...	Or married filing jointly with an AGI of ...	Subtract this percent of your contribution (up to $2,000) from your tax bill
$0–$15,000	$0–$30,000	50%
$15,001–$16,250	$30,001–$32,500	20%
$16,251–$25,000	$32,501–$50,000	10%

Your *adjusted gross income (AGI)* is your gross income minus deductions that you're allowed to list before you take off your itemized or standard personal deduction (for example, deductible IRA contributions, student loan interest payments, and so on). It is clearly marked at the bottom of the first page of your tax form.

The actual calculation of the tax credit has a few more rules that apply. Also, the amount of your tax credit may be further reduced by any plan withdrawals you (or your spouse) may receive (or have received in the past two years).

Joining is probably the most important decision you'll make regarding your 401(k) plan. Everything else is irrelevant if you don't start contributing to the plan.

Getting the most from your employer matching contribution

When you consider how much you need to save, don't forget about your employer's matching contribution. (See Chapter 2 for details on employer matching contributions and when they vest, or become yours to keep.) The amount of money you receive from your employer depends on how much you contribute, so it makes sense to contribute enough to get the most possible.

Timing is everything

How you time your contributions is important. Some people like to contribute more to their 401(k) early in the year to ensure that they reach the maximum before, say, having to think about buying holiday gifts at the end of the year. This is sometimes referred to as *front-loading* the 401(k). The potential problem with this strategy is that it can cause you to lose some of your employer match. Before you decide to go with this strategy, ask your employer about its timing for depositing matching contributions. Many employers only make these deposits during the pay periods when you contribute to the plan because it's easier for them. If this is how your plan works, you'll lose out by front-loading.

For example, say your employer matches 50¢ on the dollar, up to 6 percent of your salary. If you earn $80,000, and you contribute at least $4,800 (6 percent of your salary), you should receive an employer match of $2,400.

Now, say you want to contribute the full $12,000 permitted in 2003, and you want to do it early in the year. You fill out your form indicating that you want to contribute 20 percent of your pay every pay period. You're not allowed to contribute $16,000 to a 401(k), so you'll be forced to stop contributing partway through the year when you reach the $12,000 limit. (You'll get there after you've earned $60,000, because 20 percent of $60,000 is $12,000.) Say your employer stops making matching contributions then, because you're no longer making contributions at that time. You will have received only 3 percent of $60,000 in matching contributions, or $1,800, which is lower than the $2,400 you would've received if you had spread out your contributions evenly over the year. By using this strategy, you lose $600 of employer contributions.

In this case, it makes more sense to reduce your contribution rate so that you contribute for the entire year and still hit the $12,000 limit. In this instance, 15 percent would be the percentage to use (15 percent of $80,000 equals $12,000).

See how important it is to find out how your employer makes the matching contribution and to ask if you're receiving the greatest amount of matching contributions on what you contribute?

Your employer sets the rate at which it will match your contributions, along with the limit for how much it will match and the vesting schedule for the employer contributions. The match rate may be as little as 10¢ (or less) for each dollar you contribute, or as much as one dollar for each dollar you contribute, up to a percentage of your salary. The most common matching rates are 25¢ and 50¢ for each dollar you contribute, usually up to 6 percent of your salary. Some employers match dollar-for-dollar, and a few have even higher matches.

If you can't afford to contribute the full amount matched by your employer now, start with a lower percentage and increase your contribution rate as soon as possible to reach the full amount. You don't have to stop there, either. It always makes sense to contribute as much as you possibly can.

If you're married, you and your spouse should each contribute the maximum amount required to get the full match in your plans. If you can't afford to do so, you may want to see which plan has the higher match and best vesting schedule. You can then decide who's likely to stay long enough to qualify for the vested employer contributions and consider pooling your contributions to that plan to get the full match. You may also want to consider which plan has better investment options, and, if you expect to tap your 401(k) plan resources in the future, which one permits in-service withdrawals or loans. (Read more about these options in Chapter 7.) You can then contribute more to the plan that offers the best options.

There's no delicate way to put this, so we'll be blunt. If you think there's a chance that you won't stay married, you may be better off continuing to fund your own 401(k) to the extent possible rather than putting some of your money toward your spouse's 401(k) plan. Divvying up retirement accounts after a divorce can be tricky.

Deciding How to Invest Your Money

After you decide how much to invest, you need to decide where to invest your money. Your enrollment papers will likely include something called an *investment election form* (see Figure 3-3), which lists the investment options offered by your 401(k) plan. You need to specify what percentage of your contribution should go into each option you choose.

The percentages on your investment election form must add up to 100 percent.

If you're not sure right away what to invest in, don't use that as an excuse to put off signing up for the plan. At a minimum, find out if your plan offers a money market fund. A *money market fund* generally earns some interest and is the least likely to lose value, so it's a good short-term investment, but it doesn't have as good a potential for long-term growth as stocks or bonds. Until you decide on a plan for investing your money, you can have your contributions deposited into a money market option. (You can read more about how to select investments in Chapter 6.)

SECTION III - Investment Election

I choose to invest all contributions to my account in **whole percentages totaling 100%** as follows:

Investment Option	Investment %
Short-term bond fund	
All-bond index fund	
S&P 500 stock index fund	
Wilshire 5000 stock index fund	
Large-cap growth stock fund	
Large-cap value stock fund	
Mid-cap blended stock fund	
Small-cap stock index fund	
Small -cap blended fund (growth and value blend)	
Emerging markets growth stock fund (growth oriented)	
Emerging markets value stock fund	
International stock index fund	
International large-cap blended stock fund	
Money market fund	
Total	**100%**

Figure 3-3: Sample 401(k) investment election form.

Ask your employer how often you can change your fund elections. After you do your research, decide on an investment plan and then fill out a form to change your fund elections the next time it's possible.

Naming a Beneficiary

Another form you have to fill out is the *beneficiary designation.* This is where you list the person or people whom you wish to receive the money in your account if you die.

The 401(k) beneficiary form that you file with your employer is the primary instrument that determines who receives your plan benefit if you die. A will or trust won't control distribution of the 401(k). If you don't name a beneficiary, or the beneficiary you name isn't living when you die, the provisions in the plan document determine who gets the money. This may not be the person you intended the money to go to. Therefore, filling out the beneficiary form and keeping it up-to-date is very important.

You'll probably be able to name both a primary and a secondary beneficiary (or beneficiaries). The primary beneficiary will receive your 401(k) money if he or she is living at the time of your death. If not, your secondary beneficiary receives the money. You should be able to name more than one primary and/or secondary beneficiary. If you do name more than one, you have to specify what percentage of the account each should receive. Figure 3-4 shows what this form may look like.

SECTION I Beneficiary Designation				
Participant SHOULD complete A and B below to designate specific beneficiary(ies).				

A. **Beneficiary Designation (Please Print)**

Primary Beneficiary(ies) - In the event of my death, I hereby designate as my primary beneficiary(ies):

Beneficiary Name	Social Security No.	Date of Birth	Relationship	% Share
				Total 100%

Secondary Beneficiary(ies) - In the event my primary beneficiary(ies) should predecease me, I designate as my secondary beneficiary(ies):

Secondary Beneficiary Name	Social Security No.	Date of Birth	Relationship	% Share
				Total 100%

Signed _____ Date of this designation: _____

Participant

Figure 3-4: Sample 401(k) beneficiary designation form.

Your spouse: The go-to person

By law, your spouse automatically receives your 401(k) benefit when you die, regardless of whom you named as your beneficiary, unless your spouse signs a *benefit waiver* that is witnessed by a notary or a plan representative. (This benefit waiver form should also be in your enrollment packet.)

One of the questions Ted has received regarding the spousal waiver is what to do if you're legally married but your spouse is nowhere to be found. If you're in this situation, name your children or someone else as your beneficiary — but be aware that your spouse still has legal rights to claim your 401(k) benefit.

Another question is whether a waiver that's part of a pre-nuptial agreement will suffice. The answer isn't clear. By law, the waiver must be signed by the spouse. An individual is not a spouse before actually getting married. As a result, the spouse (*after* the wedding ceremony) can contest the prenuptial waiver (that he or she signed *before* the wedding ceremony). Ain't love grand?

Your children

If you have minor children whom you want to name as beneficiaries or secondary beneficiaries, consider naming a trust instead, for their benefit. Doing so can help avoid the legal complications that may arise when money is left directly to minor children.

A *trust* will hold the money until the date you've established for it to be distributed. The trustee will be responsible for overseeing the trust assets, including investing the funds until they're distributed. If you have minor children and have a will, it probably includes trust provisions that can be used for this purpose. A trust may also be advisable if you have a large account and don't want your children to get all the money when they reach age 18.

Payment can be made directly to adult children.

Reviewing your choices

Whenever your marital status changes, you need to review your beneficiary designation. For example, you may be single when you join the plan. If you marry, your new spouse automatically becomes your beneficiary, regardless of who's named on the form you previously filed with your employer. This is fine if you want your spouse to receive the benefit, but it isn't if you want someone else, such as your children, to receive the benefit. Remember that your new spouse remains as the primary beneficiary unless he or she signs a spousal waiver.

Part II
Finding an Investment Strategy That Lets You Sleep at Night

The 5th Wave   By Rich Tennant

In this part . . .

The best exercise routine you've ever had probably worked because it was right for *you* — you enjoyed the exercises and were able to work them into your daily schedule. You may not have become Arnold Schwarzenegger or Suzanne Somers, but you kept fit. Meanwhile, your neighbor may have invested in fancy clothing, equipment, or a health club membership for exercises that he hated and quit after a month. Although he had the best intentions, he's now back at square one, while you're steadily achieving your goal of fitness.

Retirement planning is similar. If you take the time to develop a plan that suits you and your personality, you'll have the best chance of meeting your goals for retirement. The key is finding a happy medium between spending everything today and saving nothing for the future, and putting away so much for the future that you don't have fun today. This part aims to help you find this happy medium.

Chapter 4

Developing a Savings Plan

● ●

In This Chapter

▶ Deciding when to retire

▶ Figuring out how much money you'll need and where it will come from

▶ Calculating how much to save in order to reach retirement

● ●

Spontaneity can be a lot of fun. But it's the last thing you want when you're planning for retirement. Saving for retirement involves delayed gratification, planning, and discipline, but today's sound-bite society may find this news hard to swallow. Luckily, tools like a 401(k) can help make the process less painful, because a lot of the saving is automatic after you set up the plan.

If you're young, you may wonder whether it's too soon to plan for something that's 30 or 40 years away. The truth is that the earlier you start, the better, because your savings will have more time to build up through compounding (as the earnings on money in your account continue to earn even more money). Starting to save early will give you more freedom later to decide what you want to do.

On the other hand, if you're already in your 40s or older, you may wonder whether it's too late for you to plan. The bottom line is that it's never too late. But you may find that you need to scale back some of your goals or increase the amount you save each year. This chapter aims to help you set and meet retirement goals and develop a detailed plan for achieving them. It walks you through the steps of deciding on a target date to retire, calculating how much income you'll need in retirement, developing a savings plan to achieve that amount of income, and tracking your progress as you save over the years.

Setting a Target Date for Retirement

The first step in planning for retirement is deciding when you want to retire. This can be trickier than it sounds. Attitudes about what retirement means and when it should happen have been changing over the last decade or two.

It used to be clear-cut — you worked until you were 65 (or maybe 62), and then you were forced to retire with a gold watch and a pension. Social Security checks started arriving in the mail soon after your 65th birthday. Nowadays, things are different. There's no standard retirement age that applies to everyone and every type of account. Consider the following:

- If you were born in 1960 or later, you'll only be able to take full Social Security benefits when you turn 67, rather than when you turn the traditional age of 65.

- You're *allowed* to withdraw money from your 401(k) without penalty at age 59½ (or age 55 if you leave your employer).

- You're *required* to start withdrawing money from your 401(k) when you're 70½ — unless, that is, you're still working for the company sponsoring the 401(k). Then you can wait until you retire to take out your money, unless you own more than 5 percent of the business.

Whew! With all those different ages, how can you know when to retire?

For the purposes of planning, you need to estimate when you'll have to start withdrawing the money in your retirement accounts, and whether that money will be supporting you entirely, or whether you'll have other sources of income.

Choosing an age now can help you plan how much you need to save and how much time you have in which to save it (your *time horizon*, in financial planning lingo). The advantage of estimating a retirement age now is that you can see whether that goal is reasonable. If it's not, you may have to rethink it. The key is to remain flexible.

In choosing a target date for retirement, you need to consider several factors, including

- When you can access your various sources of retirement income
- What you'll do when you retire
- Whether living to the age of 100 runs in your family

Determining when you can access retirement income

When you retire and no longer earn a paycheck, you'll need to get income from somewhere. If you plan well, that income should be available from several sources.

Social Security

The first source of income that you'll have during retirement is *Social Security,* the federal government's social insurance program that includes monthly benefit payments to retirees. Every worker who earns enough credits (by working) will be eligible for Social Security benefits in retirement.

Many people mistakenly think that they'll start receiving Social Security checks when they turn 65. In fact, for anyone born after 1938, the age to receive full Social Security benefits (called the *normal retirement age*) will be at least a couple of months past their 65th birthday. If you were born in 1960 or later, you won't be eligible for full Social Security benefits until your 67th birthday.

You can choose to receive reduced benefits at age 62 (even if you were born in 1960 or later). If you retire at age 62, your benefits will be reduced to 80 percent of the full benefit if 65 is your normal retirement age, and 70 percent of the full benefit if 67 is your normal retirement age. Keep in mind that you'll always receive the reduced benefits if you retire at age 62; they won't increase when you reach your normal retirement age.

Table 4-1 shows the full retirement age for different birth years after 1937.

**Table 4-1   Social Security Full Retirement Age and
Reduction in Benefits for Early Retirement**

Year of Birth (If you were born on Jan. 1, refer to the previous year)	Full Retirement Age	Total Reduction in Benefits if You Retire at 62 (in %)
1937 or earlier	65	20.00
1938	65 and 2 months	20.83
1939	65 and 4 months	21.67
1940	65 and 6 months	22.50
1941	65 and 8 months	23.33
1942	65 and 10 months	24.17
1943–1954	66	25.00
1955	66 and 2 months	25.84
1956	66 and 4 months	26.66
1957	66 and 6 months	27.50
1958	66 and 8 months	28.33
1959	66 and 10 months	29.17
1960 and later	67	30.00

Source: Social Security Administration Web site (www.ssa.gov).

In sum, you can't expect to receive any retirement benefits from Social Security before age 62, and you can increase the amount you receive if you wait until 65, 66, or 67 (whatever your "normal retirement age"), or even 70.

A few years ago, the Social Security Administration (SSA) began mailing annual statements to workers who are over 25 years old. These statements estimate how much money they'd receive monthly at age 62, at full retirement age, and at age 70, based on their income to date. If you threw yours away or can't find it, you can contact the SSA for a new one at www.ssa.gov/mystatement/. Or if you prefer not to send personal information over the Internet, you can download a form that you mail in to request the statement. You can also request the form by telephone, at 1-800-772-1213, or by appearing in person at your local Social Security office. The mailing address is on the form.

Social insecurity?

Social Security is what's known as a "pay-as-you-go" system. When you pay Social Security taxes out of your paycheck, the taxes don't go into an "account" in your name. The taxes go to pay the benefits of today's retired folks. In the same way, today's toddlers and teenagers will be supporting you one day — hopefully. But as the 76-million-strong Baby Boom generation starts turning 65 in 2011 (and doesn't stop until 2029), a tremendous strain will be placed on the system. In 1945 there were an estimated 41.9 workers for every retiree. By 1999, the ratio dropped to an estimated 3.4 workers for every retiree. By about 2030, the ratio is expected to drop to two workers for every retiree. Clearly, something will have to give.

The Social Security program is projected to begin running a deficit around 2017. In 2002, the U.S. government estimated that the trust fund would run out of money completely in 2041 if nothing were done to shore it up.

You can factor the estimated benefit amount into your planned retirement income, but remember that Social Security was never meant to be your only source of retirement income. What's more, the future of Social Security is somewhat uncertain. Although Social Security benefits may not disappear completely during the next 20 to 30 years, they may be reduced.

Other sources

Now, what about your other sources of income during retirement? The following list highlights possible retirement resources above and beyond Social Security:

- ✔ **401(k):** As long as you're working for the employer that sponsors the plan, you generally can't take money out before you're 59½. If your plan does permit you to withdraw money, you'll have to pay taxes and an extra early withdrawal penalty on the money you take out. If you leave your job at age 55 or older, you can withdraw the money without any penalty tax, but you still have to pay income tax. You can also roll it over into an IRA, as we explain in Chapter 8.

- ✔ **Other tax-favored retirement accounts:** Accounts similar to a 401(k), such as a 403(b) or IRA, have rules similar to those of 401(k)s. Generally, you shouldn't count on having easy access to your money before age 59½, or possibly age 55. The rules are different for 457 "deferred-comp" plans. (We explain 403(b) plans in Chapter 10, and 457 plans in Chapter 11.)

  In some circumstances, you may be able to get at your retirement account money before age 55 without paying an early withdrawal penalty. (We cover this in Chapter 8.)

✔ **Traditional defined-benefit pension plan:** If your employer offers one of these plans (see Chapter 2 for specifics), your human resources or benefits representative should be able to tell you what your expected payment will be if you qualify to receive benefits.

✔ **Life insurance:** Some people buy a type of life insurance policy that allows them to build up a cash account (a *cash value* policy) rather than buy term life insurance, which is worth nothing after you stop making payments. If you have a cash value policy (such as whole life or variable life), it should have a cash account that you can tap at retirement.

✔ **Regular taxable savings:** A taxable account is any kind of account (such as a bank account, mutual fund account, or stock brokerage account) that doesn't have special tax advantages.

✔ **Part-time work:** No matter when you retire, you may want to take a part-time job that will keep you active and give you extra income.

✔ **Inherited wealth:** You shouldn't count on any inheritance until you actually receive it. But if you do inherit a substantial amount of money, integrate at least part of it into your overall financial plan to give yourself a higher retirement income.

If you plan to retire before age 65, don't forget to factor in the cost of medical insurance. The availability and cost of medical care is a major issue if you plan to retire before you and your spouse are eligible for *Medicare,* the government-sponsored medical program for those age 65 and older.

You can take the first step toward figuring out when it'll be feasible to retire by writing down on a piece of paper your sources of income and when you can access them.

Figuring out what you'll do when you retire

Assume that your retirement begins tomorrow. What will your life be like? This is the necessary question that retirement calculators don't ask. Most importantly, what will you do six months after the novelty of retirement wears off, when you're tired of golfing, shopping, traveling, or just being a couch potato? Many people find it difficult to go straight from full-time work to full retirement — particularly when they haven't developed interests outside of work.

According to the Employee Benefit Research Institute's 2002 Retirement Confidence Survey, 24 percent of retirees said that they had worked at least sporadically since retiring. Of those, more than half said that the reason they continued to work was that they enjoy working and want to stay involved. About 25 percent of them said that they worked to keep health insurance or other benefits, while 22 percent said that they wanted money to buy extras.

Having an idea of what you'll do in retirement is important so that you can avoid these common mistakes:

- ✔ Retiring too early, realizing that your money isn't going to last, and being forced to go back to work. In the meantime, you've lost out on contributing more to your 401(k) — and possible employer contributions, as well.

- ✔ Retiring, becoming totally bored within six months, and begging for your old job back.

Keeping the family gene pool in mind

When you think about the age at which you want to retire and how long you'll need to finance your retirement, keep your genes in mind. If you have a history of longevity in your family, you should plan financially to live until 100. (If you're the cautious type, you may want to do this anyway, even if you don't think there's a chance you'll live that long.)

Calculating How Big Your Nest Egg Should Be

After you decide when to retire, your next step is to consider how you'll feel when you're retired and no longer have a paycheck. You'll probably need close to 100 percent of your income in the year before you retire in order to maintain your standard of living.

How much savings will it take to provide this level of income? The answer is "a lot."

Ted recommends trying to save 10 times the income that you expect to earn in the year before you retire. This formula is a good starting point if you plan to retire at your Social Security normal retirement age (65, 66, or 67). If you plan to retire earlier, you'll need to save more. If you have a company pension or other sources of income, or if you retire later, you may be able to get away with saving a bit less.

What goes up — or inflation-adjusted income

What is inflation-adjusted income? *Inflation* is the rate at which prices increase over time. When you plan for the future, you have to plan for prices to go up, otherwise your money will run out too soon. Inflation-adjusted income essentially refers to the *purchasing power* of your money — what your bucks can buy. It means that if over the next 25 years you want to be able to buy what will cost $30,000 today, you'll need actual dollar amounts that are higher than $30,000.

You can't know for sure what the inflation rate will be. You need to make an assumption. We use 3 percent, which is on the low side from a historical perspective but, we believe, realistic for long-range planning.

The following table shows how much income is needed to keep the buying power of $10,000 over the years. (Using $10,000 makes it easy to adjust to whatever income you think will be right for your situation.) For example, you can calculate that you'll need $60,984 in the 25th year of your retirement to buy what $30,000 will buy in the first year ($20,328 × 3).

Number of years after you retire	Annual income needed	Number of years after you retire	Annual income needed
1	$10,000	14	$14,685
2	$10,300	15	$15,126
3	$10,609	16	$15,580
4	$10,927	17	$16,047
5	$11,255	18	$16,528
6	$11,593	19	$17,024
7	$11,941	20	$17,535
8	$12,299	21	$18,061
9	$12,668	22	$18,603
10	$13,048	23	$19,161
11	$13,439	24	$19,736
12	$13,842	25	$20,328
13	$14,258		

If you're retiring in the near future

Assume that you're retiring at the end of this year, and your salary for this year is $50,000. According to Ted's benchmark, you should save $500,000 to hit the "10-times" goal.

Sound like a lot of money? It is, but it would provide approximately $30,000 a year of *inflation-adjusted income* (see the sidebar "What goes up — or inflation-adjusted income" in this chapter for more information) over 25 years, assuming

- ✔ The rate of inflation is 3 percent.

- ✔ Only a small cushion will remain at the end of 25 years.

- ✔ You invest 50 percent of your nest egg in stocks and 50 percent in bonds during this period.

A yearly income of $30,000 may not sound like much, but remember that your taxes will be lower when you retire, and you won't need to save income for retirement anymore. Your expenses will likely be less than when you were working. Your income should also be supplemented by your taxable savings and Social Security, as well as any of the other sources listed earlier in the chapter, giving you an adequate level of retirement income.

If your retirement is farther off

We can hear you calling, "Hey, a little help over here. . . . I'm not retiring tomorrow, so how do I know how much I'll be earning the year before I retire?" Not to worry. Table 4-2, Ted's Inflation Adjustment Table, is here to help.

Table 4-2	Inflation Adjustment Table				
Number of Years	*Assumed Annual Rate of Change*				
	3%	*3.5%*	*4%*	*4.5%*	*5%*
1	1.03	1.035	1.04	1.045	1.05
2	1.06	1.07	1.08	1.09	1.10
3	1.09	1.11	1.12	1.14	1.16
4	1.12	1.15	1.17	1.19	1.22
5	1.16	1.19	1.22	1.25	1.28

(continued)

Table 4-2 *(continued)*

Number of Years	Assumed Annual Rate of Change				
6	1.19	1.23	1.27	1.30	1.34
7	1.23	1.27	1.32	1.36	1.41
8	1.27	1.32	1.37	1.42	1.48
9	1.31	1.36	1.42	1.49	1.55
10	1.34	1.41	1.48	1.55	1.63
11	1.38	1.46	1.54	1.62	1.71
12	1.42	1.51	1.60	1.70	1.80
13	1.46	1.56	1.67	1.77	1.89
14	1.51	1.62	1.73	1.85	1.98
15	1.56	1.68	1.80	1.93	2.08
16	1.60	1.74	1.87	2.02	2.18
17	1.65	1.80	1.95	2.11	2.29
18	1.70	1.86	2.02	2.21	2.41
19	1.75	1.93	2.10	2.31	2.53
20	1.80	1.99	2.19	2.41	2.65
21	1.86	2.06	2.28	2.52	2.79
22	1.91	2.13	2.37	2.63	2.93
23	1.97	2.21	2.46	2.75	3.08
24	2.03	2.29	2.56	2.87	3.23
25	2.09	2.37	2.66	3.00	3.39
26	2.15	2.45	2.77	3.14	3.56
27	2.22	2.53	2.88	3.28	3.74
28	2.28	2.62	3.00	3.43	3.92
29	2.35	2.72	3.12	3.58	4.12
30	2.42	2.81	3.24	3.74	4.33

Assume that you're 41, and you want to retire when you're 62. You need to project your current income to what you think you'll be earning 20 years from now (at age 61, the year before you retire).

Decide on an average rate that you expect your income to increase — say 3 percent. Go down the Number of Years column (refer to Table 4-2) to 20, and over to the 3% column, where you see the factor of 1.80. Multiply your current income, say $50,000, by 1.8, and you'll see that your expected income at retirement is $90,000. Using the 10-times rule, your desired nest egg becomes $900,000 (10 × $90,000). This is an easy way to get a rough idea of how big a retirement account to build — regardless of your current age or income.

Using a retirement calculator

Another way to develop a workable retirement plan is by using one of the many retirement calculators and other tools available on the Internet or through the financial organization that handles your 401(k) money. Remember that each calculator uses different methods and assumptions, so different calculators can produce widely varying results. Check the assumptions each calculator uses to see if they make sense for your situation.

Here are some of the better general calculators we've seen:

- ✔ www.quicken.com/retirement/planner
- ✔ http://cgi.money.cnn.com/tools/retirementplanner/retirementplanner.jsp
- ✔ www.asec.org/ballpark/index.htm
- ✔ www.smartmoney.com/retirement (use the various "Retirement Worksheets")

The major benefit of using a retirement calculator is that it gives you an investment reality check. Will the amount that you're saving and the investment mix enable you to accumulate what you need? A good retirement calculator will answer this question and also help you decide how to close any savings gaps. Generally, you can close a gap by increasing your contributions, adjusting your investments to achieve a higher long-term return, or a combination of the two.

Some independent companies like mPower, Financial Engines, and Morningstar are excellent sources of retirement planning information and calculations. They go farther than simple calculators and actually give you specific advice on how to invest money in your 401(k) plan and other retirement accounts. We discuss this type of assistance more in Chapter 6.

In the meantime, here's where you can find mPower, Financial Engines, and Morningstar on the Internet.

- ✔ **mPower:** www.mpower.com
- ✔ **Financial Engines:** www.financialengines.com
- ✔ **Morningstar:** www.morningstar.com

Developing Your Retirement Savings Plan

After you recover from the shock of how much you'll need in your retirement account, your first thought will probably be, "How on earth do I accumulate ten times my annual income — and then some — by the time I retire?"

The key is to start as early as you can, because the earlier you start saving, the longer your money has to benefit from compounding, even if you only start by putting away small amounts.

Cutting down on your expenses

We realize that many workers barely earn enough to pay for basic necessities and can't eke out anything extra for a 401(k) plan contribution. But it's important to try. Or you may be in your 40s and want to save more to catch up, but you can't figure out where to find the money. You may be surprised at some of the places you can save money. Often, a few minor spending adjustments can free up money for savings.

Like most everything, it all boils down to making choices. Table 4-3 lists suggestions for cutting your spending. None of the expenses listed are necessities — and cutting out one or two, or reducing the cost of a few, can help begin your savings program.

Table 4-3	Ten Tips for Saving Money
Expense	*How to Save*
$1 each day or week for a lottery ticket	If you buy one ticket daily, cut back to one a week. If you buy one a week, cut back to one a month.

Expense	How to Save
$25 a year for a subscription to a magazine you never read	If you have three or four, you're approaching $100. Cancel them.
$25 for a carton of cigarettes	Cut down the number you smoke, or better yet, try to quit. Not only will you save money on cigarettes but your life insurance premiums should go down — not to mention other health-related costs.
$25 for a movie and popcorn for two at a cinema.	Pay $3 to rent a video, or better yet, see what your local library offers for free. Pop some popcorn yourself — it'll probably taste better, anyway.
$5 a day for an alcoholic beverage	Instead of going out every night with your friends, try to cut back to just weekends.
$3 a day for various other beverages of choice (bottled water, soda, coffee, and so on)	Drink what's provided at your office, or buy in bulk and bring it to work.
$5–$10 a day for lunch	Pack your own lunch a few times a week.
A $500 monthly car payment versus a $350 payment	Do you *really* need an SUV with leather seats and GPS?
A $250,000 home versus a $150,000 home	This depends on where you live. In California, add $400,000 to each price.
A $500 vacation versus a $1,000 vacation	Visit attractions close to home to avoid plane fares. Go to places that people would go if they were visiting you.

You're probably wondering whether all this nickel-and-diming is really worth it. We're not suggesting that you give up *everything* on the list — only that you look at what you spend to see if you can cut some costs without feeling too much pain. Giving up a few nonessential items today is far better than struggling *without necessities* during your retirement years.

Ted says he's never met a 401(k) participant who's claimed to have saved too much. He's never heard participants say that they wished they'd spent more money earlier. Instead, what many older participants tell him is that they wish they had started saving sooner.

This may be difficult to believe, but the important thing about money is *not* how much you earn. It's how you manage what you have.

Spenders will always spend what they have or more, regardless of how much they earn. A spender who gets a substantial increase in income will adjust his spending habits to the new level within a very short period of time.

 If you have a tendency to spend, you should automatically take a portion of any pay increase and put it into a 401(k) or similar forced savings vehicle before you get used to having it in your hot little hands. Otherwise, you may never break your spending cycle.

Considering sample plans

After you begin to save, you have to keep checking to make sure that you're on track. Certain benchmarks can generally help you gauge where you should be.

The following savings goals are designed for 25-year-olds just starting their savings programs. If you're over age 25, these benchmarks can still tell you if you're on target with your retirement planning. If you're significantly behind these benchmarks, you're certainly not alone.

Remember that these are ideals; they're not here to make anyone feel defeated. Instead, the intention is to motivate you to sit down and develop a workable plan for catching up. This may mean that you have to work longer than you'd like or substantially increase your savings rate. If you feel depressed looking at these, just be glad you're starting now. If you'd waited, imagine how much more catching up you would have to do!

   ✔ **Savings goal by age 35: One times your pre-retirement income.** Your goal should be to accumulate the amount of your annual income by age 35. Table 4-4 shows what you need to do to accomplish this goal.

Table 4-4	How to Accumulate One Times Your Pre-Retirement Income by Age 35				
Age	Your Pay	Your Contribution	Employer's Contribution	Total Return	Year End Value
25	$25,000	$1,000	$500	$68	$1,568
26	$26,000	$1,300	$650	$229	$3,747

Age	Your Pay	Your Contribution	Employer's Contribution	Total Return	Year End Value
27	$27,040	$1,622	$811	$446	$6,626
28	$28,122	$1,687	$844	$710	$9,867
29	$29,246	$1,755	$878	$1,006	$13,506
30	$30,416	$1,825	$912	$1,339	$17,582
31	$31,633	$1,898	$949	$1,710	$22,139
32	$32,898	$1,974	$987	$2,126	$27,226
33	$34,214	$2,053	$1,026	$2,588	$32,893
34	$35,583	$2,135	$1,067	$3,104	$39,199

The numbers in Table 4-4 are based on the following assumptions:

- Annual pay increases of 4 percent

- Employee contributions of 4 percent of pay the first year, 5 percent the second year, and 6 percent in subsequent years

- Employer matching contribution of 50¢ on the dollar, limited to the first 6 percent of pay that the employee contributes

- An average investment return of 9 percent

The 50 percent employer matching contribution is a big help. You have to adjust your contributions if you're in a plan that has a lower employer contribution or none at all.

✔ **Savings goal by age 45: Three times your pre-retirement income.** Assume that in the next 10 years you increase your contribution rate to 10 percent. You continue to receive a 50 percent match (equivalent to a 3 percent of pay contribution from your employer), your annual pay continues to increase by 4 percent per year, and your investment return is 9 percent per year. Table 4-5 shows the results.

Table 4-5	How to Accumulate Three Times Your Pre-Retirement Income by Age 45				
Age	Your Pay	Your Investment	Employer's Contribution	Total Return	Year End Value
35	$37,006	$3,700	$1,110	$3,744	$47,753
36	$38,487	$3,849	$1,154	$4,523	$57,279
37	$40,026	$4,003	$1,201	$5,389	$67,872
38	$41,627	$4,163	$1,249	$6,351	$79,635
39	$43,292	$4,329	$1,299	$7,420	$92,683
40	$45,024	$4,502	$1,350	$8,604	$107,139
41	$46,825	$4,683	$1,405	$9,917	$123,144
42	$48,698	$4,870	$1,461	$11,368	$140,843
43	$50,646	$5,065	$1,519	$12,973	$160,400
44	$52,672	$5,267	$1,580	$14,744	$181,991

By age 45, you'd be ahead of schedule with an accumulation of more than 3.5 times your annual pay.

✔ **Savings goal by age 55: Seven times your pre-retirement income.** Assume that everything stays the same for the next 10 years — except that you increase your contribution rate from 10 percent to 15 percent at age 50, your annual salary increases by 4 percent per year, and your investment return continues at 9 percent until age 50. The return then drops to 8 percent from age 50 to 55, because you sell some of your more risky stock investments in favor of investments that provide a more stable, but lower, return. Table 4-6 shows the result.

Table 4-6	How to Accumulate Seven Times Your Pre-Retirement Income by Age 55				
Age	Your Pay	Your Investment	Employer's Contribution	Total Return	Year End Value
45	$54,778	$5,478	$1,643	$16,699	$205,811
46	$56,970	$5,697	$1,709	$18,856	$232,073
47	$59,248	$5,925	$1,777	$21,233	$261,008

Age	Your Pay	Your Investment	Employer's Contribution	Total Return	Year End Value
48	$61,618	$6,162	$1,848	$23,851	$292,869
49	$64,083	$6,408	$1,922	$26,733	$327,932
50	$66,646	$9,997	$1,999	$26,714	$366,642
51	$69,312	$10,397	$2,079	$29,828	$408,946
52	$72,085	$10,813	$2,162	$33,235	$455,156
53	$74,968	$11,245	$2,249	$36,952	$505,602
54	$77,967	$11,695	$2,339	$41,571	$561,207

At this point, you will have accumulated 7.2 times your annual pay. As you near retirement, your goal is within reach.

✔ **Savings goal by age 60: Ten times your pre-retirement income.** Assume that your contribution rate remains at 15 percent, your employer's contribution rate remains at 3 percent of your salary, and your pay continues to increase by 4 percent per year. Your investment return remains at 8 percent. Table 4-7 gives you the numbers.

Table 4-7   How to Accumulate 10 Times Your Pre-Retirement Income by Age 60

Age	Your Pay	Your Investment	Employer's Contribution	Total Return	Year End Value
55	$81,085	$12,163	$2,432	$45,480	$621,282
56	$84,329	$12,649	$2,529	$50,311	$686,711
57	$87,702	$13,155	$2,631	$55,573	$758,130
58	$91,210	$13,682	$2,736	$61,307	$835,855
59	$94,858	$14,229	$2,845	$67,551	$920,480
60	$98,652	$14,798	$2,960	$74,348	$1,012,586

At this point, you should be in a good position to consider various alternatives — including retirement, working fewer hours at your current job, or shifting to some other income-producing activity that interests you.

These projections are based on assumptions that may differ considerably from your actual experience. Take all these figures as guidelines to help you understand the important features of investing for retirement.

Sticking with your retirement savings plan for the long haul

The purpose of the previous sample plans is to show you how a specific plan gives you a tangible way to measure your progress each year. It's helpful for you to know some assumptions in the previous savings goal examples:

- ✔ Money is saved for retirement every year. You should even add to your retirement savings during periods that you're not eligible to contribute to a 401(k).

- ✔ All the money is left in the plan until retirement. None of the money is withdrawn for other purposes.

- ✔ The assumed return requires at least 60 to 70 percent in stock investments (mutual funds or a diversified mix of individual stocks) up to age 55. After age 55, the stock holdings drop to the 50 to 60 percent range. (We explain more about this in Chapter 6.)

Your retirement nest egg comes from your own contributions and your employer's contributions, and the investment return that's earned on these contributions. Table 4-8 shows this final breakdown among the three sources, using the example of savings progress at age 60 from the previous section.

Table 4-8	Account Breakdown by Source
Source	*Amount*
Employee contributions	$226,173
Employer contributions	$57,812
Investment return	$728,601
TOTAL	$1,012,586

You've probably heard about the magic of *compounded growth* — a term used to explain how money can grow over time. It's very real, but this magic is significant only over long periods of time —

20 to 30 years or longer. This is why starting to save at an early age and sticking with your program is so important. If you wait 10 years before you start, you'll substantially reduce your investment return. The difference can be made up only by a much larger savings rate or by working and saving longer.

Figure 4-1 looks at the cost of waiting to save $1,000 a year. See how much more the person who starts at age 25 ends up with than the one who waits until age 35.

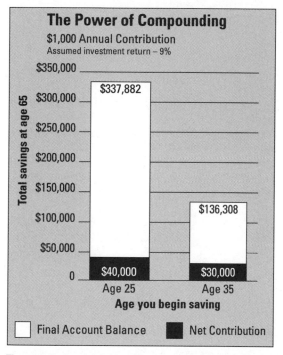

Figure 4-1: A quick look at the importance of compounding.

Chapter 5

Building Wealth by Taking Reasonable Risks

. . . .

In This Chapter

▶ Identifying some rules of investing

▶ Appreciating investment risk and how it can help you

▶ Knowing the basics of managing investment risk

▶ Understanding that risk can bring rewards

▶ Deciding how much risk you can stand

. . . .

*T*he whole reason that you invest your money is so it can earn more money. Otherwise, you may as well just lock your savings up in a safe. (Of course, inflation would eat away at the value of your money sitting in the safe. So investing your money is really the best bet.)

The bad news is that investing money involves a certain amount of risk. The good news is that you can use this risk to your advantage and score a higher return on your money.

Like many things, investment risk isn't that scary after you understand it. This chapter explains the different types of risk involved with your 401(k) investments. The goal is not to frighten you away from investing but to make you comfortable by familiarizing you with the unfamiliar. After all, the key to successful long-term investing is building a good plan and sticking to it. Finding the level of investment risk that's right for you will help you stick to your plan.

Defining Some Investment Basics

In general terms, *investment risk* refers to the fact that the value of your investment will go up and down over time. Another term often used to refer to the movement in an investment's value is *volatility*. Essentially, the more volatile an investment is, the higher its risk.

In order to fully understand these concepts, you need to grasp some investment basics. If you're already familiar with debt, equity, and the concept of diversification, feel free to skip down to the next section, which defines different types of investment risk.

Debt and equity

Debt and *equity* instruments are the two types of investments that you use to make money with your money.

When you invest in a debt instrument, such as a bank certificate of deposit (CD), you essentially loan money to an entity for an agreed period of time. In return, you receive regular interest payments, and you get your *principal* (initial investment) back at the end of the term (*maturity*).

Debt instruments also include *bonds* and *money market* securities. They're often referred to as *fixed-income* investments, because the amount you earn is fixed and predetermined. The two main investment risks that you face with debt instruments are as follows:

- ✔ **Whoever you loan your money to can *default* on the loan — in other words, miss interest payments and/or not pay back your principal.** In this case, you lose money. Bonds run the spectrum from what are considered the safest (short-term U.S. government bonds) to the most risky (high-yield or junk bonds, issued by corporations with low credit ratings). The interest paid on a short-term government bond is less than that promised on a junk bond, because the government bond is less risky. But the likelihood that you'll see your principal again is much higher with a government bond than with a junk bond. Agencies such as Standard & Poors and Moody's give credit ratings for bonds issued by companies (corporate bonds).

- ✔ **You may not get the full price back if you try to sell bonds before the maturity date.** The situation is fairly unpredictable — the essential thing to remember is that longer-term bonds are more volatile than shorter-term bonds if you try to sell them before they mature.

Equity refers to the stock market. When you put your money in equity investments, you're buying a piece of a company. The amount you gain or lose depends on how well (or poorly) the company does.

Unlike debt investments, equity provides *no* specified interest or payment.

With equity investments, the main risk is that the company you invest in will do poorly or even go bankrupt. In the first case, the value of your investment goes down; in the second, you may lose all your money. On the other hand, if the company does phenomenally well, so does your investment. That's why equities are generally considered more risky than fixed-income investments. However, the potential rewards (investment gains) of equities can be bigger than with fixed-income investments.

If a stock investment loses value, it's often referred to as a *negative return* rather than a loss. Technically speaking, it's not really a loss unless you sell the stock. If you hold on to the stock, its value may go back up over time, and you've lost nothing. However, holding on to a stock and waiting for this to happen may be a bad idea, depending on the stock.

Taking a dip in the mutual fund pool

Mutual funds are a common investment option in 401(k) plans. When you invest in a mutual fund, your money is pooled together with that of many other people and invested under the direction of a professional money manager, or in line with an index.

Mutual fund investments in your 401(k) may include the following broad categories:

- ✔ Money market funds
- ✔ Stable value funds
- ✔ Bond funds
- ✔ Stock funds (U.S. and international)

We explain these types of investments (and more) in Chapter 6. For this chapter, what you need to know is that the different categories of funds carry different levels of investment risk and expected return. In general, money market funds are the least risky and historically have had the lowest return, while stock funds are the most risky and historically have had the highest return. (Investing is all about trade-offs!)

Because of the large pool of investor money, mutual funds can invest in a number of different issues, which is known as *diversification*. Diversification benefits you by lowering your overall risk. (Read more in the "Diversification" section later in this chapter.)

Return of the mummy . . . er . . . mutual funds

Participants often ask us what return to expect on their 401(k). That's a great question, and we wish we could answer it definitively — but we can't. Why? Because the return on your 401(k) investments depends on a number of factors.

We *can* provide guidelines based on past results of different investment types and generally accepted figures. These are long-term averages based on past performance; you can't assume that your investments will turn in exactly the same return, or that they'll have the same return year in and year out, because they won't. The return will fluctuate. For example, it's reasonable to expect stocks to return an average of 9 percent over a period of about 20 years or more, but it's not reasonable to assume that this will occur over shorter periods such as five years. Historically, stocks have periodically produced a much higher or much lower return during shorter time spans.

Over the long term:

- ✔ Money market funds may be expected to return around 4 to 5 percent.
- ✔ Bond funds may be expected to return around 6 to 7 percent.
- ✔ Stock funds may be expected to return around 9 to 11 percent.

Because you'll probably hold a combination of investments, the highest overall return that you should estimate for your account as a whole shouldn't exceed 9 percent — and it should be that high only if you're holding at least 75 percent in stock investments. Otherwise, you should reduce your expected return to 7 to 8 percent (or lower if you're really conservative).

The robust stock market performance during the 1990s was great, but it created unrealistic expectations. Many investors came to expect annual returns of around 15 to 20 percent. Returns in this range should *never* be built into your retirement planning.

Diversification

The best way to reduce your risk of loss, whether you invest in bonds, stocks, or other investments, is to *diversify* your investments — in other words, spread your money around. That way if one investment does badly, the others may do well and make up for the loss. Also, if one investment does extremely well, you'll benefit.

Here's an example of how it can pay off to put your money in a combination of different investments.

Manuel and Sophia both have $5,000 in their 401(k)s. Manuel chooses to invest his entire balance in a "safe" money market fund with an average return of 5 percent a year. Sophia decides to diversify her 401(k) money by investing $1,000 in each of five different categories. Her first investment choice fails, and she loses the entire $1,000. The second option doesn't do well, and although she doesn't lose any money, she doesn't make any either. Her third, fourth, and fifth investment choices have average to above-average returns.

After 25 years, Manuel has $16,932 ($5,000 at 5 percent return for 25 years). Sophia, however, has $22,070. How did she do it? Table 5-1 shows the comparative returns.

Table 5-1	The Advantage of Diversifying Your Investments
Sophia invests her $5,000 as follows . . .	**And ends up with this . . .**
$1,000 and loses it all	$0
$1,000 at 0% return	$1,000
$1,000 at 5%	$3,386
$1,000 at 8%	$6,849
$1,000 at 10%	$10,835
Total	$22,070

If Sophia had invested her entire account in the first option, she would've lost everything. By spreading her money over different investments, she overcame that loss and even ended up making more money than Manuel did.

The most efficient way for most 401(k) participants to diversify is often through collective investment funds such as mutual funds. Mutual funds invest in a number of different companies or other investments. They're run by professional money managers who decide what investments to hold. Some mutual funds are *index funds*, meaning that they hold most or all the same stocks in an index such as the S&P 500 (which contains 500 of the largest companies in the United States). The manager doesn't pick stocks for index funds. The other types of mutual funds are *actively managed* funds in which the fund manager buys and sells stocks in order to try to get a better return than with an index.

Even investment professionals dispute whether you get more for your money with an actively managed fund or whether you're just as well off, if not better off, with an index fund. There's no firm conclusion except that you'll pay higher fees for an actively managed fund (see Chapter 2 for more about fees).

What goes up . . .

Most people have heard of the great stock market crash of 1929 that heralded the beginning of the Great Depression. That drop was 86 percent from the high point to the low point. The following table looks at the biggest market drops since the beginning of the 401(k) in 1980, as measured by the S&P 500 index of 500 of the most influential companies in the United States.

Date of market peak	Decline in S&P 500 index before recovery	Date of market peak	Decline in S&P 500 index before recovery
Nov. 28, 1980	27%	July 17, 1998	19%
Aug. 25, 1987	34%	March 24, 2000	35% as of June 27, 2002*
July 16, 1990	20%		

*No definitive recovery had begun as of the time of writing.

These percentages reflect the *average change* for the 500 companies in the S&P 500 index from a high point to a low point, usually over several months. Some stocks fare better than the general market decline, and some fare worse. Because some stocks fare worse, the stocks of some S&P companies actually dropped by a lot more than 35 percent during the decline that began in 2000. The big problem with owning a single stock is that your company may be the one that drops by 80 percent (or more) during such a period. This decline can be a big problem if it happens a year or two before you need your money.

Here's why it's useful to own a mutual fund. Say you buy shares in a mutual fund that owns only stocks. The value of that fund could conceivably *increase* on a day that a single stock drops by 30 percent, if the fund doesn't own that stock. Even if your fund does own this particular stock, your account value may drop by only a few percentage points for the day — compared to 30 percent for a person who owns only this one stock.

It's usually not enough to own just one mutual fund. In Chapter 6, we explain how to put together a good combination.

Classifying Different Types of Risk

Several types of risk come into play when you're investing in a 401(k). This section explains what those types are, but keep in mind that this isn't an exhaustive list of *all* kinds of risk.

The risk of losing more than you can stand

No one wants to lose any money, but folks are especially fearful of losing more than they can afford. You probably won't lose everything in your 401(k) account, but losing to the point of severe pain is a very real possibility (especially if you don't diversify your investments).

The amount of risk you can take depends to a large extent on how soon you'll need your money — your *time horizon*. If you won't need the money for 20 or 30 years, it doesn't matter if the stock market goes into a slump for a few years. Historically, the market has always recovered, so if you hold on to your investments, they'll probably rebound (providing that you had a good reason to buy them in the first place).

If you'll need your money in five years or less, however, you may not have time to recover from a drop in the stock market. This is when you need to move some of your money out of high-risk investments and into more stable investments that safeguard your principal, such as money market funds, stable value funds, and shorter-term bonds.

A common mistake 401(k) investors made during the late 1990s was putting too much into certain stocks that were doing extremely well — high-tech companies such as computer and software producers come to mind — instead of diversifying their investments.

(They may have thought that they were diversifying by buying a high-tech mutual fund instead of stock in a single company, but that doesn't help when the entire industry goes kaput.) When those companies' performance began to suffer, many portfolios lost a lot of value. Younger investors picked themselves up, dusted themselves off, and started all over again with diversified portfolios. But investors within a few years of retiring had a completely different outlook. They probably had to delay retirement.

Even if you put together a portfolio that contains good, solid performers, you're at the mercy of general economic conditions. This type of risk is known as *systematic risk*, or *market risk*. It's the risk that your investments will decline in value simply because current economic conditions are making most investments decline in value. These general declines have happened periodically over history and will happen again. You need to look carefully at your investments. If you decide that your investments are the right ones for you, hang on and ride it out. Historically, the stock market has always recovered, although sometimes it can take a few years. If you're an investor nearing retirement, be sure to have enough of your investments in less risky securities that'll keep your principal intact in case you need to tap it.

The risk of losing your entire investment

The stock market slump that began in 2000, combined with the much-publicized retirement savings disaster at Enron Corporation, has caused many people to worry about losing all their retirement savings. We've heard from a number of workers who want to know if they should pull their 401(k) money out of stocks and invest in something "safer."

Before you do something rash (such as pull all your 401(k) money out of stocks), you need to understand that there's no such thing as a completely risk-free investment. Even if you bury your money or hide it in your mattress, your dog can still dig it up and eat it for lunch, or the money can be stolen. Even the investments most people consider completely safe — FDIC-insured bank savings accounts and certificates of deposit (CDs) — are only guaranteed to a certain point. They still carry some risk of loss.

The *FDIC (Federal Deposit Insurance Corporation)* is federal government insurance that protects your money up to a certain amount ($100,000 per person as of 2002) should the bank where you parked your money in a savings account go bankrupt. Not all financial institutions are FDIC-insured. Mutual funds are never covered by the FDIC. What's more, the FDIC doesn't have enough resources to back its guarantees in a total economic collapse.

The important fact is that you'll probably never lose all your money, even if it's all invested in stocks. One important exception is if you have too much invested in your own company's stock or any other single stock. This type of investment can be a ticket to either riches or rags, as we explain in the next section.

The risk of owning too much company stock

A number of 401(k) investors face the very real risk of holding too much stock in their employer's company. *Company stock* may be available in a number of ways:

- ✔ Your employer can use it to make matching contributions to your account.

- ✔ Your employer can give it to you as an additional contribution.

- ✔ Your 401(k) may offer it as an investment option for your own contributions.

Employers who contribute company stock to a 401(k) as a matching contribution or other contribution may place restrictions on when you can sell that stock — you may only be able to sell it when you turn 55, for example. This restriction puts you in a difficult situation, because you won't be able to diversify that part of your account even if you want to. In this situation, remember two things:

- ✔ Your other investments need to balance out the fact that you have so much invested in your company's stock.

- ✔ You shouldn't increase your holdings by investing *your own contributions* in company stock.

The second point is very important. The fact that many companies prospered throughout the 1990s, and their stock values consistently increased, led a number of employees to invest some or all of their own contributions in company stock. Just how bad an idea this is became apparent in 2000, when the stock market began to decline and many investors lost big chunks of their retirement accounts. The old adage about not putting all your eggs in one basket couldn't be more true.

We do recognize that it can be hard not to invest a lot in your own company. After all, you work there, and you want to support the company, as well as feel that you have an ownership stake in how well it does.

What's more, you may have gotten a big sales pitch from senior management on the benefits of owning company stock. Many senior managers want employees to own as much company stock as possible.

Interesting psychology is at work here. According to at least one study, 401(k) plan participants who receive a matching contribution in company stock are more likely to also invest their own contributions in company stock if such an option is available in their plan. So, if your company matches your contribution in stock, you're more likely to direct your own contributions into company stock, when really, the rules of diversification dictate that you should put your own contributions somewhere else.

Not to be ignored is the possibility that your buddies at work may laugh at you for investing your money in mutual funds when they're making a ton of money investing in company stock. The pressure to not miss out on this "once-in-a-lifetime opportunity" can be great. One solution: Ignore your buddies.

If your employer gives you company stock, you certainly shouldn't look a gift horse in the mouth. Take it! But think twice before you invest your own money in company stock. The risk of a major loss is simply too high. It wasn't just Enron or dot-com companies that tanked during the market downturn that began in 2000. Many large, well-known companies watched their stock prices drop by more than 50 percent. Every stock's value goes down at some point — it seems to be only a question of when and by how much. It's virtually impossible for a stock to only go up for 20 years or more.

Unfortunately, many 401(k) investors with a lot of company stock learned this lesson the hard way, at the worst time — in their 50s and nearing retirement. For years they saw the value of their accounts grow as they rode the company stock rocket. Then, seemingly overnight, they watched much of what they had gained flame out and disappear.

A single stock has much more potential to move up and down than a diversified collection of investments. You should keep your ownership of company stock at the lowest level permitted by your plan in order to avoid unnecessary risk. This type of risk is called *company risk* or *unsystematic risk,* and the only way to reduce or eliminate it is to diversify your investments.

Congress wants to protect us from ourselves

Because individual stock investments are so volatile, and because participants aren't always the ones who choose whether company stock ends up in their 401(k) plans, some members of Congress introduced bills in 2002 to limit the amount of company stock that can be held in a 401(k). The catalyst for Congress was the bankruptcy of Enron Corporation, the Houston-based energy trading company that collapsed in late 2001, taking the retirement accounts of many of its employees with it. A main reason for the big losses in retirement accounts was that Enron employees held very high percentages of Enron stock, and when it became worthless, so did their accounts. Not only did the company match these employees' contributions in company stock but employees also invested their own money in the stock.

It didn't appear likely at the time of publication that any legislative changes would be enacted during 2002, but this issue will likely resurface in Congress. What is certain is that the real concern for you as a 401(k) investor is how company stock affects your overall mix of investments — your *asset allocation.* (We explain this concept in more detail in Chapter 6.) Essentially, investing a large percentage of your money in a single stock can throw your portfolio off balance. If the stock does very well, you may be fine, but if it does poorly, you risk losing a lot of money.

The risk of not having enough money to live on during your retirement

Considering the risks outlined in the previous sections, you may wonder why investing your money in anything other than a relatively safe bank savings account is even necessary. The answer is that you need to beat *inflation*, the gradual rise in prices over time. You may be able to avoid many investment disasters, but inflation isn't one of them.

If prices rise by an average of 3 percent a year — which is a conservative estimate based on past history — your money will lose more than 60 percent of its value over 30 years. This means that the $100,000 you have today will be worth only $40,000 when you need it at retirement 30 years from now. This loss is just as real as waking up tomorrow morning to find that your account value has dropped by 60 percent. Ouch!

You have to invest your 401(k) contributions — it's the only way to beat inflation.

Your 401(k) retirement nest egg must come from your savings, any employer contribution, and investment income (return). As we explain in Chapter 4, you'll probably have other sources of retirement income besides your 401(k), but it'll still be an important part of your income. The more your 401(k) investments earn, the less you'll have to contribute to the account.

Understanding the Risk-Reward Relationship

When you think about it, retirement investing is a 40- to 60-year event that includes both your working and retirement years. You can't afford to accept a "safe" return over this time period, because it may not keep up with inflation.

"Simple," you may be saying. "All I have to do is invest in something risky, and that will bring up my average return." Unfortunately, it's not that easy. Although you generally do have to take on more risk to get a higher return, or reward, that doesn't mean that every high-risk investment will give you a high return. Some may fail miserably.

You need to choose reasonable investments that are right for your goals as well as for your personal risk tolerance. Investments with the same level of risk can produce very different returns. Your goal is to find the investments that will give you the best returns for your risk level.

We explain general guidelines in Chapter 6. You can also hire a financial planner to do an analysis for you or use financial planning software and services available over the Internet. We list financial planning resources at the end of Chapter 6. A financial planner (or software) will run a number of different scenarios through the computer and come up with a combination of investments that should give the greatest potential return for a given level of risk. This would be nearly impossible to do on your own.

As an example of why it's so important to try to get the best return possible at your desired risk level, Figure 5-1 shows the impact of an additional 3 percent return on your end balance.

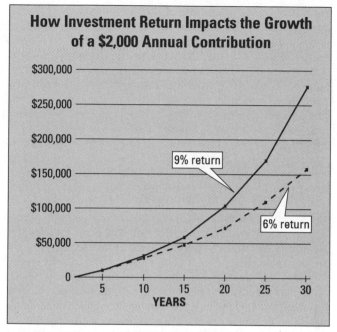

Figure 5-1: How returns affect investment growth.

As you can see, a 9 percent return results in an end balance of $273,000 after 30 years versus $158,000 at a 6 percent rate of return. The 3-percent-higher return generates a 73-percent-higher 401(k) nest egg and a 73-percent-higher retirement income. To achieve the same result over 30 years at the lower rate of return, you'd need to make an annual contribution of $3,460 instead of $2,000.

Deciding How Much Risk You Can Stand

The key to managing risk is knowing how much you can tolerate. When you know how much risk you can handle, you can find investments that you can live with over the long term. If you panic and sell your investments following a price plummet, all you'll do is lose money. If you can stick it out and not sell the investments when they're low, you'll be in better shape.

We want to clear up a common misconception. The amount of investment risk that's right for you has nothing to do with whether you like to go bungee jumping on weekends or drive race cars as a hobby. When it comes to investments, the amount and type of risk you can tolerate has more to do with your time horizon than with your personality (although personality does factor in to a degree). Your time horizon is the length of time between now and when you'll need your money. The longer your time horizon, the more time your investments have to increase in value, even if they have a bad year or two. That generally means that you can take on more investment risk, as part of a carefully thought-out investment strategy, if you have 20 or 30 years until retirement than if you have, say, 5 years until you'll need your money.

Can you handle drops of 20 percent, 30 percent, 40 percent, 50 percent, or even more in the value of your account? Answering questions like this will help you determine whether to invest in risky stocks or safer bonds. Imagine yourself with a retirement account of $100,000 that drops to $50,000 in value. Would you be able to hang on, or would you, like so many others, be tempted to sell those investments and put the money in lower-risk investments? If you do sell, you'll have to dramatically increase your contributions to make up both the loss *and* the lower investment return you'll get in the future. Many investors are comfortable owning stocks when things are going well but tend to sell when stocks are down. This is generally the wrong thing to do.

Table 5-2 illustrates the risk-reward tradeoff. It contains results of the S&P 500 stock index and the Lehman Government Intermediate Bond index over a nearly 30-year period from February 1973 through June 2002, alone and in combined portfolios. You can see how higher average return goes hand in hand with higher risk (illustrated by the worst return over a 12-month period). The table also gives you an idea how much one dollar invested in the different combinations would have grown by mid-2002.

Results Feb. 1973- June 2002	100 % S&P 500 (stock)	80% stock/ 20% bond	50% stock/ 50 % bond	20% stock/ 80 % bond	100 % Lehman Gov't. Intermediate Bond (bond)
Table 5-2 Illustration of Risk-Reward Relationship					
Average 12-month return	11.39%	11.04%	10.32%	9.37%	8.62%
Worst 12-month return	−38.93%	−31.79%	−19.84%	−6.24%	−1.75%
Return on $1.00	$28.82	$21.74	$17.97	$13.93	$11.35

The whole point of finding a comfortable risk level is that it helps you stick to your investment plan. Investing more aggressively (taking more risk) gives you a chance of getting a higher return, but it may also mean more ups and downs than you want. It's a trade-off. The bottom line is that you have to feel comfortable with the investments you choose.

Long-term investing gives you a lot of time to recover from market slumps. The important thing is to choose good, solid investments and reduce your stock holdings as you approach retirement, when you'll have to start generating an income from your investments. (Within your stock investments, you can also shift from growth stocks toward value stocks, which tend to be less volatile.) "What goes up, must come down" is an old saying, but it's one that many 401(k) investors found to be true during the continuing market slump of the early 2000s.

Chapter 6

Selecting Investments

• •

In This Chapter

▶ Understanding what all those investment names mean

▶ Finding the right combination of investments

▶ Comparing sample asset allocation pies

▶ Knowing where to go for help

• •

*W*hen you drive somewhere, what kind of ride do you like? A bumpy one that rises and dips like a roller coaster, leaving you with a stomachache by the time you reach your destination? Or a smooth one that lets you arrive feeling rested and relaxed? Unless you truly enjoy discomfort, you probably prefer the smooth ride.

Investing for retirement is a lot like car rides. And we have news for you — *diversifying* your investments (choosing a range of different ones) puts you on a smoother investing path than not diversifying. How? Different types of investments, such as stocks and bonds, tend to move up and down in value at different times. If you choose several investments, one may go down in value as another begins to go up.

You may ask, "Why not just put everything in the one investment that performs better than the others?" Great idea, in theory. But in practice, you can't possibly know which investment will perform better than others. As all mutual fund companies will tell you, *past performance does not guarantee future results.* (They don't tell you this just to be nice, either. They're required, by law, to inform you of this.) Just because a fund performed well over the last year, or even several years, doesn't mean that it will continue to do so if you invest all your money in it. (According to Murphy's Law, as soon as you put all your money into it, it will do terribly.)

Your 401(k) plan probably lets you choose from up to a dozen different investments, or possibly more. How can you choose? You can close your eyes and point or throw darts, but that's not advisable. What you need is a strategy.

This chapter outlines the main categories of investments likely offered by your 401(k) plan, how to compare and combine them so that they're likely to keep increasing in value, and where to go for more help.

Looking Over the Investment Menu

When your employer set up your 401(k) plan, it chose a selection of investments to offer. If you're new to investing, the list may appear baffling — like trying to order dinner from a menu written in a foreign language. Although making a mistake while ordering a meal may set your stomach back for a day or two (Pan-fried calves' brains? Oops, I meant to order risotto!), choosing the wrong 401(k) investments can set back your retirement plans considerably.

Most investments offered by your 401(k) plan are likely mutual funds. Mutual funds pool together money from many investors and use that money to buy a variety of investments. Different types of mutual funds exist, such as stock funds, bond or other fixed-income (non-stock) funds, and money market funds, which are generally named after the type of investment they favor. Within those broad categories are more specialized mutual funds, as we describe in the following sections. Mutual funds give you an advantage as an individual investor because they let you invest in many more investments than you probably can on your own.

Your plan may also offer non-mutual fund investments, such as company stock or a brokerage window, which we describe later in this chapter.

As you look at your list of 401(k) investment choices, you may wonder whether to invest a little bit in each fund or just choose the one that performed best during the past year. The answer is likely somewhere in between. Your job is to decide what combination makes sense for *you*.

How do you do that? First you need to understand the degree of risk and potential return of the investments. (We discuss these concepts in detail in Chapters 4 and 5.) Here, laid out roughly from lowest risk to highest (based on past performance), are broad categories of investments often found in 401(k) plans:

- Money market funds
- Guaranteed investment contracts or stable value funds
- Bond funds (short- or intermediate-term)

✔ Balanced funds

✔ Stock funds

✔ Company stock

Money market funds: Show me the money

Money market funds are considered the least risky investments. They invest in very short-term debt instruments (called *cash equivalents*) issued by banks, large U.S. companies, and the U.S. government. A fund earns interest on the instruments it holds, but the instruments themselves do not increase or decrease in value. Your money isn't expected to lose value in money market funds, and it will probably gain a bit.

These funds generally have low returns, and they shouldn't be used for long-term investing, because they probably won't beat inflation over the long run. However, they can be a good place to park your money temporarily while you try to figure out what to do with it. Also, you may want to invest in one as part of a diversified portfolio if your plan doesn't give you another fixed income (non-stock) option, or if you desire added stability, especially as you approach retirement.

Guaranteed investment contracts and stable value funds

Guaranteed investment contracts (GICs) and *stable value funds* are fixed-income investments commonly backed by insurance companies or other financial institutions. Many 401(k) plans include these as "conservative" investments, but they aren't widespread outside retirement plans. Their values don't fluctuate, such as a bond fund's sometimes does (see the next section), and you generally receive a predetermined and fixed rate of return over specified periods.

You can consider these an alternative to bonds for the fixed-income portion of your investments. But remember that even though the word "guaranteed" may appear in the name, they aren't fully guaranteed. If an insurance company (or other financial institution) backing the investment fails, or if another asset held in the portfolio is in default, you may lose money. Also, your return could decline in a period of rising interest rates and increasing inflation. The long-term return of stable value funds has generally been below that of bond funds but higher than money markets.

Bond funds: Single portfolio seeks stable relationship

Bond funds invest in U.S. government bonds and/or corporate bonds (bonds issued by companies). The risk level and potential return of the fund depends in part on whether it holds more long-term bonds (that mature in 20 to 30 years), medium-term bonds (5 to 10 years) or short-term bonds (1 to 3 years). In general, funds holding mostly short-term bonds are thought to have lower risk and lower return than funds holding intermediate- and long-term bonds. Another factor that affects your investment results is the quality of the bonds the fund owns. *Junk bonds* have a potentially higher return but also potentially greater losses.

A fund company isn't going to call its fund that invests in junk bonds a "junk bond fund." It will more likely be called a "high-yield fund." Read the prospectus or other material carefully before actually investing your money in any fund.

In a 401(k), you generally invest in a bond fund to add stability to your portfolio. Sticking to less-volatile short-term and intermediate-term bonds makes sense. The name of the fund may indicate what kinds of bonds it holds; otherwise, you can look at the list of bonds in the fund. (Short-term bond funds sometimes have "low duration" in their name.) Like stock funds, bond funds can be *index funds* or *actively managed funds*. We explain these terms in the section "Stock funds: A feather in your cap" later in this chapter.

Changes in interest rates can affect the return of a bond fund. (The relationship isn't what you may think, though — when interest rates rise, bond values may decline, and vice versa.) In addition, a company that issues a bond (a corporate bond) may go kaput. If you invested in a fund holding those bonds, it can affect your return.

Some municipal bonds are tax-free investments — the interest earned isn't taxed. Although these may be good investments *out-side* of a 401(k) or other tax-deferred account, don't buy them *in* your 401(k); you'll be wasting the tax advantage. Money in a 401(k) grows tax-deferred, but you have to pay income tax when you take money out, whether it was invested in a tax-free bond fund or not.

Balanced funds: One-stop shopping

Balanced funds are mutual funds that invest in a set mixture of stocks and bonds, and are generally designed for one-stop shopping. Investment professionals choose the balance of stocks and bonds for balanced funds. (The mix is usually around 60 percent stocks and 40 percent bonds, but the combination may vary.)

Life-cycle or *lifestyle funds* are a type of balanced fund aimed at a particular age group, based on the number of years until retirement. These funds are designed to be most effective if you choose one that's right for you and invest only in that fund rather than mix it with other investments.

Stock funds: A feather in your cap

Stock funds, also called *equity funds,* invest mostly or entirely in the stock of U.S. and/or foreign companies.

A number of factors influence individual stock prices, such as

- Political events in the United States and around the world
- Unpredictable events, such as the 9/11 attacks, or natural disasters, such as an earthquake
- The company's revenue and profits
- A change in company management
- New products recently introduced by the company
- The company's prominence within its industry
- The industry climate
- General market trends
- The opinion of large institutional investors, such as mutual fund managers
- The opinion of key analysts

Because so many things can impact the price of a stock, you may wonder why in the world you should invest your retirement savings in something so uncertain. The answer is that, historically, stocks have provided the highest average investment return over the long term. Also, by investing in a mutual fund rather than a single stock, you can reduce your risk level.

Active versus passive management

Some stock funds are *index funds* that invest in companies that make up a stock index. Many stock indexes exist; one of the best known is the *Standard & Poors 500 (S&P 500),* which is comprised of 500 large U.S. companies considered leaders in their fields (or economic sectors). Contrary to popular belief, the companies that make up the S&P 500 are not necessarily the 500 largest U.S. companies. The S&P 500 is often used as a broad measure of the U.S. economy.

Fees for index funds are generally lower than for managed funds, because index fund managers don't spend a lot of time making decisions about what stock to buy and what to sell. Index funds are sometimes referred to as *passively managed funds.* (We give more examples of indexes in the section "Mistake #2: Comparing different types of funds" later in this chapter.)

An *actively managed* stock fund is a different cup of tea. This type of fund is run by a fund manager who tries to get better returns than the index that applies to the fund. (For example, the S&P 500 is an index for measuring the performance of *large-cap* stocks; we explain large-cap stocks in the following section.) The manager of an actively managed large-cap stock fund wants to earn a better return than the S&P 500, but he doesn't worry about doing better than a bond index, for example, because that's a different type of investment. To beat the index, the manager needs to pick stocks that he expects will do especially well. Because of additional operating costs in managed funds, the manager must beat the index by 1.5 to 2.0 percent in order for your return to be the same as if you had invested in an index fund. That's a big hurdle. Studies have shown that most actively managed funds don't beat the indexes over time, but debates still rage in the investment world as to which is better — active or passive management.

You may decide to choose an actively managed fund, even if it doesn't achieve as high a return as its benchmark, if the stocks selected by the manager have lower risk than those in the benchmark. For example, Ted, at age 60, prefers to invest in actively managed stock funds that have lower risk than the S&P 500 index. The fund prospectus and third-party sources such as Morningstar or Value Line tell you how much risk the manager takes.

Capitalizing on a company's assets

Stock funds often concentrate on companies of a certain size or *capitalization.* (Capitalization, or *market cap,* refers to the number of shares on the marketplace, multiplied by the price per share. If a company has issued 10 million shares of its stock, and the stock is valued at $10 per share, the company's market cap is $100 million.)

Generally, *large-cap* refers to companies with capitalization more than $10 billion, such as Microsoft or Wal-Mart. *Small-cap* companies have capitalization under about $1.5 billion, such as Jack In The Box or Ethan Allen Interiors. (Yes, we realize that $1.5 billion is hardly small change, but these definitions are relative. Kind of like the coffeehouse whose smallest size drink is labeled "tall.") These definitions are somewhat fluid (different experts may use different cut-offs). What you need to know is that large-cap companies as a whole are considered less volatile investments than small-cap companies, which tend to be newer, less proven companies. However, small-cap companies are generally seen as having greater potential for growth (as well as for failure).

There's also a *mid-cap* category for companies that are bigger than small-caps but not big enough for the big leagues. This category is very fluid. It may not be included in an asset allocation recommendation you get from an advisor, because a mix of large and small-cap companies may give you a similar investment result.

If you want to go whole hog, you can further divide stock funds into *growth* and *value funds*. (A mutual fund that mixes growth and value stocks is often referred to as a *blend*.) Here's the skinny on growth and value funds:

✔ *Growth funds* invest in companies that are expected to earn a lot of money over a sustained period, such as some technology companies (Microsoft) or pharmaceuticals firms (Pfizer). They generally plow their earnings back into the company rather than pay dividends to shareholders. The price of these stocks tend to be high compared to the companies' earnings, but the expected revenue and profit growth attracts investors.

✔ *Value funds* invest in companies that are seen as bargains — their stock prices are low compared to their assets, revenues, and earnings per share. The stock price may be low because the company is in a *sector* (part of the economy) that is going through a slump but is expected to recover, such as energy companies or some telecommunications and technology companies in 2002 (ExxonMobil or Verizon Communications). Another reason for a low stock price may be that the company or industry has fallen out of favor with investors for a reason unconnected to its performance — similar to a fickle public's treatment of some rock stars and professional athletes.

Put all those categories together, and you end up with funds called "Company X Small-cap Growth" or "Company Y Value Equity." The first would likely invest in small-growth companies, and the second in value stocks — potentially from a company of any size.

There's obviously a lot more to a mutual fund than its name. In fact, the name may be misleading. You should look at the fund's *prospectus* (a description of the fund that you can get from your employer, plan provider, or the fund company) to see where the fund is invested. Small-cap growth funds may also have investments in bonds and cash. Why does that matter? Say you've figured out that 15 percent of your money should be in bonds, and you've already invested that much in a bond fund. If the stock fund you invest in also holds bonds, you'll end up with more bonds than you want, which probably means a lower return over the long run.

You should also check how an independent third party such as Morningstar or Value Line identifies the fund. (We explain more about these and other services in the "Seeking Help from the Pros (and We Don't Mean Julia Child)" section at the end of this chapter.)

International investing

Your 401(k) plan may offer a mutual fund (or funds) that invests in companies outside the United States. Foreign investments may move up and down at different times from the U.S. stock market, meaning that international investments can help diversify your portfolio. An "International" fund generally invests only in non–U.S. companies, while a "Global" or "World" fund may also include U.S. investments.

International funds may be named after the specific region they invest in: Europe, the Pacific Rim, Latin America, or Emerging Markets (developing economies), for example. Be sure to research any fund (before you invest in it) to find out exactly what it holds. Also, read up on the politics and economics of the countries the fund invests in — instability increases the risk to your investment. For example, Emerging Markets investments generally are riskier than investments in developed economies such as Europe.

Company stock funds: Don't get burned

Your 401(k) plan may let you invest your contributions in your employer's stock. Although doing this can seem like a good idea, especially if your company is the greatest, think twice before you decide whether to do it. Company stock isn't a diversified investment such as a mutual fund. Although your company's stock may do really well, it can also do really badly at some point. (Think Enron.)

Enron investors did very well until the year the company collapsed. Although the collapse was a big deal for Enron employees, it wouldn't have mattered so much to the rest of us if Enron were the only large company that saw its stock value tank. Unfortunately, it wasn't. WorldCom and Global Crossing were but two other big companies whose stock hit the skids. The stocks of many other employers dropped by more than 50 percent during the period from 2000 to mid-2002. Employees who thought they were winning by investing heavily in company stock for many years suffered major losses at the worst time — when they were close to retirement and needed their money. Remember your parents' admonition about not playing with matches? It's the same with company stock. Hold it too long, and eventually you'll get burned.

If you have a lot invested in your company's stock, it may pull your entire account down, even if you also have money invested in mutual funds. Many financial planners advise holding no more than 10 percent of your retirement investments in company stock (including the portion your employer may give you as a contribution), and some encourage investors to sell all their company stock and buy mutual funds instead (if their plan's rules allow them to follow this advice). See Chapter 5 for more on the risks of company stock.

Brokerage window: Don't fence me in

Like cowboys living out on the range, some 401(k) investors don't like to be fenced in. They want to invest in more than just the options chosen by their employer. To make these employees happy, some companies offer a *brokerage window*. This isn't really a class of investment, such as the others described in this section, but we include it here because it's a way of investing in a 401(k) plan that is becoming more common. The "window" may let 401(k) participants invest in any stock, bond, or mutual fund they like, not just the ones offered by their plan.

If your plan offers a brokerage window (sometimes called a *self-directed* option), you probably have to pay extra for it. Also, some companies don't give you complete freedom, because they don't want you to use a brokerage account to *day-trade* (buy and sell investments frequently, trying — and usually failing — to make a quick buck) or to invest all your 401(k) money in a single stock. Ted advises employers who offer a brokerage window to limit investments to professionally managed mutual funds.

Using a brokerage window puts more responsibility on you to research your investments to make sure that they're right for you. We recommend getting help from a reputable advisor if you choose to go this route.

Different Strokes for Different Folks

Different types of funds serve different investment *objectives*. Broadly speaking, objectives can include growth (capital appreciation), income, and capital preservation (which we explain in just a second).

Long-term investors (those with at least 5 to 10 years before they may need the money) usually invest primarily for *growth*. When you invest long-term, you don't want an immediate return such as interest or dividends. Instead, you want your investments to increase in value, so that when you're ready to sell them, they'll be worth a lot more than you paid for them. You're willing to take on a certain amount of risk for the possibility of higher return. The most common investment for this type of strategy is stocks — of all kinds.

Within 5 to 10 years of retirement, you can cut back your level of stocks by shifting into less volatile investments, such as bonds and stable value funds, in order to reduce your risk. You may also shift the remaining stock portion of your portfolio from more risky stocks (generally growth-oriented companies) to less volatile ones (generally value-oriented companies). This is a *capital preservation* strategy. You want your money to grow at a rate that will at least beat inflation, but you want to reduce your risk of losing money. The long-term return of this portfolio will probably be lower, but, at this point, you're more concerned with preserving your capital.

Some retirees who are very concerned about preserving capital during their retirement years will typically invest to generate an income through interest and dividends. A problem with this strategy is that you have little or no *hedge* (protection) against inflation. In addition, you can't count on companies that pay high dividends to always do so. Dividends are one of the first things to be cut when profits shrink. You need income during your retirement years, but you can collect it in other ways. Ted recommends using an automatic withdrawal plan from mutual funds or an annuity rather than trying to find investments that will generate enough income through interest and dividends. (We explain this strategy in detail in Chapter 9.) In any case, you should probably still keep at least 25 percent of your money in stocks, because retirement can last for 20 years or more, and your money needs to keep growing.

Baking Your Asset Allocation Pie

Figuring out the right investments for you is an important part of 401(k) investing. It requires some time at the outset, but when you're done, you shouldn't have to spend too much time on managing your account, except for periodic maintenance.

The first step is to figure out what percentage of your investments should go into the different asset classes. The five asset classes that are generally used are large-cap stocks, small-cap stocks, international stocks, fixed income (bonds, GICs, and stable value funds), and "cash" (money market funds). Pie charts are the financial planners' preferred method for illustrating *asset allocation,* or how to divide your money among different investments. Figure 6-1 shows a sample allocation for someone 25 years from retirement who is a moderate investor (not too conservative, not too aggressive).

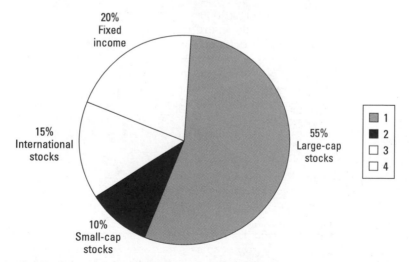

Figure 6-1: Pie chart with 55% large cap, 20% bonds, 10% small cap, and 15% international.

Everyone's situation is unique, and the sample allocation that we show here may not necessarily represent the right strategy for your situation. You may need or want something more aggressive (risky) or less risky. These are guidelines to put you in the ballpark — whether you end up sitting behind home plate, in the bleachers, or somewhere in between is up to you.

The right asset allocation for your situation depends on a number of factors, including your time horizon, retirement goals, and comfort level with investment risk, which are concepts we discuss in Chapters 4 and 5. It also depends on whether you expect your 401(k) to be your principal source of retirement income, or whether you have other substantial resources to rely on, as well. (If you have other resources, you may be able to take less risk with your 401(k) and still meet retirement goals.) You and your next-door-neighbor may both be 25 years away from retirement, but she may require a more conservative portfolio, while your situation may warrant one that's more aggressive.

For example, someone with a 25-year time horizon who doesn't mind investment risk may decide on a 401(k) allocation that's 100 percent stocks, as shown in Figure 6-2.

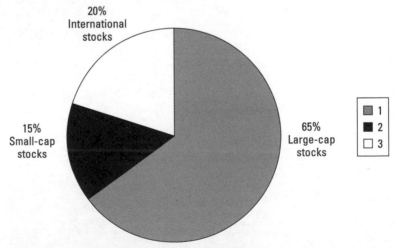

Figure 6-2: Pie chart showing 65% large cap, 15% small cap, and 20% international.

Someone else with the same time horizon who is risk-averse may move more into bonds and even a money market (cash) investment, as shown in Figure 6-3.

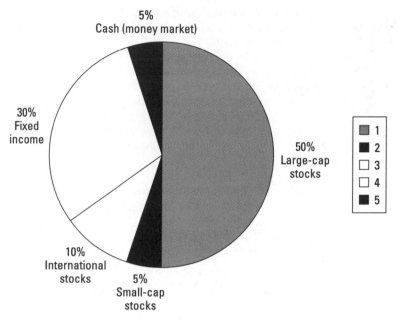

Figure 6-3: Pie chart with 50% large cap, 5% small cap, 10% international, 30% bonds, and 5% cash.

After you determine an appropriate asset allocation for you, the next step is to determine which funds in your 401(k) plan match up with the *asset classes* that you want to invest in, and decide which funds to invest in. The following section, "Check your ingredients and avoid these common mistakes," gives some tips for choosing investments.

How you go about completing these steps depends on whether you prefer to do things yourself or seek professional advice, as well as on what resources are available to you at work. In the "Seeking Help from the Pros (and We Don't Mean Julia Child)" section at the end of this chapter, we give suggestions for where you can go for help.

Check your ingredients and avoid these common mistakes

When you decide on an asset allocation, you need to split your money among the funds available in your 401(k) to achieve the desired allocation. If you have already contributed money to your

401(k), you may need to move it into different funds to achieve the mix that you want. You should also make your new contributions in these proportions.

With a 401(k), you can move money among investments without paying fees. Most plans let you move money when you want to, although some may restrict you to a few dates per year.

When choosing specific funds, be sure to focus on the right information. Following are some common mistakes 401(k) investors make.

Mistake #1: Basing investment choices on the past performance of the investments

Good results are often fleeting. Many of the funds that appear on "Top 10" lists aren't repeat stars.

Many technology funds were top performers prior to 2000. They then dropped into the worst-performing category in 2000 and early 2001. One mutual fund that invested in small Japanese technology companies gained 100 percent during the first six months of 1999, and 114 percent in the second half of 1999. If you were shopping around for a fund back then, boy, would that have looked like a winner. But (there's always a "but," right?) when technology companies took a dive in 2000, the fund dropped by 71.8 percent. If you'd been paying attention to analyst predictions about the tech sector and had looked at the companies held by the fund, you would've been forewarned. You probably would have chosen another fund and ended up better off. That said, we recently ran across an Internet message board with entries from three investors who were in the fund in April 2000, when the fund was nosediving. Two of the three said that they were hanging on to the fund because they thought it would go back up. (The fund no longer exists, by the way.)

Mistake #2: Comparing different types of funds

You can't compare apples with oranges, and you can't compare stocks with bonds. You must compare a fund's performance to that of others in its *peer group* (similar types of funds).

Identifying a fund's type can be difficult. The name won't always help you. Looking at a prospectus for the fund should help you figure out a fund's type, but it still may not be totally clear. An independent source such as Morningstar, Value Line, or Schwab can be your best bet for finding out what the fund invests in.

To measure your mutual fund's performance against a standard, use an *index*. Indexes are made up of a large number of companies that fall into the category being measured, so they provide a good indication of how the category is doing. Several financial institutions have created indexes to measure different categories of investments. The main companies with indexes are

- Standard & Poors (S&P); www.standardandpoors.com
- Barra; www.barra.com
- The Frank Russell Co.; www.russell.com
- Wilshire Associates; www.wilshire.com
- Morgan Stanley; www.morganstanley.com
- Lehman Brothers (for bonds); www.lehman.com

You need to make sure that you measure the mutual fund's performance against the appropriate index. In general, you can measure

- Large-cap stock funds against the S&P 500 or Wilshire 5000
- Small-cap stock funds against the Russell 2000
- International funds against the MSCI-EAFE (Morgan Stanley Capital International Europe, Australasia, Far East Index)
- Bond funds against the Lehman Brothers Aggregate Bond Index

The financial institutions listed also have a number of more specialized indexes for measuring performance of specialized funds such as large-cap growth, small-cap value, and so on.

Mistake #3: Failing to look at both short- and long-term performance

You should compare the fund's most recent returns, and also longer-term (three- to five-year) performance, with that of other funds from the same category. Looking at long-term results helps you tell whether the fund is relying on one good year for its overall good performance.

Mistake #4: Assuming that the fund with the highest average return will give you the most money

This is not necessarily the case, believe it or not. For proof, look at the year-by-year comparison of two different funds in Table 6-1.

Table 6-1   Net Annual Return Comparison (In Percent)

Fund	Year 1	Year 2	Year 3	Year 4	Year 5	3-Year Avg.	5-Year Avg.
A	35.3	22.4	(–8.7)	18.5	(–7.6)	16.33	11.98
B	21.1	17.3	(–0.5)	13.2	2.7	12.63	10.76

The natural assumption from looking at the numbers listed in Table 6-1 is that Fund A is better because its five-year average return is 11.98 percent, which is higher than Fund B's return of 10.76 percent. However, you arrive at a different conclusion when you look at Table 6-2, which shows the dollar amounts you'd accumulate in both funds if you invested $10,000 in each at the beginning of each year.

Table 6-2   Amount Accumulated With $10,000 Annual Investment (In Dollars)

Fund	Year 1 (end)	Year 2 (end)	Year 3 (end)	Year 4 (end)	Year 5 (end)
A	$13,530	$28,801	$35,425	$53,829	$58,978
B	$12,110	$25,935	$35,755	$51,795	$63,463

Looking only at percentage returns (Table 6-1), Fund A would have appeared in the winner's circle after the first three years, with a 16.33 percent average annual return, while Fund B's 12.63 percent average three-year return probably would have attracted little or no attention. But Fund B accumulated a slightly larger amount than Fund A after three years (Table 6-2). The difference is even more dramatic after five years.

After five years, Fund A achieved an 11.98 percent average return compared to 10.76 percent for Fund B, but the dollar amount accumulated in Fund B is 7.6 percent more than Fund A!

Here are the essential things to know from this example:

✔ A fund that has less dramatic ups and downs can perform better than a more volatile fund.

✔ Average performance results are of limited value.

> ✔ Don't consider "Top 10" listings the final word. Find the funds that can sustain top performance.
>
> ✔ It can take a long time to get back to where you were after a bad year.

The last point of the list is especially important. Assume, for instance, that you have $100,000 invested in a fund that drops 20 percent to a value of $80,000. A 20 percent gain the next year brings your value up to $96,000. But you're still 4 percent behind. If you're counting on a 12 percent annual return to get you to your retirement goal, you have a lot of ground to make up. Your $100,000 at the beginning of this two-year period would have to be worth $125,440 to be on track, but it's worth only $96,000 after the recovery. You need a 46 percent gain the third year to get on track, which is highly unlikely.

The combination of setting unrealistic return expectations and picking funds that don't do well during down markets may eventually result in a serious gap between what you need to save and what you actually have in your account. Somewhere along the way, you need to make up for the investment gains that didn't occur. This is another reason why it makes sense to pick funds with less dramatic ups and downs.

In the final analysis, the funds you choose must meet your personal objectives. You're not always going to follow conventional wisdom — you need to make informed investment decisions that are right for you.

Open the oven door once in a while to check your progress

After you develop your asset allocation pie, you should leave it alone, but don't ignore it completely. Check it at least once a year to see whether you need to *rebalance*, or bring your investments back in line.

To take a simple example, say you have 75 percent in stocks and 25 percent in bonds. Say stocks take off and do really well. The stock portion of your account increases in value at a much faster rate than the bond portion, to, say, 85 percent of your total account. The bond portion is now worth only 15 percent of your total account. You're in a position to lose a lot of money if the stock market drops — more than if you had 75 percent in stocks. You need to sell some stocks and use the money to buy bonds to move your account back to a 75/25 split, if that's the right asset allocation for you. You may not want to do this, because your stocks have been doing so well, but it's the right thing to do.

Studies have shown that many participants have never rebalanced their 401(k) accounts. Many workers over age 55 entered the market slump that began in 2000 with a higher percentage invested in stocks than ever in their careers. They lost a lot of money from their accounts because they hadn't rebalanced. In fact, at their stage in life, they should have actually gone one step further and *reallocated,* or changed, their fundamental asset allocation. They should've reduced their stock investments to a lower level than when they joined their plans. For example, a 50/50 split of stocks and bonds would be more appropriate for a 60-year-old than a 75/25 split. If the participant had 85 percent in stocks, the unfortunate result would be greater losses than they should have had.

After you determine an appropriate asset allocation, you probably shouldn't change your allocation pie unless a major life change event occurs, such as inheriting a million dollars or winning the lottery, or you're approaching retirement age.

Make sure that your pie complements the rest of the meal

One of the cardinal rules of planning a menu is that, if you serve a main dish with a crust (such as Beef Wellington or quiche), you shouldn't serve pie for dessert. Otherwise, you have too much crust for one meal. Likewise, make sure that your 401(k) investments go well with other investments you have. They should balance as a whole.

For example, say your company matches your 401(k) contribution in company stock, and you've built up quite a lot of it — 50 percent of your 401(k) balance. Assume that you can't change this distribution, because your employer requires you to hold the stock until you turn 55, and you're only 40. You also buy additional shares through a stock purchase plan. What can you do? You should count the company stock as a high-risk stock investment when you decide how to invest your own contributions to your 401(k), and try to use your own contributions to adjust your overall risk to a more comfortable level.

You should also take into account how you're investing in your IRA or outside savings account. If you're married, you can look at your 401(k) and your spouse's as one investment and compensate for the aggressive company stock investment in yours with more conservative investments in your spouse's account.

You should also take into account any guaranteed retirement benefit payment that you expect from your employer with either a defined-benefit or cash balance pension. With these plans, your employer takes the investment risk rather than you. With a defined-benefit plan, you receive a regular defined payment when you retire. Having either of these plans gives you room to invest your 401(k) money somewhat more aggressively, but only if you've been, or expect to be, with your employer for enough years to qualify for a significant pension payment. (That may be quite a few years.)

Of course, things can change very quickly. Your company may change or terminate the plan, the company may be sold or go out of business, and so on. Your investments should be re-evaluated if changes such as these occur.

Seeking Help from the Pros (and We Don't Mean Julia Child)

A common mistake 401(k) participants make is to randomly pick their investments without any idea of what they're investing in or why. Becoming informed about investing doesn't necessarily require a major time commitment.

Finding books and publications

You can buy, or borrow from the library, a number of books that cover the basics of investing, starting with *Investing For Dummies* and *Mutual Funds For Dummies,* both by Eric Tyson (Wiley Publishing). Another good one is *401(k): Take Charge of Your Future,* by Eric Schurenberg (Warner Books). Many public libraries also carry investing resources, such as mutual fund reports from Morningstar and Value Line, which are packed with information, including various funds' holdings, risk levels, and past returns. You may also want to talk to friends who seem to be successful investors, and ask them what resources they find helpful.

Consulting a real live person

Investing is like any other life experience — the result usually depends on the effort you're willing to put into it. If you're like us and most other 401(k) participants, you don't have a lot of time to manage your investments. (That's why you're reading this book and not a 500-page tome on the theory of investing, right?) Consider getting professional investment advice. Your plan may offer advice, or you can also get advice independently from outside your plan.

An advisor can analyze the funds offered by your 401(k) plan and match up a specific investment recommendation with your risk tolerance and goals. The advisor will recommend exactly how much you should invest in each option and also whether you need to move around what's already in your account.

 You should determine if the advisor makes money by advising you to invest in a particular fund or funds. Some are independent, or fee-based, while others earn a commission on what they sell. Possible sources for finding a good advisor include

✔ Word of mouth — but make sure that you ask people who seem to be doing well, not your colleague who's always asking to borrow a stick of chewing gum or five bucks.

✔ Professional associations or companies, such as

- The National Association of Personal Financial Advisors (www.napfa.org), 1-800-366-2732

- The Financial Planners' Association (www.fpanet.org), 1-800-647-6340

- Dalbar, Inc. (www.dalbarinc.com for company information, or http://moneycentral.msn.com/investor/dalbar/main.asp for the Advisor Finder)

Going online for info

Many resources for retirement investors are available online. For asset allocation and fund allocation advice, you can look at independent online advice providers. At publication, the top online advice providers were

✔ mPower (www.mpower.com for company information, or http://money.msn.com/retire/planner.asp for the mPower retirement planner)

✔ Morningstar (www.morningstar.com)

✔ Financial Engines (www.financialengines.com)

Each online advice provider has a different presentation, fee, and technology, but they all gather information about you and make a specific recommendation for how to invest your money. You can either take the recommendation as is, or compare it with one you've come up with on your own.

mPower and Morningstar give you a general asset allocation recommendation for free. If you want specific advice on how much to invest in particular funds in your 401(k) plan, you pay a fee. In order to get the free asset allocation pie chart, both Web sites require registration. Financial Engines charges for providing a basic asset allocation pie chart, as well as for more detailed advice. (Information about these services was correct at the time of writing, but it can always change, of course.) The beauty of all three is that they provide independent advice — they don't stand to gain a commission by recommending one fund over another.

mPower provides easy-to-understand retirement investing information on its mPower Cafe Web site (www.mpowercafe.com). (Yes, that's a shameless plug for the Web site Brenda manages and Ted writes a column for, but heck, the site *has* been recognized for excellence.)

You can also find mutual fund reports by Morningstar and Value Line on their Web sites. Value Line charges a subscription fee, and Morningstar asks you to register with its site. (Morningstar also charges for certain services.) Both companies rate mutual funds, but keep in mind that the ratings are based on past performance, which is no guarantee of how the funds will perform in the future. Another resource for mutual fund information is Charles Schwab, the large online broker. Go to www.schwab.com and click on "Mutual Funds" to see how Schwab classifies various funds.

Whatever you do, remember that investing is not an exact science. The important thing is to do *something,* and make sure that what you do is reasoned. Even when you use an advisor, you should know enough about investing to determine whether the advice you're getting makes sense.

Part III
Getting Your Hands on Your Money

The 5th Wave   By Rich Tennant

STEVE IRWIN, THE CROCODILE HUNTER, PICKS AN INVESTMENT STRATEGY FOR HIS 401(k) PLAN.

"Og-look at this one. This one's reeeally dangerous! In fact, it's potentially fatal! It's a beauty though. I could definitely live with this one."

In this part . . .

Believe it or not, saving money in a 401(k) is the easy part. Taking it out is hard. You need to plan carefully to avoid squandering your hard-earned money on taxes and penalties. Uncle Sam gives you a tax advantage with these plans, but in return, he expects you to use the money to help pay for your retirement. Using it for something else can be difficult, not to mention expensive; depending on your plan, it may even be impossible. After you retire, you still need to be careful about how you manage your money to make sure it lasts.

This part explains the rules for taking money out of a 401(k) when you're working, when you change jobs, and when you retire, and how to avoid paying unnecessary taxes and penalties. It also explains basic rules for Individual Retirement Accounts (IRAs), an integral part of many retirement strategies.

Chapter 7

Putting Your Hand in the 401(k)ookie Jar

*L*ife is so unpredictable. Just when you think you have everything under control . . . wham! An unexpected expense jumps out of a dark alley, bops you on the head, and runs off with your wallet. At times like that, it's nice to know that you may be able to tap your 401(k) plan funds to tide you over.

Uncle Sam permits two ways for getting money out of your 401(k) while you're still working — hardship withdrawals and loans. However, your employer isn't *required* to allow you to do either one. Before you go any farther with this chapter, check your summary plan description (summary of your plan's rules) to see what your plan allows. It may permit both loans and hardship withdrawals, only one or the other, or neither.

You're probably wondering why you can't get your money any time you want. After all, it's your money, right? Yes, it is, but remember that Uncle Sam gives you big tax breaks to help you save in a 401(k). He really wants you to use this money when you retire, so he makes it difficult to take it out earlier.

If you *are* allowed to take a loan or make a hardship withdrawal, you'll be much better off if you understand the rules and how much you may have to pay in taxes and penalties, before doing so. You may decide that it's better for your long-term future to look for another source of emergency funds first.

The rules we discuss in this chapter apply if you're still working for the employer that sponsors your 401(k) plan. The rules are different for taking money out after you leave your employer. We discuss those details in Chapter 8.

Hey, Self, Can You Spare a Dime?

Most 401(k) plans allow hardship withdrawals, but not all of them do. Why *wouldn't* a plan let you withdraw money to pay for an emergency? Your employer may want you to use the money only for retirement — period. In the rest of this section, we assume that your 401(k) plan offers a hardship withdrawal possibility.

Defining a hardship

Hardship withdrawals are only permitted if you have an *immediate and heavy financial need.* This doesn't mean that you'll be able to take a withdrawal if your yacht broke down and you need to buy another one before the spring thaw, or you need a little extra to buy the winery that you've always wanted to run as a hobby.

Two different approaches can determine immediate and heavy financial need. One is the *facts and circumstances test,* which requires you to prove that you've exhausted all other resources. You have to give your employer substantial personal financial data to prove this. In fact, the requirements are so extensive and invasive, that most employers choose the other method, called the *deemed hardship method*, in which withdrawals are limited to a list of hardship situations that have the IRS stamp of approval. These situations are

- ✔ Costs related to the purchase of your primary residence

- ✔ Payment of post-secondary tuition and related educational expenses for the next 12 months for you, your spouse, a dependent, or nondependent children

- ✔ Medical expenses for you, your spouse, or dependents not covered by insurance

- ✔ Payments necessary to prevent either eviction from your principal residence or foreclosure on the mortgage for your residence

Using the deemed hardship method, your employer doesn't have to ask you for personal financial data to show that no other resources are available. By the way, we didn't dream up these rules — the government did.

Participants who are unhappy with their 401(k) investments frequently ask whether they can take their money out of the plan as a hardship withdrawal, while they're working, and roll it into an IRA. The answer is "no." You can only transfer your money to an IRA under the conditions explained in Chapter 8.

Withdrawing the money: How much?

You can withdraw only the amount you need to meet your hardship expense. Because you have to pay tax on a hardship withdrawal, you can include the taxes you'll owe in this amount. We provide an example in the next section, "Calculating the tax you owe," that includes taxes.

The money you're allowed to withdraw for a hardship may be limited to the money you've contributed (excluding investment gains), or it may include vested employer contributions and money you have rolled into the plan from an IRA or another retirement plan. Your employer decides the rules. Many employers don't permit their contributions to be withdrawn for a hardship, because they want this money to stay in the plan and be used to provide retirement benefits.

If your plan lets you borrow money from your 401(k), you may be required to take a loan before taking a hardship withdrawal. It depends on your plan's rules. In this case, you take the maximum loan allowed to you, and then if you still need money, you take the rest of what you need as a hardship withdrawal. We discuss loans in more detail in the section "Both a Borrower and a Lender Be" later in this chapter.

Calculating the tax you owe

You need to pay federal income tax, and state income tax if applicable, on the amount of your hardship withdrawal. (You didn't think you'd be able to avoid taxes, now, did you?) Additionally, if you're under 59½ years old, you may have to pay a 10 percent early withdrawal penalty on the amount you take out (we list circumstances when you don't have to pay the penalty, later in this section). Some states also impose an early withdrawal penalty of a few percentage points. In total, you'll probably have to pay 25 to 40 percent of the amount withdrawn, and you may sometimes have to pay even more.

For example, say you need $10,000 for a down payment on a house, your federal tax rate is 27 percent, and you're under 59½. Because of your age, you'll also owe a 10 percent early withdrawal penalty. Without taking into account state and local taxes, you'll need to withdraw $15,873 in order to have $10,000 after paying 37 percent tax. (The extra $5,873 is what you'll owe when you file your income tax return.)

Don't spend all the money you withdraw without first determining how much you owe in taxes! Your employer will normally withhold 10 percent of the hardship withdrawal. However, this mandatory tax withholding has no relationship to the amount of federal and state tax you'll owe — it's simply a deposit to the IRS. You'll determine the actual taxes owed when you figure your taxes for the year you receive the distribution, and you'll have to pay the difference. Determine how much tax you'll have to pay — and pay it — before you do anything else. Many participants fail to do this and end up with an unexpected, whopping tax bill.

Participants often ask us whether withdrawing money to buy a home or to pay for college expenses exempts them from the 10 percent early withdrawal penalty. The answer is "no." The confusion arises because you *can* avoid this penalty if you withdraw money from an IRA to buy a home or pay for higher education expenses. We discuss rules for IRAs in Chapter 8.

In some situations, money withdrawn from your 401(k) while you're working won't be subject to the 10 percent early withdrawal penalty (although income tax will still be due). These situations include

- ✔ If you become disabled, as defined by the IRS

- ✔ If you owe medical expenses that equal more than 7.5 percent of your income

- ✔ If you set up a special schedule for receiving equal payments over a number of years (not all plans allow this)

- ✔ If a court order requires you to withdraw the money to give to a divorced spouse, a child, or other dependent

Wait, there's more: Anticipating longer-term consequences

As if the consequences we've talked about so far weren't enough, Uncle Sam has a few other rules you need to know about.

For one thing, if you take a hardship withdrawal using the deemed hardship approach, you have to wait six months before you're allowed to begin contributing to your 401(k) again. You also have to wait six months to contribute to all other deferred compensation plans your employer offers, including stock purchase plans.

Also, your contributions in the year following the hardship withdrawal will be limited to the federal maximum, which we explain in Chapter 2, *minus* the amount that you contributed during the year you took the hardship withdrawal. This rule is a bit tricky, so here's an example.

Assume the following:

- ✔ You take a hardship withdrawal on May 14, 2003.
- ✔ You contribute $4,500 pre-tax during 2003, before taking the withdrawal.
- ✔ You start to contribute to the 401(k) again on January 1, 2004.

You'll be allowed to contribute only $8,500 to your 401(k) in 2004, even though the federal maximum limit is $13,000 for that year. Why? Because your contributions for 2004 must be reduced by the $4,500 contributed during 2003 (the year you took the hardship withdrawal). When you figure the math, you have $13,000 minus $4,500 equals $8,500.

Another consequence from hardship withdrawals is that your retirement savings will be disrupted. Say you withdrew $15,873 in order to end up with $10,000 after paying taxes (as in the earlier example). You wouldn't just lose the $15,873 from your 401(k); you'd lose what this money would've been worth by the time you retire. If that money had stayed invested for 30 years with a 9 percent return, it would've been worth $210,598. You'll have to substantially increase your contributions to make up this loss by the time you retire.

Dipping into Your 401(k) Money to Buy Your First Home

The tax bite and disruption to your retirement account are two good reasons to avoid a hardship withdrawal, unless, of course, the withdrawal is absolutely necessary. But withdrawing money to buy your first home may be a smart financial decision.

Investing in a home can bring you a good return. Assume that you take a hardship withdrawal of $15,000 at age 35 to buy a $180,000 home with a 30-year mortgage. Assume that the value of your home appreciates at a rate of 3 percent per year. After 30 years, your house would be worth $435,000. Of that, $255,000 is capital appreciation ($435,000 – $180,000).

If you had left the $15,000 in your 401(k) plan and it had earned a 9 percent return until your retirement age of 65, it would've grown to $199,000, which is less than the capital appreciation on your house. This is a simplified example to show you the potential value of home ownership.

If you're using some of your 401(k) money to purchase your first home, here's a smart approach that will either eliminate or substantially reduce your tax bite. Essentially, you need to buy your home as close to the beginning of the year as possible, as the following example shows.

Assume the following:

- Your first home costs $180,000.
- You have to withdraw $15,000 to help cover the initial costs.
- The property taxes are $2,500 per year.
- The mortgage will be $162,000 at a 6.5 percent interest rate.
- The settlement date is January 15.

In the year you buy the home, the property taxes you pay will be $2,395, and the mortgage interest will be $10,100, because you will have owned the home for only 11½ months. You start to receive the tax benefits of first-time home ownership by deducting the interest and taxes — $12,495 of deductions that will largely offset the impact of having to add the $15,000 withdrawal from your 401(k) to your total income.

But this strategy only works if you withdraw the $15,000 during the same year that you buy the home. You get less of a benefit the later in the year that you buy the home, because you have to include the full withdrawal in your income, but you can deduct interest and tax payments only for the period that you own the home. The worst case would be to buy your home in December, because you get the tax break related to home ownership only for part of one month. In this case, you'd have a $15,000 taxable distribution minus a $1,000 tax break, meaning that $14,000 is taxable income.

You may have to borrow the money, rather than withdraw it, if your plan gives you both options. Again, this is one of those crazy government things.

Both a Borrower and a Lender Be

Most 401(k) plans allow loans, but your plan may limit your ability to borrow from your 401(k). Your employer may not want you to squander your retirement money on something that's not really a necessity.

Following are general rules for loans. Keep in mind that the rules for your specific plan may differ.

Give one good reason . . .

You can take out a loan only if your 401(k) plan document allows you to borrow for the specific reason that you have in mind. Some plans permit borrowing for any reason, but another common approach is to permit loans only for the reasons included on the hardship withdrawal list that we discuss earlier in this chapter (see the section, "Defining a hardship," earlier in this chapter for more info). You can get specific details about account loans from your summary plan description or from your benefits office or 401(k) plan provider.

Figuring out how much you can borrow

The government sets the limits on how much you can borrow. Generally, you're allowed to borrow no more than 50 percent of your account value up to $50,000 maximum. The other half stays in the account as collateral. However (there always seems to be a "however"), government rules theoretically permit borrowing 100 percent of an account up to $10,000. For example, if your account value is $15,000, you may be able to borrow $10,000, even though 50 percent of $15,000 is only $7,500. Most plans don't allow this, though — they limit all loans to 50 percent of the account value for the sake of simplicity. Some plans also impose a minimum loan amount, because it's not worth the hassle for them to administer a loan for only a few bucks.

Determining how much interest you pay

The interest that you pay on your 401(k) loan is determined by your employer and must be a level that meets IRS requirements. It's usually the *prime rate* (the interest rate that banks charge the most creditworthy companies) plus 1 or 2 percentage points. In most plans, the interest that you pay goes back into your account, so you're in the interesting position of being both the borrower and the lender (what would Shakespeare have said about *that*?).

Paying the piper: Repayment rules

You normally have to repay the loan within five years, but you can repay it faster if your plan permits. Also, your employer may permit a longer repayment period if the money is used for a home purchase.

Employers usually require you to repay a loan through deductions from your paycheck. The loan repayments are taken out of your paycheck after taxes, not pre-tax like your original contributions. Then, when you eventually withdraw this money in retirement, you pay tax on it again. We repeat: *You pay tax twice on money used to repay a 401(k) loan.*

The fact that most employers require you to pay back the loan with payroll deductions means that if you're laid off or you quit your job, it becomes impossible to keep repaying the loan. What happens then? You have two choices: Either repay the entire outstanding loan balance right away, or take the amount as a taxable *distribution* (payment from the account).

If you don't have the money to repay the loan, you must declare the entire unpaid loan balance as income on your tax return. Adding insult to injury, if you're younger than 55 when you leave your job, you'll probably have to pay an early withdrawal penalty of 10 percent (or more). As we explain in the earlier section, "Calculating the tax you owe," this withdrawal penalty hurts.

If you take a loan, you should be pretty sure that you're going to stay with your employer long enough to repay it. At the very least, try to have a "Plan B" in the works (other than robbing the nearest bank) to help you scrape together enough money to repay it in full if you're laid off.

To Loan or Not to Loan (to Yourself, That Is)

Although the ability to take a loan is nice in an emergency, it shouldn't be used lightly. Taking a loan from your 401(k) rather than from another source has definite disadvantages.

The most attractive feature of a loan is that it isn't taxable when you receive the money.

However, you eventually have to pay tax on the loan. You have to repay the loan and interest with after-tax deductions from your paycheck, so you simply pay tax on the loan every pay period rather than all at once. And when you withdraw money at retirement (including those repayments that were already taxed), you pay income tax again. You're taxed twice on the amount of a loan.

If you can't afford to continue making pre-tax contributions to the 401(k) at the same time that you're repaying the loan, your eventual account balance will be lower than if you hadn't taken the loan.

Say you're contributing $1,800 a year pre-tax to your 401(k), and you receive an employer matching contribution of $900. If you stop contributing for five years, you lose out on $9,000 of your own contributions ($1,800 × 5) and also on $4,500 in employer matching contributions ($900 × 5). If those amounts are invested in the 401(k) plan over 30 years, with an average return of 9 percent, they will grow to $139,340.

If you take a loan, try to continue making pre-tax contributions to your 401(k) while you're repaying the loan. Doing so will help build up your 401(k) balance over the long run.

Deciding Whether to Take a Hardship Withdrawal or a Loan

You may come up against a situation where you're required to tap your 401(k), either by using a hardship withdrawal or a loan, because you have no alternative.

Table 7-1 compares the end result of a loan and a hardship withdrawal on the balance of a hypothetical account after five years. In this case, the person repaying the loan isn't making new contributions to the account.

Table 7-1	Impact of Loan versus Hardship Withdrawal on Account Balance	
	Loan	*Hardship Withdrawal*
Beginning account balance	$20,000	$20,000
Amount borrowed or withdrawn	$10,000 (borrowed)	$15,873 (withdrawn to have $10,000 left after tax)
Monthly repayment (loan) or contribution (hardship withdrawal)	$202.76 monthly loan repayment for 60 months	$277.75 monthly contributions for 54 months (after six-month suspension)
Annual investment return	9 percent	9 percent
Balance after five years without employer contribution	$30,603	$24,736
Balance after five years with employer contribution of 50¢ on the dollar	$30,603	$33,930

You can see that the decision whether to take a loan or hardship withdrawal isn't cut-and-dried. If your employer makes a matching contribution, the hardship withdrawal may work out better for you in the long run, because you can start benefiting from those contributions earlier. However, if you can afford to keep making pre-tax contributions to your account while paying back a loan, the loan may be a better long-term solution. A loan may also work out better if your employer doesn't make matching contributions.

Using 401 (k) Money for Other Things — Good Idea?

The bottom line is that both loans and hardship withdrawals are much less attractive than they first appear for most purposes. As a result, you should use them only when absolutely necessary rather than as a convenience.

By taking a loan or hardship withdrawal, you're most likely reducing the eventual balance of your retirement account. We explain earlier in this chapter why it may make sense to take money out of your 401(k) to buy a first home. Doing so may give you a good return on your investment. We know people who have borrowed from their 401(k)s to start businesses, also. Like buying a house, this could be a smart move if the business does well — but not if it flops.

People also often ask whether to take money out of a 401(k) to pay off credit card debts charging high interest rates. The thinking is that it's better to pay 9 percent interest to yourself (with a 401(k) loan) than 22 percent interest to a credit card company. This may be true, but the danger is that you'll simply rack up more debt, and you'll have no 401(k) to bail you out. If you do use 401(k) money to pay off credit card debt, make sure that you cut up your credit cards so that you don't dig yourself back into the same hole.

Warning for employers

Employers must administer hardship withdrawals and loans according to the plan document and the applicable regulations. Not long ago, a controller told Ted that his company permits hardship withdrawals for any reason. This approach may make some participants happy, but it will lead to big trouble if the IRS or Department of Labor (DOL) audits the company's plan. The primary penalty for violating the law is to disqualify your plan, which creates major tax problems for your company and all participants. The company loses the tax deductions it received (for the matching contributions and employee pre-tax contributions it made), and employees lose the benefits, such as the tax-deferral for investment earnings and the opportunity to roll the money over to an IRA, that come with a qualified plan. Disqualification is rare, but that doesn't mean that a company can feel comfortable in blatantly violating the law. Short of total disqualification, other fines and penalties may apply.

Both the IRS and the DOL are likely to review both your hardship withdrawal and loan procedures if they audit your plan. Here are steps you should take to protect yourself as an employer:

✔ Keep the application and other paperwork for each hardship withdrawal or loan on file.

✔ Be sure to get documentation from the participant to support the reason for the withdrawal. For example, if the participant is buying a home, be sure to get a copy of the contract.

✔ Make sure that all loan applications include the math showing that the amount of the loan doesn't exceed the applicable limits (for example, 50 percent of the account balance).

Many service providers offer streamlined processing for hardship withdrawals and loans. This processing makes both types of transactions faster and easier for your participants, but you're still required to follow the procedures outlined in your plan document. A few years ago, the DOL audited one of Ted's clients. The agent spent weeks on-site going through all the employer's files. Subsequently, the agent sent a letter to the company's CFO, citing a loan violation. The amount that one participant borrowed supposedly exceeded the 50 percent limit. The CFO was very upset, because the letter from the DOL made it sound like his company had committed a horrible crime. We discovered that the agent was wrong and we were right — but getting to that point was a big hassle. The agent wasn't very polite about the whole thing, either — Ted's client didn't receive an apology letter after the agent was informed of his error.

You should operate your plan with the awareness that these audits do occur and are not fun. They're exhaustive and exhausting, and they take you away from important business. Do everything you can to avoid an audit. Some audits are random, but others are triggered by red flags, such as an employer that consistently takes much longer than permitted to put employees' money into the plan.

Chapter 8

Weighing Your Options When You Leave Your Employer

• •

In This Chapter

▶ Making smart decisions about your 401(k) when you change jobs

▶ Keeping your 401(k) tax advantage by doing a rollover

▶ Looking at all your options

▶ Understanding how to handle company stock in your 401(k) when you leave your employer

• •

*W*hen you stop working at the employer that sponsors your 401(k) plan, as if by magic, some restrictions on your money drop away. Except in a few extreme cases, you're allowed to withdraw your money for any reason at all (it doesn't have to be a hardship), although you still have to pay applicable taxes and penalties.

This newfound freedom makes about one-third of 401(k) participants giddy enough to do something silly — that is, take the money and run. That's a bad idea — we explain why later in the chapter. Fortunately, there's an easy way to avoid pillaging your 401(k) — do a *rollover.* You can transfer your 401(k) money directly from your former employer to an Individual Retirement Arrangement (IRA) or to your new employer's retirement plan (if it allows rollovers), without owing tax. In the new account, the money continues to grow tax-deferred, with no income tax on annual earnings.

If you don't do a rollover right away, you can most likely leave the 401(k) money in your old employer's plan while you consider your options. This chapter explains how to preserve your 401(k) tax advantage when you change jobs and how to avoid costly mistakes with your retirement money. Chapter 9 explains your options when you retire, which may be slightly different.

A Rolling 401 (k) Gathers No Taxes

When you leave your job, one of the many forms that you'll likely have to fill out is a 401(k) *distribution election form*. (*Distribution* is employee-benefit-speak for the payment to you of your vested 401(k) money.)

The most sensible thing to do with your 401(k) from a tax-management point of view is a *direct rollover* (also known as a *trustee-to-trustee transfer*) of the money. With this type of rollover, the money goes directly from your 401(k) plan into another tax-deferred account — an Individual Retirement Arrangement (IRA) or your new employer's 401(k) plan, 403(b) plan, or 457(b) plan. (We discuss 403(b) plans, generally used by educators and nonprofit employees, in Chapter 10, and 457(b) plans, generally offered by state and local governments, in Chapter 11.) By doing a direct rollover, you don't have to pay any tax on the money when it comes out of your old employer's 401(k). The money also continues to grow tax-deferred in the new account.

Instead of transferring the money directly to the new plan or IRA, your employer may give you a check for the 401(k) balance. With a direct rollover, the check should be made out to the financial institution that runs the account where you want the money to go. If the check is made out to you personally, things get complicated.

If the check is payable to you, your former employer is required to withhold 20 percent of the account value as federal withholding tax. So, if you have $10,000 vested in your account, you'll receive a check for only $8,000. In order to avoid paying income tax and an early withdrawal penalty, you'll have to deposit the $8,000 check *plus* $2,000 of your own money into an IRA or new employer's plan within 60 days of receiving the distribution. (The IRS will return the $2,000 to you when you file your tax return if you do the rollover correctly.) The amount that you *don't* deposit in the new account will be considered a cash distribution on which you'll owe applicable tax and penalties. The IRS is firm on this 60-day limit.

Account size matters

If your account balance is less than $5,000, you may be forced to take the money out of your employer's 401(k) plan when you leave. If it's more than $1,000 (and less than $5,000), and you don't tell your employer what you want to do with the money, your employer can automatically roll the money into an IRA on your behalf. If the balance is $1,000 or less, your employer can simply issue a check to you for the entire amount without giving you any alternatives, but you'll owe tax and penalties on the money. You should really let your employer know right away that you want to do a *rollover* if your balance is less than $1,000.

If your vested 401(k) balance is $5,000 or more, and you're younger than the normal retirement age specified in the plan document (usually 65), your employer is required to let you leave your money in the 401(k) if you want to. Leaving your money in the plan can be a useful strategy, at least as a temporary measure. See the section "Never Can Say Goodbye: Leaving Money in Your Old Employer's Plan" later in this chapter for details.

Getting the skinny on IRAs

Many participants wonder whether it's better to roll their 401(k) into an IRA or into another employer's plan. It really depends on your situation. We look at those two options in the "Rolling over into an IRA" and "Rolling over into another employer's plan" sections later in this chapter. In the meantime, this section explains rules for IRA investing that you should know before making your decision.

Traditional IRAs

Most IRA holders have traditional IRAs because (as their name suggests) they've been around longer — since 1974. Roth IRAs, described in the next section, have been available only since 1998.

You can make two types of contributions to a traditional IRA:

- ✔ *Deductible,* meaning you can deduct your contributions from your income for tax purposes

- ✔ *Nondeductible,* meaning — you guessed it — you *can't* deduct your contributions (Who said this financial stuff was complicated?)

In both types of accounts, you don't pay income tax on your earnings until you withdraw money from the account. You owe income tax when you withdraw the money at retirement. With deductible contributions, you owe tax on the contributions plus the earnings. With nondeductible contributions, you owe tax only on the earnings. As you can well imagine, if you make both types of contributions to an IRA, you need to keep meticulous records in order to know what's what when you start withdrawing the money, which could be many years from now.

For more information about IRAs, we suggest that you take a look at IRS *Publication 590, Individual Retirement Arrangements,* which you can download for free from the IRS Web site at www.irs.gov/pub/irs-pdf/p590.pdf. (The IRS home page is www.irs.gov.)

The deductible IRA is a better deal because you get the extra tax break of being able to deduct your contributions from your taxable income. The catch is that if you have a 401(k) or any other employer-sponsored tax-qualified plan, you can deduct your contributions to an IRA only if your *income* is below the limits illustrated in Table 8-1. (By "income" we mean *modified adjusted gross income, MAGI,* which is your gross income minus certain deductions. This is defined in detail in IRS Publication 590.) If your income is in the ranges indicated in the table, you can deduct only a part of your contribution. If your income is above the upper limit, you can't deduct any part of your contribution. However, you can still make a nondeductible IRA contribution for the portion that you can't deduct.

If you participate in a 401(k) plan, you *are* allowed to contribute to an IRA. Every worker with earned income can contribute to an IRA, and so can their spouses (even if they don't work). The only question is whether your contributions will be deductible.

Table 8-1	Income Limits (MAGI) for Deductible Contributions to a Traditional IRA (for 401(k) Participants)	
Tax Year	*Single Filer*	*Married Filer*
2002	$34,000–$43,999	$54,000–$63,999
2003	$40,000–$49,999	$60,000–$69,999
2004	$45,000–$54,999	$65,000–$74,999

Tax Year	Single Filer	Married Filer
2005	$50,000–$59,999	$70,000–$79,999
2006	$50,000–$59,999	$75,000–$84,999
2007	$50,000–$59,999	$80,000–$99,999

If you're married, filing jointly, and you have a 401(k), but your spouse isn't covered by a retirement plan at work, the limits in Table 8-1 apply only to you. Your spouse can make a fully deductible IRA contribution to his or her IRA if your joint taxable income (MAGI) is under $150,000. From $150,000 to $159,999, a partially deductible contribution is allowed. If your income is $160,000 or more, the contribution isn't deductible.

Roth IRA

A Roth IRA adds a new dimension. You can never deduct your contributions to a Roth, so in that sense, it's like a nondeductible traditional IRA. However, the advantage of a Roth is that you don't pay tax on your investment earnings — ever. The money grows tax-deferred in the account, and you can withdraw it tax-free at retirement, providing you follow the rules.

You may wonder why anyone would bother with a nondeductible traditional IRA, where you have to pay tax on withdrawals, when they could have a Roth IRA. Good question. The answer is that you can't contribute to a Roth IRA if your income is over a certain limit.

In order to qualify for a full Roth contribution, your MAGI (remember, that's modified adjusted gross income, not an ancient king or philosopher) must be below $150,000 if you're married filing jointly, or below $95,000 if you're single. You can make a partial contribution if your income is between $150,000 and $160,000 for married filing jointly and between $95,000 and $110,000 for singles.

Contribution limits for traditional and Roth IRAs

Federal law limits the amount you can contribute to an IRA (or to all your IRAs combined, if you have several) in a single year. For many years, the limit was stuck at $2,000, but in 2002 it began rising. It will reach $5,000 in 2008. In addition, if you're age 50 or older in any year, you may make an additional "catch-up" contribution. Table 8-2 shows the limits that apply to both traditional and Roth IRAs.

Table 8-2	Traditional or Roth IRA Contribution Limits	
Year	*Regular Limit*	*Age 50+ Catch-Up*
2002–2004	$3,000	$500
2005	$4,000	$500
2006–2007	$4,000	$1,000
2008	$5,000	$1,000

These limits don't apply to amounts you roll over from a retirement plan. If you have a 401(k) balance of $50,000 or $500,000, for example, you're allowed to roll it all into an IRA when you leave your employer.

Roth conversion: No, it's not a new football play

If you have money in a traditional IRA, and you'd rather have it in a Roth, you can do what's called a *conversion* of the traditional to a Roth. You can do this only in a tax year in which your income (MAGI) is less than $100,000. Here's one case where it doesn't pay to be married — that limit is the same whether you file a single return or you're married filing jointly. (Don't put off the nuptials just because of that, though. Believe it or not, there are more important considerations.) If you're married but file your return separately, you can't convert your traditional IRA into a Roth IRA.

A conversion is kind of like a rollover, except you have to pay tax on the amount you convert. You can either have your IRA custodian (the bank or other financial institution where you have your IRA) make a check out to you, which you deposit in the Roth within 60 days, or do a direct transfer of the money to the new Roth IRA custodian. If you're keeping the Roth IRA at the same custodian as your traditional IRA, the process is even simpler — the institution can simply transfer part or all of the traditional IRA balance into a Roth IRA. You have to pay income tax on the amount transferred, but there's no early withdrawal penalty.

Some investors do a Roth conversion because they like the idea of having tax-free income at retirement. But you take a big tax hit in the year you do the conversion. One strategy is to do a conversion in a year your IRA investments haven't done too well: The value is down, so you pay tax on a lower amount.

Rolling over into an IRA

You can roll money from your 401(k) into a traditional IRA, but not directly into a Roth IRA. (This is because a Roth IRA is treated differently for tax purposes.) What you may be able to do, however, if you really want a Roth, is convert your traditional IRA into a Roth after doing the rollover. Check out the sidebar "Roth conversion: No, it's not a new football play" for an explanation.

 When rolling over into an IRA, you can do a *partial rollover,* rolling over only part of your 401(k) while leaving the rest in your 401(k) account or cashing it out. For example, you may not want to roll over employer stock if you receive shares as part of your distribution. (We explain the details of this strategy in the "Special Company Stock Considerations" section at the end of this chapter.) Or, you may withdraw some of your 401(k) money right away to pay for an expense, but roll the remainder into an IRA to keep it working for your retirement. Likewise, you can do a partial conversion of a traditional IRA into a Roth — leaving some of the traditional IRA intact. (Because you pay income tax on the converted amount, reducing the amount you convert lowers the tax you pay for the conversion.)

If you already have a traditional IRA, you can roll your 401(k) money into that account. However, it's probably a better idea to open a separate IRA just for your rollover money. This will make keeping track of the funds easier. This type of account is often referred to as a *conduit IRA,* because it can act as a conduit between your old 401(k) and a new employer's plan or a *rollover IRA.* Read the sidebar, "Conduit or rollover IRAs — still necessary?" for more details.

IRAs have different rules from 401(k)s. Be aware of the following before you do a rollover:

- ✔ You aren't allowed to take a loan from an IRA. If you roll your 401(k) into an IRA, you won't be able to take a loan as you may be able to with a 401(k).

- ✔ You can always withdraw your money from an IRA. You don't have to apply for a hardship withdrawal as with a 401(k). However, you will owe income tax on money you withdraw from a traditional IRA, in addition to a 10 percent early withdrawal penalty if you're under 59½. Also, you can't replace the money in the account like you can with a 401(k) loan. You can put in only as much as the permitted annual IRA contribution.

✔ You can avoid the early withdrawal penalty with an IRA if you take money out to

- Purchase a first home (you're limited to $10,000 over your lifetime)

- Pay higher education expenses for you, your spouse, or relatives such as the children or grandchildren of you or your spouse

✔ An IRA generally offers more investment choices than a 401(k). Depending on how much choice you like to have, this can be good or bad!

✔ If you have money in a 401(k) plan, you can be forced to withdraw the money when you reach the plan's normal retirement age, usually 65, unless you're still working for that employer. With a traditional IRA, you're required to start taking minimum distributions only after you turn 70½. A Roth IRA never requires you to take withdrawals (unless you inherited the Roth IRA).

✔ Money held in a 401(k) may be more secure from your creditors than money in an IRA. IRA protection depends on state law, while 401(k)s are protected by federal law. We explain this idea in more detail in Chapter 1.

To qualify for the tax advantages, your IRA must be held by a qualified *custodian* or *trustee*. Many financial institutions — a bank, brokerage, mutual fund company, trust company, and so on — may act as qualified *trustees* for your IRA.

In choosing one, you need to decide how much investment choice and what level of service you want.

Along with brokerage firms, just about any financial organization can now sell you stocks and bonds, including banks and insurance companies. If you buy a mutual fund from a bank, keep in mind that it's *not* guaranteed or insured like other more traditional bank investments, such as certificates of deposit (CDs) or plain old savings accounts. While we were writing this book, Ted heard from a 48-year-old woman who'd taken her bank's advice and invested in two mutual funds. The investments dropped in value by more than 35 percent, and she was deeply troubled by this, because she thought banks were a safe place to invest. She didn't realize that the mutual funds weren't guaranteed investments. Keep in mind that stocks, bonds, and mutual funds involve the same level of risk whether you buy them from a bank, stockbroker, or other financial institution.

Conduit or rollover IRAs — still necessary?

Money in an IRA can come from two sources: your own contributions made directly to the IRA each year, or a rollover of money in a 401(k) or similar plan from a former employer. You can also roll money in the other direction — from an IRA into a 401(k) or other employer plan.

Now for a history lesson. Before 2002, you were allowed to do a rollover from an IRA into a 401(k) *only* if the money in the IRA came from a 401(k) at a previous employer. If any money in the IRA came from your own contributions (even if it was just one dollar!) or from a different type of plan than a 401(k), you couldn't roll it over. If you wanted to keep your options open, you had to keep it in a special IRA untainted by any other money — a conduit IRA.

Conduit IRAs seemed to become less important in 2002, because Congress eased the rules to allow you to roll *any* traditional IRA money into a 401(k), whether it comes from a former employer's 401(k), 403(b), or 457(b) plan, or from your own contributions. The problem is, you never know what those guys and gals in Congress are going to do next. The rules can change. In fact, the legislation allowing the rollover rule change and many other retirement saving changes (EGTRRA) is due to expire in 2010. Congress has to renew all these provisions. Otherwise, in 2011, we'll be back to the pre-2002 situation.

The bottom line: It's easy to open a rollover IRA, and it may save you a lot of heartache in 2011.

Rolling over into another employer's plan

You don't have to roll over your 401(k) into an IRA. You may be able to roll the money over into your new employer's plan. You may decide to do this for a number of reasons, including

- ✔ Your new employer has a terrific plan with great funds and low expenses.
- ✔ You want to consolidate all your retirement savings in one place for ease of management.
- ✔ You think you may want to take a loan someday (remember, you can't take a loan from an IRA).

Before you decide to roll over your 401(k) into the new employer's plan, make sure that you get a copy of the new plan's summary plan description to find out all the rules your money will be subject to. Remember, after the money is in the 401(k) plan, you may not be able to withdraw it and move it into an IRA unless you leave your job, so be certain about the rollover before you do it.

You also need to find out whether your new employer's plan accepts rollovers. In theory, you're allowed to roll a 401(k) plan into another 401(k) plan or into a 403(b) plan or 457(b) plan. In practice, though, not all employer plans accept rollovers. If yours doesn't, you can leave your money in your old 401(k) or roll it into an IRA to preserve the tax advantage. (See the sections, "Getting the skinny on IRAs" and "Never Can Say Goodbye: Leaving Money in Your Old Employer's Plan," in this chapter for more information about these options.)

Federal law was changed in 2002 to allow rollovers from 401(k) plans directly into 403(b) and 457(b) plans, and vice versa. Previously, money could be rolled only from one type of plan into the same type of plan — for example, 403(b) to 403(b). One reason your new employer may not accept a rollover from a different type of plan is that the employer may not have adopted the new federal rules yet.

Your new plan may require you to wait until you're eligible to participate before accepting a rollover from your old 401(k). For example, if your new employer has a waiting period of one year before you can contribute to the 401(k), you have to wait one year to roll the money into the 401(k). In that case, you can either leave your money in your former employer's plan or move it to a conduit IRA, ready to be transferred into the new 401(k) when the time comes.

Playing the waiting game

After you decide to roll over your 401(k) money into an IRA or a new employer's plan, the transaction may take a while to happen. We've heard from participants who've had to wait months (or in extreme cases, years) before their former employer would release their money.

Your plan is allowed to retain your money as long as it wants, but no longer than the "normal retirement age" specified in the plan document. We've heard of companies restricting money in this way for up to five years after an employee leaves. One reason that an employer may set up a plan this way is to help retain good employees. Delaying distributions will prevent an employee from quitting simply to access 401(k) money. Employees in this situation usually ask us whether their former employers can legally hold on to the money. The answer is "yes." Amazingly (and somewhat frighteningly), under federal law, a plan is only required to distribute your money when you reach retirement age. (More specifically, it must be paid no later than 60 days after the end of the plan year when you reach the plan's normal retirement age, which is often 65.)

The good news is that most employers want to get rid of the responsibility of administering an account for someone who's no longer an employee, so most plans provide for immediate distribution of your money.

Another rule that the employer has to follow is to treat employees in *a uniform and nondiscriminatory manner.* In other words, your former employer has to handle your benefit distribution the same way it handled those of other employees who left under similar circumstances. Benefit distributions may also be delayed for administrative reasons. Employers that make profit-sharing contributions typically do so just before filing their corporate tax return, which can be 9½ months after the end of the year.

Never Can Say Goodbye: Leaving Money in Your Old Employer's Plan

Leaving your money in your old 401(k) plan may be a good temporary solution while you figure out your next step, but it's probably not the best long-term solution.

Leaving the money in the 401(k) may have advantages for some investors because

- ✔ Some people don't want to make new investment decisions. If you're satisfied with your 401(k) investments, this strategy is fine. However, be aware that an employer can change the investments offered by the plan at any time. If your money is in your former employer's 401(k), you have to go along with the change. During the switchover period, which can take several weeks or months, you won't be able to access your account.

- ✔ Money in a 401(k) generally has more protection from creditors than that in an IRA should you declare personal bankruptcy.

But, here are some drawbacks to consider about leaving your money in your former employer's 401(k):

✔ After you leave a company and are no longer an employee, you'll be low in the pecking order for service if you request a distribution from the 401(k) plan, or if you have questions or complaints. Companies can change a lot over time, including being acquired or restructured. The level of support you receive as an ex-employee usually drops dramatically if this happens.

✔ While the money is in a former employer's 401(k) plan, you can't take a loan. (Remember, you have to pay these back through payroll deductions.) Taking a withdrawal will also probably be difficult.

✔ You can no longer contribute to the old 401(k) plan, but you can rebalance the investments.

Withdrawing the Money with a Lump (Sum) in Your Throat

We hesitate to mention this, but you need to know all your options — when you leave your employer, you may withdraw all the money in your 401(k) account. This type of withdrawal is called *a lump-sum withdrawal.* Surveys show that about one-third of participants who change jobs withdraw all the money in their 401(k) account. Often, they have small account balances and probably figure that it's just not worth it to bother with a rollover.

Unless you have a serious financial need, cashing out the money and spending it is something you should avoid. Even if your account balance is small, it's worth leaving the money alone. If you take cash, you'll have to pay income tax on it. You'll also owe the 10 percent early withdrawal penalty if you're under 55 when you leave your employer and you don't meet any of the exceptions explained in Chapter 7.

While you're still with your employer, the magic age for withdrawing money from the plan without a 10 percent early withdrawal penalty is 59½. This is also the magic age if you have an IRA. However, the IRS lets you avoid the penalty if you're at least 55 when you leave your job (the job with the employer who sponsors your 401(k) plan). The reasoning is that if you lose your job at age 55 or older, it can be particularly hard to find a new one, so you may need the money. Imagine that — for once, the IRS gives you a break.

Moving out of the country

We often receive questions from non–U.S. citizens who work for a time in the United States, build up a 401(k) balance, and then wonder whether they can transfer it overseas and preserve the tax advantage.

You should consult an international tax expert for details about your specific situation, because the answer may depend on tax treaties between the United States and the country where you want to transfer your money.

But even if you can't do the equivalent of a rollover when you depart the United States, it may still be worthwhile to save in a 401(k) while you have the chance, particularly if you will get an employer matching contribution. When you leave your employer, you can leave the money in the 401(k) or (better yet) transfer it into an IRA to preserve the tax advantage. When you reach age 59½, you can withdraw the money without a 10 percent penalty, either all at once or little by little. (If you were at least 55 when you left your employer, you don't have to pay the penalty.) In any case, you'll still owe U.S. income tax, so you should try to withdraw the money in a year, or years, when you have no other taxable U.S. income. Your tax rate should be lower then.

Some people take a cash distribution and spend the money, figuring it's such a small amount that it won't matter. This is a mistake. An amount as small as $5,000 when you're 25 can grow to $157,047 by the time you're 65, assuming a 9 percent rate of return. That additional income could mean puttin' up at the Ritz rather than puttin' up a tent during your retirement travels.

What's more, you wouldn't even get the full $5,000. After paying income tax and penalties, you may just be able to afford a big-screen TV. (And you'll be working so hard trying to make up for lost time in your retirement savings that you probably won't have time to watch it!)

Special Company Stock Considerations

If you have company stock (stock in your employer's company) in your 401(k), you need to know a few things about taxation before you decide what to do with it.

One option is to convert the stock to cash and then transfer it along with your other 401(k) money into an IRA. This gives you an opportunity to diversify your investments by selling the stock (a single investment) and using the proceeds to buy a variety of investments. That's good. However, if you're willing to take on the increased risk of holding company stock outside your IRA, you can get an additional tax break on the company stock. (We discuss risk and company stock in Chapter 5.)

Here's how it works. If you take a distribution of the company stock from your 401(k), but you don't roll it over into an IRA, you'll pay tax on the value of the stock at the time you acquired it — not at the time you withdraw it from the plan. This special provision of the tax law provides your first tax break, because the stock is most likely worth more now than when you received it. (Your employer is responsible for letting you know the total taxable value of the stock when you receive the distribution.)

Assume that you have $50,000 worth of company stock in your 401(k) when you take a distribution, but it was valued at $20,000 when you received it. At the time of your distribution, you'll receive $50,000 worth of stock but pay tax on only $20,000 of it. Later, when you sell the stock, your investment gain (whatever the stock is worth over $20,000) will be taxed as a capital gain, a lower rate than the income tax rate.

If you hang on to the stock for a long time and still own it at the time of your death, your heirs will benefit. They'll have to pay tax only on the gain that occurs after they receive the stock. Say it's worth $100,000 when they get it, and they sell it at $110,000. They pay tax only on $10,000 — the difference between the value when they received it and the sale price. They never pay income tax or capital gains tax on the $50,000 gained while you held the stock.

This is a big tax break, but it's only useful if you don't need the money during your retirement years. You must also be willing to take on the higher investment risk of having a chunk of money invested in a single stock for a number of years.

Chapter 9

Living Beyond the Gold Watch

*W*hen you retire, your investment job isn't over. In some ways, the job's just beginning. You have to convert your account balance (your *nest egg*) into a healthy income stream that will last the rest of your life. This means that you not only have to decide how to invest your money, you also have to decide how and when to spend it.

It'd be great if you could invest the money in a way that would let you live off the investment income without touching the *principal* (the amount in your nest egg before withdrawing any money), but for most people this isn't possible. You have to slowly spend the principal, as well. Spending your account's principal is often referred to as *drawing down* your account. The trick is spending just enough to make things comfortable but not using everything up before you go to the great beyond.

This chapter helps you decide what to do with your 401(k) money when you retire from your job, and how to manage it during your retirement to give you comfort and peace of mind (and maybe even have a little something left over for your heirs).

Note: All the recommendations that we provide in this chapter are directed toward individuals, not couples. That's because both you and your spouse need to do your own retirement planning — unless you operate on a combined income. If you and your spouse have joint accounts and a "what's yours is mine" attitude, a combined plan is fine. But remember that, unless you have other resources, both incomes need to be replaced to maintain your lifestyle.

Decisions, Decisions: What to Do with Your 401(k) Money

One of your first decisions as a retiree will be what to do with the money in your 401(k). You'll essentially have two choices:

- ✔ Leave it in the plan.
- ✔ Take it out of the plan.

Well, okay, the choices are a bit more complicated than that. On the first point, you can leave it in the plan if your vested balance is more than $5,000, and you haven't reached the plan's normal retirement age, usually 65. Leaving your money in your former employer's plan is probably fine if you like the 401(k) plan investments, and if you're not going to need the money soon. However, remember that the employer can change the plan investments at any time, and you have to go along with it. Also, most plans won't let you take installment payments, so if you need to withdraw some money from the plan, it'll be all or nothing.

That brings us to the second option — taking it out of the plan. When you take money out of a 401(k), you have to act carefully to keep taxes and penalties in check. The amount you take out has to be added on top of your other taxable income for that year. This additional income can push you into the highest tax bracket if you have a healthy account balance that you withdraw all at once. If your plan lets you take installment payments, you can arrange to take out what you need and pay income tax only on that amount each year. (This works until you hit age 70½, when you must start taking a *required minimum distribution* each year.) We explain these distributions in the section "Paying Uncle Sam His Due: Required Withdrawals" later in the chapter.

However, most plans have an "all-or-nothing" policy — either leave it in the plan, or withdraw a *lump sum* (the entire amount). With all-or-nothing plans, the best solution is generally to transfer some or all of the money into an IRA, to preserve the tax advantage, and withdraw money periodically from the IRA as you need it. Again, you pay income tax only on the amounts that you withdraw, which works out to be less than paying tax on the entire amount all at once. (See Chapter 8 for more on IRAs.)

What you decide to do, and when you decide to do it, should depend largely on two factors:

- ✔ Your age when you leave your employer
- ✔ When you plan to start using the money

Being older can save you money

Your age when you leave your employer is important, because it determines whether you have to pay a 10 percent early withdrawal penalty on money you withdraw from the 401(k), in addition to taxes.

If you're at least 55 years old when you leave your employer, you won't have to pay the penalty on money withdrawn from that employer's plan. You still have to pay income tax on any withdrawals, though.

The exemption from the 10 percent early withdrawal penalty doesn't apply to any 401(k) money you may still have with employers you once worked for but left before turning 55.

If you're under 55 years old when you retire, you *will* owe a 10 percent early withdrawal penalty on any 401(k) money you withdraw, in addition to taxes. (There are a few exceptions called *72(t) withdrawals*, which we explain in the following section.) When you reach age 59½, though, you can withdraw your 401(k) money without a penalty, even if you retired from your employer before age 55.

Just to complicate matters, remember that your plan can refuse to let you withdraw money until you are the plan's "normal retirement age," which is often 65. Make sure to find out the rules for your plan before you do anything drastic, like retire.

No matter how old you are, you can avoid the early withdrawal penalty tax by rolling over your 401(k) money into an IRA. Remember, though, that after it's in the IRA, you'll generally owe a 10 percent early withdrawal penalty on any money you withdraw before you turn 59½. (The mysterious *72(t) withdrawal* exception, which we explain in the following section, applies here, too.)

Foiling the dreaded early withdrawal penalty

But what if you need your money before age 55 or age 59½? Here's where the *72(t) withdrawals* (distributions) come into play — you can use them to avoid the early withdrawal penalty. These distributions are a list of exceptions to the penalty, such as being disabled or having medical expenses exceeding 7.5 percent of your income (see Chapter 7 for the complete list). However, one of the exceptions, called a *SEPP*, can be used by anyone. (SEPP stands for substantially equal periodic payments.)

When you use SEPP withdrawals, you set up a schedule of annual payments that continue for five years or until you're 59½, whichever is longer. Each year, you withdraw the same amount. (You determine the amount using an IRS formula that is based on your life expectancy. Several approved methods exist. The simplest is the same one used to determine required minimum distributions, described in the section "Paying Uncle Sam His Due: Required Withdrawals.") You can set up SEPP payments with your 401(k) if your plan allows these periodic payments. If it doesn't allow periodic payments, you can roll your 401(k) balance into an IRA and take the SEPP payments from the IRA.

Use a SEPP to avoid the 10 percent penalty tax if you retire before age 55 and start withdrawals from your 401(k) before age 59½, or if you need to make withdrawals from your IRA before age 59½.

If you move your 401(k) money into an IRA, remember to have it transferred directly. Don't accept a check made out to you personally. If your employer makes the 401(k) check out to you, your employer has to withhold 20 percent of the amount for taxes. You have to make up this difference when depositing the money in the IRA, otherwise it will count as taxable income. See Chapter 8 for more information.

Here's an example of a situation requiring SEPP withdrawals. Say you stop working at age 56 and leave your money in your 401(k). Everything's fine for two years, and then you decide you need money from your 401(k). You don't have to worry about the 10 percent early withdrawal penalty, because you were at least 55 years old when you left your employer. However, you still have to think about income tax. If you withdraw the entire 401(k) balance, you'll have a big tax hit. Your employer may allow you to take installment payments from your 401(k) in the amount of your choosing, which would solve your problem. However, if your employer lets you take only a lump sum withdrawal, what do you have to do? (If you've read the earlier chapters, we expect you to belt out this refrain like a Broadway chorus by now.) That's right, roll over the 401(k) into an IRA to preserve the tax advantage.

There's one complication, though. (There's always something.) If you take a distribution from an IRA before you're 59½, you'll have to pay the 10 percent penalty tax. It doesn't matter that you were over 55 when you left your employer. To get the money out of the IRA without the penalty tax, you need to take a Section 72(t) distribution that must continue for at least five years — until you're 63, in this example.

An alternative is to take a partial distribution from your 401(k) for just the amount you need right away, and roll over the rest of the money into an IRA. For example, assume that you have $200,000 in your account, and you need to use $35,000 before you turn 59½. You can take $35,000 (plus enough money to cover the tax) from your 401(k) plan and transfer the rest of the money directly to the IRA.

After retiring, we recommend having the bulk of your savings in an IRA, because IRAs give you greater withdrawal flexibility after age 59½ and more investment flexibility than a 401(k).

Leaving money with your former employer

If you don't need to use any of your 401(k) money for retirement income, and your account exceeds $5,000, you can leave the money in your 401(k). Your employer can't force you to take the money out prior to your plan's normal retirement age. Participants who are comfortable with the investments they have in their 401(k) and/or who don't like making decisions are more likely to leave their money in the plan. Those who aren't thrilled with their 401(k) investments usually can't wait to get their money out of the plan and into other investments that they think are better.

There is no right or wrong decision. Either arrangement is fine if your 401(k) investments are satisfactory. One thing to remember is that money in a 401(k) may have somewhat greater protection from creditors than money in an IRA, depending on your state of residence, should you declare bankruptcy. (IRA protection depends on state law where you live, whereas 401(k) protection is afforded by federal law.)

On the other hand, an IRA offers much greater investment flexibility. An IRA also gives you greater flexibility in naming a beneficiary. (You don't have to get your spouse's approval before you can name someone else as beneficiary, as you have to with a 401(k).)

As you decide whether to leave your 401(k) money with your former employer, you should also consider the fact that the corporate landscape changes constantly. In a continuous merger-and-acquisition climate, Ted usually advises participants to get their money out of the 401(k) plan as soon as they can. Not only can former employers be elusive but they can also change your plan investments at any time. Your money can be moved from one set of investments to another without your approval.

Paying Uncle Sam His Due: Required Withdrawals

In the previous sections, we talk about when you're allowed to take money out of your 401(k). Now we switch gears and explain when you're *required* to withdraw money from your 401(k).

You must begin taking your money out of the 401(k) plan by the time you're 70½, unless you're still working for the employer that maintains the plan. (If you own more than 5 percent of the company, you must start taking distributions by age 70½, even if you're still working.) The government wants to collect tax on your money at some point, which is why you can't leave it in a 401(k) forever.

The amount that you're required to withdraw each year is called your *required minimum distribution,* or *RMD.* The first one you have to take applies to the year when you turn 70½, even though you have until April 1 of the following year to take the installment. You then have to take required distributions by December 31 of each year.

You have a few extra months to take your first required distribution (until April 1), but because that distribution is for the previous year, you still have to take a second required distribution for the current year before December 31 of that same year. Be aware that this will increase your taxable income for that year. You may want to take your first withdrawal earlier.

Here's an example. If you turn 70½ in 2003, you have to take your first RMD by when? That's right, April 1, 2004. But you can take it sooner, in 2003, if you'd like. Why would you do that? Because you'll also have to take a distribution by December 31, 2004, for the year 2004. If you put off your 2003 distribution until 2004, you'll have a higher taxable income that year, all else being equal.

Calculating your RMD isn't terribly difficult if you have the right information available:

✔ **You need to know your account balance as of December 31 of the year before the one that you're taking the distribution for.** In other words, if you're calculating your 2003 distribution, you need to know your account balance as of December 31, 2002.

✔ **You also need to get hold of the IRS life expectancy tables that apply to you and find the correct number for your age.** You can find these tables in a supplement to Publication 590 for 2002, available at www.irs.gov/pub/irs-pdf/ p590supp.pdf. Beginning in 2003, the tables should be included in Publication 590, which can be found on the IRS Web site (www.irs.gov.) Use Table III if your spouse is less than 10 years younger than you, if you're single, or if you're married but your spouse isn't your named beneficiary. Use Table II if your spouse is more than 10 years younger than you. Don't worry about Table I — it's for beneficiaries who inherit an IRA.

For example, if you're 70 and married, and your spouse is 65, you'll use Table III. On that table, the distribution period for a 70-year-old is 27.4. You divide your account balance by that number, and the result is your required minimum distribution. Say your account balance on Dec. 31, 2002, is $500,000. Your required minimum distribution is $18,248.18 ($500,000 divided by 27.4). That's how much you have to take out the first year. For the following year, you do a new calculation with your updated account balance and the next distribution period number on the table.

If you think that's complicated, you should've seen the rules before the IRS simplified them in 2001! You can always ask your plan provider or IRA custodian to calculate the RMD for you. In fact, IRA custodians are required to help you calculate it, so don't be shy about asking for help.

By the way, the rules for calculating required minimum distributions are the same whether your money is in a 401(k) or an IRA. And you can always take out more than the required minimum. However, if you take out less, the IRS will fine you 50 percent of the required amount that you didn't withdraw.

Developing a Strategy to Deal with the Tax Man

It would be nice if taxes disappeared when you retired, but unfortunately they don't. The earlier sections of this chapter talk about minimizing taxes when you first move your money out of your 401(k), but you need to look at a few other situations, too.

Which comes first: Plucking the chicken or emptying the nest egg?

You most likely have some money saved in "taxable" (non-tax–advantaged) accounts as well as in your 401(k). How do you decide which money you should spend first?

Historically, many professional advisors had recommended keeping as much money as possible in a tax-deferred account, even during retirement. The rationale was that you would continue to benefit from the fact that no interest, dividends, or gains would be taxable while the money was in the account.

But the game changed when Congress revised the tax rules regarding Social Security benefits. Although this tax-deferred advantage is still true, you also have to factor in taxation of your Social Security benefits. When you start receiving Social Security, your benefits will be taxed if your income is over certain limits. Distributions from a 401(k) or traditional IRA are taxable retirement benefits that are included in the income that must be counted to determine what portion, if any, of your Social Security benefits will be taxable. So, if you take money out of your 401(k) or IRA when you start receiving Social Security benefits, you may have to pay tax on your Social Security benefits. It would be wise to do some basic planning before deciding on withdrawals. For up-to-date rules, contact a tax attorney and look at the Social Security Administration Web site at www.ssa.gov.

If you retire a few years before taking Social Security benefits, you may want to use up your tax-deferred accounts first, rather than your other savings.

Here's an example. Assume that you

- Retire at age 60

- Plan to start receiving Social Security benefits when you reach age 62

✔ Have $100,000 of personal savings

✔ Have $250,000 in your 401(k) account

✔ Will need $35,000 of income (after taxes) each of your first two years of retirement (before Social Security kicks in)

You could either use your personal savings or withdraw approximately $40,000 from your retirement account during each of these two years. (We're assuming that a $40,000 withdrawal will leave you about $35,000 after paying taxes. If you have other taxable income, your tax rate might be higher.) Withdrawing the money from your 401(k) right away will reduce the size of the taxable distributions you'll receive after you become eligible for Social Security. It reduces your taxable income after you start to collect Social Security benefits, so perhaps you won't have to pay as much, or any, tax on your benefits. This may be a better tax deal than the tax break you receive by keeping more money in your retirement account. And you'll still have your personal savings available, which has already been taxed.

You need to do some fairly complex calculations to see what's better in your situation, so we strongly encourage you to consult an experienced tax attorney or other qualified adviser who does this type of planning.

More on that darned company stock

You also need to consider taxes when you decide what to do with the company stock you may have accumulated in your 401(k) account or other employer-sponsored plan, such as an Employee Stock Ownership Plan (ESOP). As we discuss in Chapter 8, you get a special tax break when you receive company stock as a distribution. You pay tax only on the value of the stock when it was credited to your plan account, not on its current value. You pay a capital gains tax on the difference whenever you eventually sell the stock. These capital gains taxes are lower than the income taxes you would otherwise pay. Finally, if you pass the stock to your heirs when you die, they won't pay tax on any gains that occurred before it was given to them.

This type of estate planning is feasible only if you don't expect to use the stock during your retirement, and you're willing to take the risk of having a chunk of money tied to one stock for many years.

Holding stock in an individual company is much riskier than investing in a number of different investments. If you're not sure why, check out Chapters 5 and 8.

If you roll your company stock into an IRA, you can sell it and diversify into other investments. You will have to pay income tax on your eventual withdrawals. If you take your distribution of stock, you must pay tax on the value of the stock when you received it in the plan. You can then sell the company stock, paying only capital gains tax on the gain, and use the money to invest in more diversified mutual funds or a portfolio of stocks. However, returns on these "taxable" investments will be subject to income tax every year. Still, the benefits of diversification probably make either one of these strategies more palatable than holding on to the company stock, unless you really aren't going to need the money during your lifetime.

Don't let the tax tail wag the dog. Passing company stock on to your heirs is an instance when tax planning for them may get in the way of good investment planning for you.

Managing Your Investments in Retirement

Investing to build up an adequate retirement nest egg takes most people an entire working career. But, believe it or not, managing your investments is even more critical *during* your retirement years, because what took many years to build can go "poof" in an instant, like one of those big soap bubbles kids blow. When you're younger, you can do some really dumb things and still have time to recover. If your investments lose 20 percent or more when you're 30, it's a non-event. When you're 70, it can be a disaster.

As a retiree, you really have to pay attention to your investments so that you can convert your retirement account and other resources into an income stream that will last for the rest of your life.

As you decide how to manage your nest egg during your retirement years, we can't emphasize enough the importance of consulting a professional. This is probably the best investment you can make for your retirement. Ask co-workers, friends, or family members for recommendations on financial professionals in your area. A couple of good resources are www.napfa.org, the Web site of the National Association of Personal Financial Advisors, or www.fpanet.org, the Web site for the Financial Planners' Association. You can also try Dalbar, Inc.'s Advisor Finder at http://moneycentral.msn.com/investor/dalbar/main.asp.

Live long and prosper

Maintaining an income stream that will last for the rest of your life is more difficult now than it used to be. A generation or two ago, retirees commonly converted all their available funds into *income-producing investments.* For most retirees, this meant converting their funds into bank certificates of deposit (CDs). Those who owned stocks typically stuck to the ones that were popular for widows and orphans — in other words, stocks such as utilities that paid high dividends and had a history of steady income with low price fluctuation and modest long-term growth.

Keeping up with inflation wasn't a big deal when the average retiree lived for only 10 to 12 years after retiring. A 3 percent inflation rate reduced the amount of income a retiree could spend by only 23 percent after 10 years.

Today, if you retire during your 50s or early 60s, you need to plan for at least 30 years of retirement income. Your buying power will be reduced by 58 percent after 30 years of inflation at 3 percent. You've probably read that you have to keep some money invested in stocks during your retirement years to help offset the impact of inflation. This advice makes sense, because stocks have produced a higher level of return on average than other investments over 20- to 30-year time periods. But you also need to know how much stock, and which types of stock, to own.

When you do your retirement planning, don't expect an annual 15 percent or higher return. Unfortunately, too many 401(k) investors came to expect just that during the high-performance 1990s. But as the market plummeted in the early 2000s, these investors learned the hard way that the stock market has never produced a return in this range for more than a few years. Expect your return to average 7 percent to 9 percent per year during your retirement years — even with stock investments.

Be realistic about your expectations

In the previous section, we tell you what *not* to expect. Now, to help you plan, here are some rules about what investment return to expect. In general, stocks have produced about a 10 percent average return, and fixed income about a 6 percent average return over a 20- to 30-year period. The return for your overall portfolio will depend on your mix of stocks and bonds. For example:

- ✔ If 75 percent of your money is invested at 6 percent and 25 percent is invested at 10 percent, you can expect an average portfolio return of 7 percent.

- ✔ If your money is split 50/50, expect an average portfolio return of 8 percent.

- ✔ If 25 percent of your money is invested at 6 percent, and 75 percent is invested at 10 percent, expect an average portfolio return of 9 percent.

Remember that these are simply guidelines to help you establish realistic investment expectations for your retirement years and decide how to split your money among different types of investments. They outline *average returns* that could be expected during a *20- to 30-year period.* The year-to-year returns will vary — with even larger variances — when you have a large amount invested in stocks. You also have to consider the fact that these are average long-term expectations. You won't get these returns every year. Your return will be higher for some years and lower for other years. They may even be negative for some years.

Many professional investment advisors recommend investing less than 75 percent of your money in stocks during your retirement years. This means that you should expect an average return in the 7 to 8 percent range if you follow the most commonly recommended mix of stocks and fixed-income investments for retirees. This mix includes a stock allocation of around 40 to 60 percent, depending on your age and risk tolerance. For example, a 60 percent stock allocation may be appropriate during the early years of your retirement, but in most instances, you should reduce the percentage as you get older.

Managing Risk and Maximizing Return

Why so much talk of risk during your retirement years? After all the years you worked hard to reach your retirement goal, you probably want, and deserve, a break that's free of investment stress. We wish we could tell you how this sort of break is possible, but we can't, because it's not. At this point, you need to withdraw money from your account to live. The combination of a low or negative return for a couple of years and regular withdrawals can really disrupt your carefully laid plans.

Imagine that you have a retirement nest egg worth $250,000. You withdraw 6 percent, or $15,000, for living expenses the first year. The next year you withdraw $15,450 to keep up with 3 percent inflation. Now say the value of your investments drops 10 percent the first year and another 4 percent the second year. Finally, assume that you based your plan on an 8 percent return during your retirement years.

An 8 percent return may have looked like a sure thing when you retired, but the market hasn't done well during the first two years of your retirement. Table 9-1 shows how much the value of your nest egg drops after two years of retirement, and where you are compared to your original investment plan.

Table 9-1   How Actual Results Can Differ from Your Plan

	Your Plan (Assumes 8 % Return)	Your Results with 100 Percent Stock	Your Results with 50/50 Split Stocks/Bonds
Beginning amount	$250,000	$250,000	$250,000
Withdrawal year 1	$15,000	$15,000	$15,000
Withdrawal year 2	$15,450	$15,450	$15,450
Investment gain (or loss) year 1	$19,400	–$24,250	–$4,850
Investment gain (or loss) year 2	$19,734	–$8,121	$2,224
Ending balance year 1	$254,400	$210,750	$230,150
Ending balance year 2	$258,684	$187,179	$216,924

This example assumes that you withdraw money monthly. Although no one can predict when the market will go up and down, you do need a predictable stream of income during your retirement years. But withdrawing money when the value of your investments is declining can be gut-wrenching.

One way to avoid having to sell stocks when they're down is to invest about 20 percent of your nest egg in low-risk, fixed-income investments, such as a money market fund or short-term bond fund. Hold these investments in your regular IRA or in a separate

IRA. Use this money as a special cash reserve fund during down periods. You can tap this fund rather than become forced to sell stocks when their value is down.

You can reduce the risk of a loss in any retirement year by increasing the amount you invest in bonds and other fixed-income investments. In the example illustrated by Table 9-1, if you had invested 50 percent in stocks and 50 percent in bonds rather than 100 percent in stocks, the overall loss in the first year would've been only 2 percent, and you actually would've gained 1 percent in the second year. This amount would still be different from your target, but it would, nonetheless, substantially soften the blow.

We can hear you asking why you shouldn't simply put your entire account into fixed-income investments during your retirement years. The answer is that dreaded "I" word: inflation. In Chapter 4, we discuss how inflation makes things cost more over time. In the example in Table 9-1, the amount of money that you'll need to withdraw during the 20th year of your retirement will have increased from $15,000 to $26,300. (That's assuming a 3 percent inflation rate, which is on the low side, historically speaking.)

If you're particularly thrifty, you may think that you don't need to adjust for inflation. Don't fool yourself. You're not living on the same income now that you had 20 or 30 years ago, and you won't want to live on today's income 30 years from now. Some argue that, despite inflation, expenses decrease during retirement years. That's true for some expenses, but medical expenses usually increase, and you may ultimately need to cover the cost of an assisted-living facility. Keeping some of your investments in stock should help you make up the gap that inflation causes.

Living within Your Means for Your Lifetime

Some people think that they'll never run out of money if the amount they withdraw from their retirement account each year never exceeds their investment return. But how can you do this in years when your return is low or negative? Would you be able to live on 1 percent of your account? (Even with an account of $500,000, that would be $5,000 for the entire year.)

Achieving an investment return such as 8 percent is not a given every year. Stock returns can be almost nonexistent even during extended periods. Living through one of these longer-term market funks when you're building your nest egg isn't easy — but it's much more painful when you're retired and watching your account shrink. In addition to good planning, a favorable economy during most of your retirement years will certainly help — but of course, you can't control that.

If you have a $500,000 nest egg, a realistic amount to withdraw each year to avoid running out of money would be around $30,000 per year (adjusted for inflation). If you find that difficult to believe, take a look at Table 9-2, which shows the effect of those annual withdrawals on the account. After 25 years, you've only got enough left for two more years. That's not a very big cushion.

Table 9-2	Managing Your Nest Egg During Your Retirement Years			
No. of Years	Beginning of Year Balance	Annual Withdrawal (Assumes 3% Inflation)	Investment Return (7%)	End-of-Year Balance
1	$500,000	$30,000	$33,950	$503,950
2	$503,950	$30,900	$34,195	$507,245
3	$507,245	$31,827	$34,393	$509,811
4	$509,811	$32,782	$34,539	$511,568
5	$511,568	$33,765	$34,628	$512,431
6	$512,431	$34,778	$34,653	$512,306
7	$512,306	$35,822	$34,610	$511,094
8	$511,094	$36,896	$34,485	$508,683
9	$508,683	$38,003	$34,278	$504,958
10	$504,958	$39,143	$33,977	$499,792
11	$499,792	$40,317	$33,574	$493,049
12	$493,049	$41,527	$33,060	$484,582
13	$484,582	$42,773	$32,424	$474,233
14	$474,233	$44,056	$31,654	$461,831

(continued)

Table 9-2 *(continued)*

No. of Years	Beginning of Year Balance	Annual Withdrawal (Assumes 3% Inflation)	Investment Return (7%)	End-of-Year Balance
15	$461,831	$45,378	$30,740	$447,183
16	$447,183	$46,739	$29,667	$430,111
17	$430,111	$48,141	$28,423	$410,393
18	$410,393	$49,585	$26,992	$387,800
19	$387,800	$51,073	$25,358	$362,085
20	$362,085	$52,605	$23,505	$332,985
21	$332,985	$54,183	$21,413	$300,215
22	$300,215	$55,809	$19,062	$263,468
23	$263,468	$57,483	$16,431	$222,416
24	$222,416	$59,208	$13,497	$176,705
25	$176,705	$60,984	$10,445	$129,166

If that's not enough to convince you, and you want more information on this topic, you may want to look at a widely reported study by three finance professors at Trinity University in San Antonio, Texas (the "Trinity Study").

The study showed that portfolios with a stock/bond mix, rather than 100 percent stocks or 100 percent bonds, are most likely to provide an income for the longest period of time. It also found that withdrawing more than 6 to 7 percent of your retirement account per year substantially increases the chance that you will outlive your savings. Your chance of *not* running out of money is even better if you withdraw only 3 to 4 percent each year.

More detailed information about the Trinity Study appears in the book, *Retirement Bible,* by Lynn O'Shaughnessy (Wiley Publishing, Inc.). An article by the study's authors (including results tables) was also available at www.aaii.com/promo/mstar/feature.shtml at the time this book was written.

Row, Row, Row Your Boat, Gently Down the Income Stream

When you're living off your retirement accounts, you need to come up with a strategy to provide a stream of income that's as predictable as your paycheck was. You'll have expenses that need to be paid, trips you want to take, and activities you want to participate in, and they will all cost money.

You can structure your retirement account in several ways to provide a monthly stream of predictable income.

IRA withdrawals

One way to develop a monthly stream of predictable income is to take monthly withdrawals of a specific amount from mutual funds held in an IRA. You can even have the money automatically deposited directly to your checking account.

For example, assume that you have $250,000 in your IRA, and you want to withdraw a total of 6 percent per year. This would be $15,000, divided into monthly payments of $1,250. If your investments are split evenly between a bond fund and a stock fund, you can ask to have $625 transferred from each account into your checking account every month.

When you invest in mutual funds, you may receive dividends, interest, and realized capital gains (gains on stocks that the mutual fund sells). You can elect to have these amounts paid directly to you, but having them reinvested into new mutual fund shares is easier. The mutual fund company sells enough shares each month to generate the payment you've requested.

You can increase or decrease your withdrawal amount if you absolutely have to, but you should try hard to stick with your plan. Remember that your nest egg doesn't provide a guaranteed lifetime income stream: The checks stop when your account balance hits zero. For example, you can increase the amount you withdraw annually by 3 percent, or whatever inflation rate you've built into your plan; however, it's wiser to keep the withdrawal amount at the same level until you really need the additional income.

Keeping your withdrawal amount steady gives you a cushion for later. Your plan for managing your nest egg during your retirement years includes many variables, including a "guesstimate" of when you will exit your earthly existence. It's highly unlikely that everything will happen exactly as you plan. Living somewhat more frugally during the early years of your retirement reduces the potential that you'll outlive your nest egg.

The annuity option

Another way to get a monthly check in retirement is by purchasing an *immediate annuity,* a financial product that protects you if you live beyond a normal life expectancy. To buy an immediate annuity, you pay a lump sum (which can be rolled over from a 401(k), for example), and in return you are guaranteed income for life — no matter how long you live. How much income you receive depends on the terms of your annuity. An annuity is a good option if you have a limited amount of money that has to last you for many years.

Evaluating the pros and cons

A major disadvantage of an annuity, besides additional fees, is the fact that, depending on the terms of your annuity, the insurer may keep your money if you die sooner than expected. You can guarantee payments for a certain number of years beyond your death or for the life of another beneficiary, but doing so reduces your monthly payments while you're alive. Financial organizations that sell annuities aren't in the business of giving money away. To put it bluntly, annuity-holders who die early pay for those who live longer than expected.

Another risk of an annuity is that the insurer that is guaranteeing the annuity might fail. You should only buy an annuity from a company that has a top rating. Companies that rate insurers include A.M. Best (www.ambest.com), Standard & Poors (www.standardandpoors.com), and Duff & Phelps (www.duffllc.com).

A possible solution, if you like the guarantee offered by an annuity, is to split your retirement money between an annuity and other investments. This solution can be the best of both worlds for some people — they can count on a certain amount of life income from the annuity, plus a monthly withdrawal from the mutual funds or other investments that they make outside the annuity.

The July 2002 issue of *Money* magazine features an article titled "Income for Life" that's a good reference if you want more information about topics discussed in this chapter. You should be able to find it at your local library.

After you buy an annuity, you can't change the payment structure for some unexpected need. Because of this inflexibility, you should avoid putting all of your money into an annuity. Also, make sure that you completely understand the terms of the annuity before purchasing it.

Varying your annuity

Immediate annuities exist in *fixed* or *variable* types. With a fixed annuity, the insurance company guarantees you payments of the same amount each year. Your payments don't increase to keep up with inflation. A variable annuity lets you invest in mutual funds to try to boost your payments and keep up with inflation. However, investing in these mutual funds through a variable annuity is more expensive because of the income guarantee. Plus, your payments may drop if your investments don't do well.

If you do buy a variable annuity, be sure to choose one that gives you access to mutual funds you prefer. You can buy an annuity directly from most mutual fund companies. Remember to split your annuity investment between stocks and fixed-income investments, as you do with the rest of your portfolio.

One word of caution: Consult a trusted financial planner or other professional adviser to make sure that either type of annuity is right for your situation. It's very difficult, if not impossible, to get out of an annuity after you've bought it.

Your home is your asset

When you consider financial resources to fund your retirement, you may also wonder whether you should convert your home into an income-producing asset. In some cases, this makes sense, but many people are emotionally attached to their family home and don't want to sell it. You may have to try to take a less emotional look, however, because you may need the equity from your home to achieve a comfortable level of retirement income.

It may be better to sell your home and use the proceeds to generate income, and then find a place to rent. Why rent if you own a home without a mortgage? Consider that a home is indeed an asset, but it doesn't produce money — it eats it up. It costs a lot of money to live in your home, even if you don't have a mortgage. Assume that you own a $150,000 home. The real estate taxes are probably in the $2,500 range. Your routine annual maintenance costs are probably in the $2,000 range. (Check all your expenditures for a year if these estimates seem high.) You also have to factor in major periodic repairs, such as a new roof. You probably spend at least $5,000 per year for the privilege of owning your $150,000 home — even with the mortgage fully paid. This additional expense is okay if you have adequate retirement income, but it's not wise if your retirement resources are limited.

You can probably find a nice place to rent for $800 per month in the same area as your $150,000 home. The rental will cost you $9,600 per year compared to the $5,000 it may cost to live in your present home. You're paying almost double for the rental, but you don't have the hassle of home ownership. Most importantly, you can reinvest the money from the sale of your home and make up the difference.

Assume that you have $135,000 left after you sell your home and move. (Also assume that you don't owe capital gains tax.) You can reinvest this money in a 50/50 stock and fixed-income portfolio that may generate an average 8 percent investment return of $10,800. You will need $4,600 of this "profit" to make up the difference between the rent you pay and the housing expenses that you've eliminated. This leaves you with $6,200 of additional annual retirement income that may enable you to do some things that would not otherwise be possible. You also have access to the $135,000 for emergencies.

The same logic applies if you live in an area where housing costs are very high. If you have limited retirement resources, it makes sense to relocate to a lower-cost area so that you can unlock the equity in your expensive home.

Part IV
Floor Plans of the Other Types of "4" Plans

The 5th Wave   By Rich Tennant

"I think it's time to institute a 401(k) Plan, Robin. The men aren't looking too merry as of late."

In this part . . .

*D*oes your employer offer a retirement plan that starts with "4" but ends with something other than "01(k)"? This part looks at 403(b) plans (offered by public schools, hospitals, and many nonprofits) and 457 "deferred comp" plans (offered by state and local governments and their agencies). These plans are moving closer to 401(k)s in their rules and regulations, but important differences remain.

Chapter 10

Making Sense of the Bizarre 403(b)azaar

- -

- -

*I*f you're a public school employee, hospital worker, member of the clergy, or employee of a 501(c)(3) nonprofit organization, chances are that you have a 403(b) plan for your retirement savings. Although these plans are often similar to 401(k)s, they're not exactly the same.

 This chapter gives a basic overview of 403(b) plans. For more detailed information about your plan, we recommend consulting your 403(b) provider. In the meantime, two Web sites that provide a lot of information about 403(b)s are mPower Cafe (www. mpowercafe.com) and 403(b)wise (www.403bwise.com). Another good resource is IRS Publication 571, available free at www.irs.gov. (The direct link is www.irs.gov/pub/irs-pdf/p571.pdf.)

Different Name, Same Tax Breaks

403(b) plans let you put off until tomorrow what the tax man would have you pay today. In other words, they offer the same tax advantages to you as 401(k) plans. Specifically,

- ✔ Your contributions to a 403(b) are deducted from your salary before taxes, reducing your taxable income.

- ✔ Money grows tax-deferred in the account — you don't pay income tax on your contributions, any employer contributions, or earnings in your account until you withdraw money from the account.

What's in a name?

The name *403(b)* comes from the section of the Internal Revenue Code that made these plans possible. You may have heard 403(b) plans referred to as tax-sheltered annuities (TSAs) or tax-deferred annuities (TDAs). These names come from the earliest retirement plans of this type — first created in 1958 — which only allowed participants to invest in annuities (see the section "Trekking Through Your Investment Options" later in this chapter for details).

In addition, many rules and contribution limits are the same for both 403(b) and 401(k) plans. (This wasn't the case before the tax laws changed in 2002; luckily, we don't have to explain what 403(b)s used to be like!) But some 403(b)s are very different from 401(k)s, because the employer isn't very involved. See the section "Understanding ERISA versus non-ERISA 403(b) Plans" later in the chapter for more details.

Stashing Away As Much As You Can: Contribution Info

Contributions to a 403(b) may come from the employee only, the employer only, or a combination of the two — for example, an employee contribution plus an employer matching contribution.

The 403(b) regular contribution limits and age-50 catch-up limit are the same as for 401(k)s. An individual can contribute up to $11,000 before taxes to a 403(b) in 2002; the limit rises by $1,000 a year until 2006 (see Chapter 2, Table 2-1 for a table with limits for each year). Additionally, contributions to the 403(b), including employer contributions, can't be more than 100 percent of pay or $40,000, whichever is less.

Workers who are age 50 and over can contribute an additional $1,000 as a catch-up contribution in 2002 if the plan has been amended to permit this type of contribution; this limit rises by $1,000 a year until 2006. Table 2-1 in Chapter 2 has these limits, too.

Playing catch-up

Certain employees qualify for *another* type of catch-up contribution, often referred to as the "15-years-of-service" catch-up. (Guess how many years you have to work at your employer before you're eligible?) The following requirements apply:

- ✔ You must be employed by a qualified organization, such as a public school system, hospital, health and welfare service agency, church, or church organization.

- ✔ You must have at least 15 years of service with your employer (the years don't have to be consecutive, and you can get some credit for part-time work).

If you meet these conditions, and you haven't contributed the full amount to your 403(b) in past years, you can contribute up to $3,000 extra per year. After you make contributions of this type totaling $15,000, you can't make any more. The formula for calculating how much extra you can contribute is complicated, so you should ask your employer or 403(b) provider to help you figure it out.

 You're allowed to make both types of catch-up contributions in the same year if you qualify for both. After you exhaust the 15-years-of-service contributions, you can continue to make the age-50 catch-up.

Mix 'n match: Combining a 403(b) with other plans

Some employers offer a 403(b) along with another plan, either a 401(k) or 457. (What's a 457? Don't worry, just turn to Chapter 11.)

If you're eligible for a 401(k) and 403(b), the most you can contribute to both plans, combined, is the federal maximum limit for a single plan — $11,000 for 2002, $12,000 for 2003, and so on (not counting catch-up contributions). We explain these limits further in Chapter 2.

If you have a 403(b) and 457, though, the plot thickens (along with your retirement account, we hope!). You can contribute the federal maximum to *each plan*, for a total of $22,000 in 2002, $24,000 in 2003, and so on (not counting catch-up contributions).

Trekking Through Your Investment Options

One big difference between 403(b)s and 401(k)s is the types of investments commonly offered. Many 403(b) plans only offer *annuities*, a type of investment sold by insurance companies. Annuities come in many different forms; 403(b) plans generally offer *variable annuities*. With variable annuities, your investment choices usually include either mutual funds or *separate accounts,* or *subaccounts*, which are like mutual funds but are run by the insurance company. Variable annuity accounts don't guarantee any return, nor do they necessarily guarantee your principal. You may have an option called a *fixed account* that guarantees your principal and a certain return. Annuity investments often carry higher fees than mutual funds outside an annuity.

Some 403(b) plans, called 403(b)(7) accounts, offer mutual funds. Mutual funds entered the 403(b) arena years after annuities did, so fewer employers have traditionally offered them. However, as more employees demand mutual fund choices, employers are increasingly looking for 403(b) providers to offer mutual funds.

You can't invest in individual stocks and bonds within a 403(b). You're only allowed to invest in mutual funds or an annuity contract.

Your 403(b) may have a fairly short list of providers, which are pre-selected by your employer. Or, it may have a laundry list of many providers, which are not screened by your employer, offering dozens of possible investments. Either one is possible with a 403(b).

You should research exactly what's available to you *before* making a decision about what to invest in. Yes, we know that this takes time, but the saying "act in haste, repent at leisure" couldn't be more true when it comes to 403(b)s. If you invest in the first thing that comes along, you may spend a lot of time regretting it.

Investing tips in Chapters 4, 5, and 6 can help you decide how to invest after you know what your options are.

Withdrawing Money: Watch Out for That Fee!

While you're working, withdrawal rules for 403(b)s are generally as restrictive as for 401(k)s. Getting your money out is difficult, but if you have a hardship, you may be able to take a hardship withdrawal. Some plans also allow loans.

With a hardship withdrawal, you generally owe a 10 percent early withdrawal penalty if you're under 59½, in addition to the income tax.

If your 403(b) money is in an annuity, you may be charged an *exit fee* (or *surrender fee*) for withdrawing money, if you're even allowed to take it out. If you want to withdraw or transfer money from an annuity, find out how much the exit fee is. (Better yet, find out before you invest in the annuity!) Remember the cartoon character George of the Jungle? He always slammed into trees because he didn't look where his vine was swinging. Don't get caught in the same trap, slamming into fees because you don't look where you're investing.

After you retire, you may receive your money in one of several ways. Be sure to find out what all your options are. For example,

- ✔ If you have an annuity investment, the insurance company offers you the chance to convert the annuity into a stream of payments. You should have a choice of how the payments are structured — whether they're for your lifetime, for yours and your spouse's jointly, and so on.

- ✔ Some annuities may offer a lump-sum payment or installment option, which you can roll over into an IRA. With a lump-sum option, you may have to pay a surrender charge; you can usually avoid this by withdrawing the money in installments. You can set up an annuity payment to last for your lifetime, but if you choose installment payments, the payments will end after a specific number of years. Confusing? You bet it is, which is why you may want to get help from a professional advisor before you make your decision. You usually can't change your mind after you pick your distribution method.

If you have a mutual fund account, your options at retirement should be similar to those with a 401(k) (we describe the 401(k) options in Chapter 9.) You may be able to leave the money in the 403(b) and eventually set up a schedule of withdrawals from that plan, or you can roll the 403(b) into an IRA.

Taking Your 403(b) on the Road

In theory, 403(b) plans are as portable as 401(k) plans. When you change jobs, you can transfer your 403(b) money into an IRA or another employer's 403(b), 401(k), or 457 plan. Like 401(k)s, though, you can only transfer a 403(b) into a new employer's plan if that plan accepts rollovers.

Before 2002, you weren't allowed to roll a 403(b) into a 401(k) or 457 plan when you changed jobs. You could only roll it into an IRA or another 403(b). Because the 401(k) and 457 rollovers are relatively new, employers may be slow to adopt them. If you change jobs, be sure to ask your new employer whether it will accept a rollover of your 403(b). If not, you can always roll it into an IRA (see Chapter 8 for more on how to do that).

Vesting

If your 403(b) includes an employer contribution, you may be required to work for the employer for a certain period of time before the contributions vest. Vesting rules for employer contributions in 403(b) plans are the same as for 401(k) plans (see Chapter 2 for details).

Understanding ERISA versus Non-ERISA 403(b) Plans

Now comes the tricky part. One important thing you need to know about your 403(b) plan is whether it is governed by the *Employee Retirement Income Security Act* (ERISA). 401(k) plans are governed by ERISA, but not all 403(b) plans are. We explain ERISA in Chapter 2, but to refresh your memory, it's the federal law that sets standards that these plans have to follow.

ERISA: Employer + plan provider

Whether a 403(b) plan is governed by ERISA depends on the level of employer involvement in the plan. A 403(b) plan that is covered by ERISA is essentially an agreement between the employer and plan provider, and it requires significant employer involvement. The employer selects a menu of investment options for participants to choose from, and it may make a matching contribution. If your 403(b) is covered by ERISA, it must follow ERISA rules outlined in Chapter 2. Your employer has fiduciary responsibility for running the plan in your best interests, you must receive an account statement at least once a year, and so on.

Non-ERISA: You + plan provider

However, a number of employers do not participate to this extent. Their plans are not covered by ERISA. Public schools often fall into this category. In this case, the 403(b) agreement is between you and the plan provider. Your employer simply agrees to send your 403(b) contribution each pay period to the plan provider that you've chosen. These employers give you a list of possible investments, but they aren't involved in pre-selecting the menu of investment options. It's often simply a list of 403(b) providers who've asked the employer to put them on the list. These providers may be (and often are) insurance agents selling annuities. (They can't just walk into a teacher's lounge and start signing up employees — they need the employer's permission.)

One disadvantage of the second type of plan is that it can be very hard to decide how to invest your money. There can be dozens of names (or in the case of the Los Angeles Unified School District, more than 100) on that list. A common criticism is that participants — usually lacking free time to research investments — may invest in a product simply because the vendor happens to hold a seminar on a day they can attend, or because a representative comes to see them at home. Frankly, that's no way to choose an investment.

If you're in this situation, the first thing you may want to do is talk to co-workers to see what they've invested in. Don't run out and invest in the first thing they mention, though; see if the same name comes up a few times. If so, it may be worth further scrutiny, particularly if your co-workers like the results.

Why can't a (b) be more like a (k)?

Congress created 403(b)s for nonprofits in 1958 and extended them to educational institutions in 1961, long before the arrival of 401(k)s. Because annuities were their only form of investment for many years, 403(b) plans have a very different history than 401(k)s.

Insurance companies had a lock on the 403(b) business during the 1950s and 1960s. There wasn't any competition from other financial organizations — mutual funds were generally sold only to individuals for personal investing, and banks only managed retirement money for employer-run retirement plans, such as defined benefit pension plans.

The idea of employees saving for retirement through salary reductions actually started with tax-sheltered annuities (TSAs — the original 403(b)s) rather than 401(k)s. Ted's experience selling TSAs was one of the reasons he was able to put the pieces together to build the first 401(k) savings plan. Without TSAs, the Treasury Department would never have issued 401(k) regulations that supported the salary reduction approach that Ted included in the first 401(k) savings plan. Permitting employees to use this technique to make pre-tax contributions to a 401(k) gave employees of for-profit companies an opportunity similar to the one many employees of nonprofit employers had been enjoying for years, with a couple of significant differences:

✔ The first distinction is the special nondiscrimination test for 401(k)s, linking the amount that *highly compensated employees* (see Chapter 2) may contribute to the amount the non-highly compensated employees contribute. TSAs weren't subject to these tests, because few, if any, employees of nonprofit employers were highly paid at the time. As a result, achieving a high level of participation was never an issue with TSAs. Today, 403(b)s aren't subject to this test either, although they have to fulfill other nondiscrimination requirements for employer contributions, employee after-tax contributions, and overall plan participation opportunities.

✔ The second distinction involves investment products. Because 401(k)s weren't limited to annuities, insurance companies never controlled the 401(k) market. Certain products offered by insurance companies, such as *Guaranteed Investment Contracts (GIC)*, were used whenever appropriate during the early days of 401(k)s, but mutual funds were also used. (We explain GICs in Chapter 6.) Senior-level managers also had a much higher level of interest in 401(k) investments than was the case with 403(b)s. One reason was the desire to achieve a high level of participation in a 401(k) in order to pass the nondiscrimination test. This desire to achieve high levels of participation led to better investment selections and, frequently, to employer-matching contributions to help drive participation.

Things have changed in a number of ways. The need for employees to save for retirement is widely accepted, regardless of the type of employer. Due to the large number of employees who are now managing their own retirement savings, the level of investment awareness and knowledge is much higher than it was years ago. Competition among financial organizations to capture and retain retirement savings is intense. All these factors have resulted, and will continue to result, in better investment products for 403(b)s and 401(k)s. The 403(b) business is no longer limited to insurance companies. Their control will continue to decline as the investments under these plans move in the same direction as 401(k)s.

After you've narrowed your choices, do research as you would for any investment. The information about risk and investing in Chapters 5 and 6 pertain to you, also.

 If you're thinking of investing in an annuity, be sure that you find out all the fees you'll be charged, including the *surrender fee* if you eventually want out of the annuity. You should get this information in writing — don't rely on verbal assurances from the salesperson.

 You may be able to get your employer to add a provider you like to the list of choices, particularly with a non-ERISA plan. Then you can use that provider's investment options. In any 403(b) plan, you should definitely let your employer know if you're not happy with the investments. For example, if you want your plan to offer mutual funds, ask your employer. Mutual funds are becoming more common in 403(b) plans precisely because more employees are requesting them.

For example, the California State Teachers Retirement System tapped a large financial institution during 2002 to provide 403(b) services, including investment advice and a self-managed account with access to more than 3,000 mutual funds.

Finding Out Rules for Church Plans

403(b) plans offered by churches and church-related organizations aren't required to follow ERISA rules, and most don't. Further, in addition to annuities and mutual funds, church plans can offer something called a Retirement Income Account (RIA) that offers more investment possibilities beyond what 403(b)(7)s offer. However, not all church plans offer RIAs. Churches may also offer 401(k) plans and may choose not to follow ERISA rules.

IRS Publication 571 contains a section explaining rules for 403(b) plans for ministers and church employees.

Chapter 11

The Wonderful World of 457 Plans

*T*o know 457 "deferred comp" plans is to love them. Unfortunately, these plans have been put together in such piecemeal fashion, that it hasn't always been that easy to get to know them.

457s are tax-deferred retirement savings plans for employees of state and local governments as well as some tax-exempt (nonprofit) organizations. So how come everybody knows about 401(k) plans, but when they hear 457 they say, "Huh?"

The answer may be that the 457 isn't necessarily the retirement lifeline for public-sector employees that a 401(k) is for private-sector workers. Workers with 457 plans also generally have a defined-benefit pension plan (which means they'll receive a specified amount each month after they retire), and the 457 is the icing on the cake.

Firefighters, police officers, and other workers in potentially hazardous jobs often retire early, and a 457 can provide a cushion to tide them over until their regular pension benefits kick in.

If you have a 457 plan, you should take advantage of it to gain tax breaks now and, potentially, a bigger nest egg. We've never heard anyone complain about having too much money in retirement!

A little history about the 457

457s are named after the section of the Internal Revenue Code that was added in 1978 to govern them. Here's a piece of cocktail-party trivia (although it may make you wonder what kind of cocktail parties we attend): The same tax law of 1978 that created 457 plans also contained the legislation that led to the creation of the 401(k).

The Scoop on Two Types of 457 Plans

457 plans are often referred to as *deferred compensation* or *deferred comp* plans, because you actually defer receiving part of your compensation until a later date in order to put off paying income tax.

These plans come in two flavors: 457(b) and 457(f). What's the difference? Take a closer look.

- ✔ The 457(b) is very similar to a 401(k) in terms of contribution limits and other rules, and it is offered to employees of state and local governments (governmental plans) as well as to rank-and-file employees of some nonprofits. Technically, 457(b)s are known as *eligible* plans, which means that they follow certain rules in order for employees to get certain tax breaks similar to those offered by 401(k)s.

- ✔ 457(f) plans, known as *ineligible* plans, are offered by some nonprofits, but only to selected highly paid employees as a way of letting them defer some of their compensation (and put off paying taxes on that compensation) until a later date. They're basically *golden handcuffs* (the promise of a certain sum of money for working at the employer for an agreed period of time).

457(f) plans have different rules from 457(b)s. For example, you can't roll over money from a 457(f) into another type of retirement plan — only into another 457(f) — if you change employers. Also, you may have to pay tax on the 457(f) money while you're still working rather than wait until you take money out of the account. With a 457(f), there aren't really "contributions" per se, usually just a promise from the employer to pay a certain amount after a set number of years. ("Work here for five years, and we'll pay you $100,000 for retirement," for example.)

Originally, 457 rules dictated that for both types of plans, assets in the plan would remain the property of the employer until they were distributed. The problem with this arrangement was that the money could go to the employer's creditors in case of bankruptcy, instead of to the retirees and future retirees to whom it belonged. After Orange County, California, declared bankruptcy in 1994, affecting the county's 457 retirement plan, the rule was changed for governmental 457(b) plans — now the money has to be kept in a separate trust, custodial account, or annuity contract. This rule is intended to keep it safe from the employer's creditors. (By contrast, in 457(f) plans it remains part of the employer's assets.)

In mid-2002, the IRS published proposed regulations for 457 plans for the first time since 1982. These rules included changes and clarifications to 457 plans made over the years in various tax bills. The proposed regulations are expected to be adopted largely without changes.

Because 457(b) plans are more common than 457(f) plans, the rest of this chapter is limited to 457(b)s. For more information about all kinds of 457 plans, some great resources are

- National Association of Government Defined Contribution Administrators (www.nagdca.org)
- ICMA Retirement Corporation (www.icmarc.org)
- mPower Cafe (www.mpowercafe.com)
- BenefitsLink (www.benefitslink.com)
- BenefitsAttorney (www.benefitsattorney.com)

Coughing It Up for the Coffers

With a 457(b) plan, you decide how much salary should be deposited into the account each pay period. The money is invested as you choose from the options available in your plan — usually mutual funds (Chapters 5 and 6 explain more about these investments). You don't pay income tax on your contributions or the earnings until you withdraw money from your account. You also get the added benefit of saving through deductions from your pay each pay period — the easiest way to save.

The federal limit on how much salary you can contribute pre-tax to a 457(b) plan is the same as for 401(k) plans ($11,000 in 2002, $12,000 in 2003, and so on, or 100 percent of your salary, whichever is less, as outlined in Chapter 2). Before you take these contribution limits for granted, note that 2002 was the first year that the limits were the same. Before 2002, rules were very different and the source of much confusion.

Approaching the retirement finish line? Get your second wind

457(b) plans may also offer an age-50 catch-up contribution with the same limits for 401(k)s explained in Chapter 2.

Another type of catch-up contribution, unique to 457(b) plans, is allowed for workers who are within three years of the plan's normal retirement age. This catch-up contribution has been around from the start. A qualified worker who hasn't contributed the maximum possible in previous years can contribute up to double the regular limit, depending on how much he or she didn't contribute in the past.

A new twist in the 2002 regulations enables you to utilize the catch-up contribution more than once, at more than one employer, if you qualify. Also, qualifying police officers and firefighters can choose a lower retirement age than other plan participants, but it can't be lower than age 40. The rules are fairly complicated, so if you think you qualify, ask your plan provider for help.

You can only make one type of catch-up contribution in a given year, even if you meet the requirements for both. For example, if you're 57 in 2003 and plan to retire in three years, and you didn't contribute the maximum possible in past years, you would meet the requirements for both. But you have to choose one. You're allowed to figure out how much you can contribute with either one and choose the one that lets you contribute more. For example, the maximum age-50 catch-up in 2003 is $2,000. If you could contribute more than $2,000 using the other type of catch-up, then you would select the one that allowed you to contribute more than $2,000. However, if the other one only allowed you to contribute, say, $1,000, then you would go with the age-50 catch-up of $2,000.

Employer contributions: A double-edged sword?

Employers are allowed to offer a matching contribution in a 457(b), but most don't. Unlike in a 401(k) or 403(b), an employer matching contribution in a 457(b) is counted toward the overall limit. For example, in 2003, the maximum contribution allowed is $12,000.

If your employer contributes $3,000 to your plan, the most you can put in is $9,000 (excluding any catch-up contributions) to reach the $12,000 maximum.

Some employers make contributions to a separate tax-deferred plan, called a 401(a), to avoid this complication. The 401(a) is essentially a 401(k) without any contributions from you, the employee. You may or may not be able to decide how the contributions are invested.

Combined plans: The sky's the limit

Some employees are lucky enough to have a 401(k) or 403(b) available to them, as well as a 457, allowing them to make cumulative contributions. For example, a schoolteacher may have a 403(b) plan through the school district and also be eligible for the county 457 plan. What's so lucky about that? It opens the possibility of quite a bit of retirement saving. You are allowed to contribute the maximum to both plans separately, for a total of $22,000 in 2002, $24,000 in 2003, and so on. (And you can contribute even more if you qualify for catch-up contributions.) This is a big change from the rules before 2001, when you could only contribute the 457 maximum, which was less than for the other plans.

A worker who has a combined 403(b) and 401(k) doesn't have the same opportunity. The maximum contribution limit for those two plans combined is equal to the limit for one plan.

Investing Your Money

A 457 plan generally offers a selection of stock, bond, and money market mutual funds as well as guaranteed investment contracts. For information about risk and choosing investments that are appropriate for you, check out Chapters 4, 5, and 6.

Taking Money Out of a 457

You can usually take money out of your 457 when you change employers or retire. You have to pay income tax on the withdrawal, but there's no 10 percent early withdrawal penalty as with a 401(k) or 403(b). (We discuss the early withdrawal penalty in Chapter 7.)

When you change jobs, you can roll over your 457(b) into another 457(b) or a 401(k), 403(b), or IRA. The rollover rules we discuss in Chapter 7 apply to 457(b)s, as well. (However, a governmental 457(b) can only be rolled over into another governmental 457(b), not into a 457(b) of a tax-exempt organization.) Remember that if you roll your 457(b) into an IRA, you won't be able to withdraw the money before age 59½ without paying an early withdrawal penalty unless you qualify for an exception (also listed in Chapter 7). Rolling into a 401(k) plan or 403(b) plan will make the money subject to withdrawal rules for those plans, which we discuss in Chapters 7 and 8 for 401(k)s, and Chapter 10 for 403(b)s.

You may also be able to withdraw money to pay for "unforeseen emergencies" while you're working. These rules have been stricter than rules for 401(k) withdrawals (discussed in Chapter 7). For example, buying a house or paying for higher education won't normally qualify as unforeseen expenses. Your best bet is to ask your employer what the rules are for your plan.

Loans are permitted in 457 plans, but not all plans allow them. You need to check with your employer to find out whether your plan allows loans.

When you turn 70½, you're required to start taking minimum distributions from your 457 each year. You calculate these as you calculate required distributions from an IRA or other tax-deferred retirement plan. We discuss required distributions in Chapter 9. More-detailed rules are available in IRS Publication 590, at www. irs.gov.

How you take your money out of the plan depends on what your plan offers. You may have to take a lump sum payment (which you can roll over into an IRA), or your plan may let you take installment payments. Plans are also allowed to let you make withdrawals on demand, but this is a new rule in 2002, and many plans may be slow to adopt it because it's an administrative hassle for them.

Part V

From the Employer's Perspective: Finding the Right Plan

The 5th Wave   By Rich Tennant

"The first thing we should do is get you two into a good 401(k). Let me get out the 'Magic 8-Ball' and we'll run some options."

In this part . . .

*E*mployers have their hands full trying to run a suc-cessful business and keep their top-notch employees happy. Keeping employees happy requires offering great benefits, especially a retirement plan, but setting up a retirement plan is no cakewalk.

As an employer, you're responsible for making sure that the plan complies with all the rules; depending on what kind of plan you offer, there may be a lot of 'em. Despite their popularity, 401(k) plans aren't always the easiest or best option, particularly for small-business owners with 25 or fewer employees.

This part outlines different retirement plan options and explains how employers can select the plan that makes the most business sense while making sure that their workers get the best possible investment deal for their retirement savings.

Chapter 12

Meeting the Small Employer's Challenge

● ●

In This Chapter

▶ Understanding how to set up a retirement plan for a small business

▶ Comparing different types of plans

▶ Deciding which plan works for you — it may not be a 401(k)!

● ●

So, you just started a small business with a couple of employees, and you're looking to set up a retirement plan. Not only do you want to save for your own retirement, but you also know that your top-notch employees may move to another company with better benefits if you don't set something up soon.

Should you run down to your local financial services provider and set up a 401(k) plan? Not necessarily. Starting a retirement plan is a bit more complex than buying your favorite brew at the local gourmet coffee shop. You may be surprised to find out that the 401(k) is not your only retirement plan option — nor is it necessarily your best option. Other types of plans are easier to operate and make more sense for many small companies.

For a small employer, the cost and effort involved in establishing a retirement plan can be daunting. The typical small-business owner wears many hats in the start-up stages — which often include human resources manager and chief financial officer — and is usually the one responsible for developing a retirement plan.

As a small-business owner, you need to be extremely well informed before you set up a retirement plan. *You* will be responsible for complying with the law, not the person who sells you the plan or the organization that manages it. If you take time to find out about your retirement plan options — paying special attention to basic legal requirements — you should be able to avoid costly mistakes.

Running a retirement plan, particularly a 401(k), can require a lot of your precious time. You shouldn't trust salespeople who tell you otherwise. Beware especially of some Internet-based providers who offer to design and get your plan up and running in five minutes — any plan that's hatched in five minutes isn't likely to meet your specific needs and is likely to be fraught with compliance problems. Remember, you're dealing with a bunch of IRS rules, so it can't be that easy!

This chapter is for owners of small businesses (from one to about 25 employees). It will help you determine which retirement plan will most benefit you and your employees. In the interest of keeping this easy to read, we give only general information about the main types of plans, not comprehensive, precise profiles. You'll need to get more detailed information later from an organization that will help you set up and manage the plan.

Some good resources for small businesses are IRS Publication 560 (available from your local IRS office or online at www.irs.gov; type "Publication 560" in the search window) or the Profit-Sharing/ 401(k) Council of America (www.psca.org; click on "Start a Retirement Plan").

Meeting Regular 401(k) Requirements Is a Pain in the Pocketbook

Regular 401(k) plans used by larger companies can be a real pain for a small employer.

The *compliance* requirements for *tax-qualified* retirement plans such as 401(k)s are very complex. A tax-qualified plan is one that gives the employer and employee special tax benefits. In return for these advantages, the employer has to follow (or comply with — hence the term *compliance*) certain rules about how the plan should be operated.

Compliance issues are the dark clouds that hang over any retirement plan. The plan you choose will depend on your tolerance for fulfilling various requirements. The first compliance issue relates to employer contributions. This is a big issue for small-business owners, particularly for start-ups. When you have more expenses than revenues, you may not want to make contributions to your employees' retirement plan. But, depending on what plan you choose, you may be required to.

Dieting won't help "top heavy" plans

Technically, employers don't usually have to contribute to their employees' 401(k)s. However, small-business owners are sometimes forced to make employer contributions to a 401(k) plan. This happens when a plan becomes *top heavy* (yes, that's the official term), meaning that more than 60 percent of the money in the plan belongs to the owners of the company and other key employees.

Say you own a small business, and you contribute at least 3 percent of your pay to the 401(k) plan. If the plan is top heavy, your company is required to contribute money into each *eligible employee's* 401(k) account, equal to 3 percent of his or her pay. You even have to do this for eligible employees who don't contribute to the plan on their own. (If the highest contribution for an owner is less than 3 percent, the required contribution to each eligible employee's account is also less than 3 percent. For example, if the highest contribution for an owner is 2 percent, your company is required to contribute the equivalent of 2 percent of each eligible worker's pay into the 401(k); if it's 1.5 percent, the required contribution is 1.5 percent, and so on.)

An *eligible employee* is one who has met the eligibility requirements for participating in the plan — for example, one who has worked at the company for the required amount of time. Just because an employee is eligible doesn't necessarily mean that he or she is actually participating in the plan. We discuss eligibility requirements in more detail in Chapter 2.

Many organizations that sell 401(k)s to small employers ignore the issue of employer contributions. In Ted's opinion, the first thing that you should consider when choosing a plan is whether you're likely to end up with a top-heavy plan because more than 60 percent of the money in the 401(k) plan belongs to the owners. The probability that you will end up with a top heavy plan is high when a company has one or more owners and only a few other employees. If this is the case with your company, you should consider another type of plan, as we explain in the section, "Finding Alternatives to the Standard 401(k) Plan," a little later in this chapter.

Sticking up for the little guy: Nondiscrimination tests

You also need to know that 401(k) plans must pass special nondiscrimination tests at the end of each *plan year.* (Most plan years run from January 1 to December 31; however, some companies use a different 12-month period.) The amount contributed by *highly compensated employees* (HCEs) must be compared to the average percentage of pay contributed by those who aren't highly compensated (non-HCEs). (See Chapter 3 to determine whether an employee is highly compensated.)

In Chapter 3, we explain that the average percentage of pay contributed by HCEs can't be more than 2 percentage points higher than the average percentage of pay contributed by non-HCEs. If non-HCEs as a group contribute 4 percent of salary on average, HCEs may contribute no more than 6 percent. Also, HCE contribution percentages on average can't be more than double non-HCE contribution percentages. So, if non-HCEs contribute 1.5 percent on average, HCEs can contribute only 3 percent (1.5 percent × 2) and not 3.5 percent (1.5 percent + 2 percent).

The nondiscrimination test can result in higher-paid employees not being able to contribute the maximum permitted by federal law ($11,000 for 2002, increasing by $1,000 each year until hitting $15,000 by 2006). This catches a lot of people by surprise, because they assume that they can always contribute the maximum allowed.

Assume that you're a small-business owner (which makes you an HCE, because you own more than 5 percent of the company), and the eligible non-HCEs in your plan contribute an average of 4 percent of pay. This means that you're permitted to contribute only 6 percent of pay (the non-HCE percentage + 2). If you earn $90,000, you can contribute only $5,400 (6 percent of $90,000) for the year. This amount may be much less than what you wanted to contribute — and it's less than the maximum amount permitted by federal law.

Before you start a 401(k), ask your non-HCEs how much they plan to contribute. This will give you a rough idea of how much *you* will be permitted to contribute to this type of plan. Typically, the average non-HCE contribution range is 2 to 8 percent of pay. You should have realistic expectations before you decide to go ahead with a plan.

You also need to consider employer contributions. Plans that don't have an employer matching contribution tend to have significantly fewer employees who participate, and those who do participate contribute less than employees in plans that offer a match. Typically, no more than half of eligible employees contribute when no match is available, while 70 percent or more of eligible employees participate in plans with an employer match of 25 cents on the dollar.

Participation levels are important, because *all eligible employees* — even those who don't participate in the plan — must be included when the nondiscrimination tests are performed. Employees who don't contribute pull down the average and reduce the amount that HCEs can contribute.

Another important point is that all eligible employees must be included in the nondiscrimination testing regardless of how many hours they work — unless your plan document has a provision that excludes employees who work less than a specified number of hours. The law requires that you include employees who work at least 1,000 hours during any year, which is an average of only 20 hours per week. This rule usually doesn't help boost contribution rates, because part-time employees are less likely to contribute.

Calculating the bottom line on employer contributions

A matching contribution of 25 cents on the dollar, up to 4 or 6 percent of pay, will actually cost you only 1 percent or less of the total payroll. Assume that all your eligible employees combined earn a total of $200,000 per year and contribute an average of 4 percent of pay. Your matching contribution equals one-quarter of the employee contributions, or 1 percent of pay. Now say that only 75 percent of your employees participate. You will pay less than 1 percent — 0.75 percent, or $750 for every $100,000 of pay. If your eligible employees earn a total of $200,000 a year, the matching contribution will cost you a total of $1,500.

Also, you can make the employer contribution vest over a period of up to three years for cliff vesting or six years for graded vesting. (Check out Chapter 2 for more detailed explanations of cliff and graded vesting.) When employees leave your company with unvested contributions, they forfeit those contributions. You can use the forfeited contributions to make matching contributions to your remaining employees' accounts. Doing so saves you money.

Deciding on other bells and whistles

When starting a plan for your business, you need to decide on a few other things as well, such as whether to offer loans and hardship withdrawals, and what vesting schedule to use for employer matching contributions.

Ted generally advises employers who are just starting plans to stay away from loans initially. First, they're hard to administer. Second, no one will have much money to borrow during the first few years. Finally, Ted always tells employers that they should leave room to improve benefits in the future, so they shouldn't give everything away when they start the plan. Employers get little (if any) benefit from including loans at the outset, but it can be a nice enhancement to add later.

Virtually all employers permit hardship withdrawals from the start, but they may not let employees withdraw employer contributions. Ted agrees with this approach and usually advises employers to keep their contributions in the plan, rather than let employees withdraw them early, to provide retirement benefits.

As for vesting, Ted generally recommends immediate vesting if the matching contribution is 25 cents on the dollar or less. Otherwise, he recommends a three-year cliff-vesting schedule (0 percent vested for the first three years, and then 100 percent vesting).

Finding Alternatives to the Standard 401(k) Plan

Major providers are often interested only in existing plans with lots of money already in them. (That's how they earn their money!) For this reason, you should consider alternatives to the standard 401(k) plan.

In the following sections, we discuss a couple of the most attractive alternatives to the standard 401(k) plan.

SIMPLE Simon met a pie man . . .

The SIMPLE IRA is a very good plan for small employers, particularly during the first couple of years of a new business. (By the way, SIMPLE stands for *Savings Incentive Match Plan for Employees.*)

You can establish a SIMPLE IRA by completing a one-page form from any financial organization that offers this type of plan. You shouldn't have to pay any set-up fees, administrative fees, or compliance fees. Avoiding these costs and headaches is a big plus.

As an employer, though, you do have to make a mandatory contribution to each employee's account. You may make either a dollar-for-dollar *matching contribution* to the accounts of only those employees who participate or a *nonmatching contribution* for all eligible employees, whether or not they participate in the plan. (The matching contribution generally goes up to 3 percent of pay, although it may be only 1 percent during certain years, which may include the first two years. The nonmatching contribution, which covers more employees, must be 2 percent of pay.)

You may not like having to make this contribution, but it can be less than what it would cost you to set up and administer a 401(k). With a SIMPLE IRA, employer contributions are fully vested at all times.

Some employers feel that the SIMPLE IRA plan is a good starting point; they use it to begin with, and then change to a 401(k) after two years so that they aren't required to make any more contributions.

The maximum amount that you as an employee can contribute to a SIMPLE IRA is $7,000 for 2002, plus a $500 catch-up contribution if you're 50 or older. Because the 2002 maximum contribution to a 401(k) is $11,000 plus a $1,000 catch-up contribution, this may not seem like a good deal ($7,500 versus $12,000).

But the SIMPLE IRA doesn't require nondiscrimination testing, so you (the owner) and other HCEs can contribute the maximum regardless of what amount the lower-paid employees contribute. You don't have to worry about HCE limits or a top heavy plan. (See the section, "Meeting Regular 401(k) Requirements Is a Pain in the Pocketbook," earlier in this chapter, for more on HCE limits and top heavy plans.) Another advantage of using the SIMPLE IRA is that you receive the mandatory employer contribution on top of these contribution limits. Also, contribution limits will rise each year until 2006, as shown in Table 12-1.

Table 12-1	SIMPLE IRA Maximum Contribution Limits	
Year	*Regular Limit*	*Age-50 Catch-Up Limit*
2002	$7,000	$500
2003	$8,000	$1,000
2004	$9,000	$1,500
2005	$10,000	$2,000
2006	$10,000 (or indexed to inflation)	$2,500

Aside from the different contribution limits, other rules for SIMPLE IRAs are the same as for traditional IRAs. One exception is that if you withdraw money within two years of starting the account, you pay a 25 percent early withdrawal penalty rather than the usual 10 percent penalty.

Also, you can make contributions to a traditional or Roth IRA even if you have a SIMPLE. However, your contribution to the traditional IRA won't be deductible if your income is over the limits we discuss in Table 8-1 of Chapter 8. (Chapter 8 also has more general explanations of traditional and Roth IRAs if you want to check them out.)

Choosing a safe harbor in a storm of requirements

A *Safe Harbor 401(k)* plan can eliminate the top heavy and nondiscrimination problems associated with a standard 401(k). All you, the employer, have to do is make a mandatory contribution to the plan. You can choose between two options: a nonmatching contribution of at least 3 percent of pay for every eligible employee, or a dollar-for-dollar matching contribution of up to 3 percent of pay, plus a 50 percent matching contribution on the next 2 percent of pay, deferred by participating employees. Remember, the number of eligible employees is generally higher than the number of participating employees.

You have to include provisions in your plan document qualifying your plan as a Safe Harbor plan, and you must notify your employees that it's a Safe Harbor plan. With a Safe Harbor 401(k), the business owner(s) can contribute the federal maximum, regardless of how much the other employees contribute.

The maximum limits for regular and age-50 catch-up contributions to a Safe Harbor 401(k) are the same as for the regular 401(k) (see Chapter 2 for details). Although this is more than you can contribute to a SIMPLE plan, remember that the Safe Harbor 401(k) requires a larger employer contribution. As an owner, you receive this contribution in addition to the amount that you can contribute from your salary before taxes are taken out. Employer contributions are immediately vested. The cost of setting up and running this type of plan is similar to a 401(k), as shown in Table 12-2.

You may have heard of something called a SIMPLE 401(k). This is a variant of a SIMPLE IRA, but it lost its usefulness when the Safe Harbor 401(k) was introduced. A Safe Harbor 401(k) has many of the same advantages as a SIMPLE 401(k) and also lets employees contribute more.

Selecting a Plan That's Right for You

Most small businesses want one of the plans that are primarily funded by employee contributions. (Other types of plans are funded primarily by the employer; check out the next section for more on these plans.) Each plan has pros and cons. Table 12-2 summarizes the main features of the different plans funded primarily by employee contributions.

Table 12-2	Popular Retirement Plans for Small Businesses (As of 2002)		
Feature	*Regular 401(k)*	*Safe Harbor 401(k)*	*SIMPLE IRA*
Maximum employee contribution	$11,000	$11,000	$7,000
Minimum employer contribution	None	3 percent of salary	1 percent of salary*
Vesting	Over time or immediate	Immediate	Immediate
Loans	Yes	Yes	No
Nondiscrimination testing	Yes	No	No
Subject to top heavy rules	Yes	No	No
Plan design flexibility	Yes**	Yes	Some

(continued)

Table 12-2 *(continued)*

Feature	Regular 401(k)	Safe Harbor 401(k)	SIMPLE IRA
Set-up fees	$1,000	$1,000	None
Estimated minimum annual administration fees (total for plan)	$1,000–$3,000 minimum	$1,000–$3,000 minimum	None

*Must be increased to 2 percent of pay nonmatching, or 3 percent of pay matching, after two years.

**Design flexibility may be adversely impacted by top heavy and nondiscrimination test requirements.

So how do you choose? Answer the following questions (you may want to write your answers down on a piece of paper), and then look at the key to help narrow your search.

1. Do you want to contribute more than $8,000 ($9,000 if over age 50) per year?

2. As the owner, are you willing to contribute 1 percent of each eligible employee's pay?

3. Are you willing to contribute 3 percent of each eligible employee's pay?

4. Are plan fees and administrative simplicity important?

5. Are you and the other business owners likely to contribute more than 60 percent of the total plan assets?

The following answer key should be able to point you in the right direction:

✔ If you answer yes to question 1, you'll need a 401(k) or Safe Harbor 401(k).

✔ If you answer no to question 1, consider the SIMPLE IRA.

✔ If you answer yes to question 2 and no to question 3, consider the 401(k) or SIMPLE IRA.

✔ If you answer no to question 2, consider a 401(k).

✔ If you answer yes to questions 1 and 3, consider the Safe Harbor 401(k).

✔ If you answer yes to question 3 and no to question 1, consider the SIMPLE IRA.

✔ If you answer yes to questions 2 and 4, and no to question 1, the SIMPLE IRA is probably best for you.

✔ If you answer yes to questions 3 and 4, consider the SIMPLE IRA and the 401(k) Safe Harbor.

✔ If you answer no to questions 3 and 5, consider a SIMPLE IRA or 401(k).

✔ If you answer yes to question 5, consider the SIMPLE IRA or Safe Harbor, regardless of any of your other answers.

Looking Out for Number One

Some retirement plans may only make sense for businesses that don't have full-time employees other than the owner, the owner's spouse, and any partners. When eligible employees enter the picture, these plans become expensive for the employer, because it's required to make contributions to the employees' accounts. This section looks at two such options.

Going it alone: The one-person 401(k)

If you're a small-business owner with no full-time employees (and no intention to hire any), and you earn less than $160,000, a possibility you may consider if you really want to sock away a lot of money is a one-person 401(k). Tax laws that took effect in 2002 made the one-person 401(k) more attractive by raising the contribution limit considerably. You can contribute the employee pre-tax maximum ($11,000 in 2002, $12,000 in 2003, and so on), plus the business can contribute up to 25 percent of your W-2 pay as an employer contribution, up to a $40,000 combined maximum. If you're 50 or older, you can add the catch-up contribution on top.

You can use this type of plan for yourself, your spouse, and any business partners, but when employees enter the picture, it may become a hassle. You should use a one-person 401(k) only if you're not planning to hire any full-time employees or if you're willing to contribute at least 3 percent of pay for each eligible employee when you have them. Your business must make the required

3 percent of pay minimum contribution for each eligible employee as soon as you hire employees, because the plan will be top heavy, and you must satisfy nondiscrimination testing. Unless you use a Safe Harbor 401(k), your salary deferral amount will be limited by how much the employees contribute.

In 2002, a number of providers launched products with names like Personal(k), mini-K, Uni-K, and so on. Advertised set-up fees range up to several hundred dollars — investment fees and annual fees are extra.

A one-person 401(k), rather than an easier-to-administer profit-sharing plan, makes the most sense for someone earning less than $160,000, who wants to contribute more than 25 percent of pay to a retirement plan. Here's why: An employer is allowed to contribute 25 percent of salary (up to $40,000) to a profit-sharing plan. If you earn $160,000 or more, 25 percent of your salary will be $40,000 or more, so the business can contribute the full $40,000 for you. However, if you earn less than $160,000, 25 percent of your pay that the business may contribute will be less than $40,000. With a 401(k), the business may contribute 25 percent of your pay as a profit-sharing contribution, and you may make a pre-tax 401(k) contribution (up to $11,000 in 2002, $12,000 in 2003, and so on), to reach the $40,000 limit. If you're 50 years old or older, you can add the age-50 catch-up contribution on top of the $40,000 limit. (We discuss these limits in detail in Chapter 2.)

Amounts *you* contribute to a one-person 401(k) are subject to Social Security tax but amounts *the business* contributes aren't. Social Security taxes are a major point to consider if you are a small-business owner with an income that is less than the Social Security maximum taxable wage base ($84,900 for 2002). Assume you earn $70,000 from your business after all expenses and you want to save $10,000 of this amount for retirement. If you set up a one-person 401(k) and contribute this amount yourself, both you and the business will have to pay FICA (Social Security) tax on this $10,000 contribution. The combined employee/employer Social Security tax will be 15.3 percent if the business is incorporated, for a total of $1,530. On the other hand, a $10,000 employer contribution isn't subject to Social Security tax.

You should consult a knowledgeable tax advisor before setting up this type of plan.

Simplify, simplify: Simplified Employer Plan (SEP)

Another choice to consider is a Simplified Employee Pension (SEP), also known as a SEP IRA. This type of IRA may be a good solution if you are your company's only employee, or if your company has a number of owners and only one or two employees.

A SEP is *not* your best alternative if you have more employees and/or you expect to expand your work force in the future, because it will become very costly for you, the employer.

A SEP is funded entirely by *employer* contributions. Employees don't make pre-tax contributions of their own. Because contributions are made entirely by the employer, they're exempt from FICA and other payroll taxes. This is significant if your earnings are less than the *Social Security maximum taxable wage base* ($84,900 in 2002). (For more explanation of why this is significant, see the example in the previous section, "Going it alone: The one-person 401(k).") You should consider whether the payroll tax savings will help you fund any contributions for the SEP for other employees. If so, this would make the SEP a good choice for your company, because you can avoid these payroll taxes and the costs of setting up and running a more complex plan.

To set up a SEP, you just need to choose a mutual fund company, bank, brokerage, or other IRA provider that offers SEPs, and fill out a one-page form. You shouldn't have to pay set-up fees or annual fees, or fulfill compliance regulations. You just have to send in the money to be invested in the IRA.

The amount that can be contributed to the SEP is very flexible — up to a maximum of 25 percent of pay (not exceeding $40,000) — and there's no required contribution. The employer can make the contribution during the year, or wait until the end of the year to determine how much to contribute.

Employees who are at least 21 years old, worked for you in at least three of the last five years, and received at least $450 in compensation for the year are eligible for the SEP (as of 2002). You can use less restrictive rules, but not more restrictive ones.

Rules for withdrawing money from a SEP are the same as those for traditional IRAs. With a SEP you don't have to set up a trust to hold the assets, which frees you from the fiduciary concerns of other plans.

Hey, it's my treat: Employer-funded plans

The SEP isn't the only plan available that's funded entirely by the employer. You may have heard of a Keogh plan, also known as an H.R. 10 plan, which is available to businesses that aren't incorporated. Keogh plans come in two flavors: defined-contribution plans and defined-benefit plans. Both are more complicated to administer than a SEP. Defined-contribution Keogh plans allow the employer to contribute up to 25 percent of employees' pay (same as a SEP). A *defined-benefit* Keogh plan may offer the opportunity to make larger contributions than a SEP, but a defined-benefit Keogh plan is more complex to administer.

If you're interested in setting up one of these types of plans, you should consult a retirement plan professional. For background information, you can look at IRS Publication 560, *Retirement Plans for Small Business,* which is available free of charge from your local IRS office or on the IRS Web site (`www.irs.gov/pub/irs-pdf/p560.pdf`).

A Word about Cost

Many employees have a general perception that a 401(k) doesn't cost their employer anything, because the employer gets a tax deduction for its contribution. It's true that the employer can deduct a retirement plan contribution from its taxable income, if it has any, but that covers only a small portion of this cost. And if a business isn't profitable, the employer pays the entire cost of any employer contributions to the 401(k).

Still, retirement plans aren't too expensive for small employers. Just about every employer can find an affordable alternative. In some instances, you can't afford *not* to have a plan, because you have to hire and keep top-notch employees in a highly competitive environment.

Considering Real-Life Examples of Different Plans

Even with all this comparative information, choosing among the retirement plan options is probably still difficult. The following examples of how other small-business owners have found attractive and affordable plans may help.

Meeting a small business's needs with a SEP

Larry and Helen run a hunting and fishing lodge. They have only one employee, who works less than 10 hours per week.

Larry and Helen each have annual earnings that are less than the Social Security maximum taxable wage base ($84,900 in 2002). As a result, any contributions they make to either a 401(k) or SIMPLE IRA would be subject to *FICA* (Federal Insurance Contributions Act; the law that requires Social Security tax on earned income) and other employer payroll taxes. Contributions to a SEP would not be subjected to these same taxes.

They decide to establish a SEP through a mutual fund company. All they have to do is complete one easy form and an IRA application for each of them. Contributions to the plan are deposited into the IRAs set up for this purpose. Larry and Helen can invest in any of the mutual funds the company offers for retirement plans. The plan has no set-up fee, no annual fees, and no compliance hassles.

Larry and Helen's business can make contributions during the year, or wait until the end of the year to determine how much to contribute. The contribution amount is flexible (up to a maximum of 25 percent of gross pay), and no contribution is required.

Reaching personal contribution goals with the SIMPLE plan

Manoj and Sarla are medical professionals who have three full-time employees. Manoj and Sarla each have earnings of $100,000, which exceeds the FICA maximum wage base. The total gross annual pay for their three employees is $82,000.

The two doctors want to contribute around $10,000 each to a retirement plan. The three employees are willing to contribute a total of $4,400 to the plan. This means Manoj and Sarla will be contributing more than 80 percent of the total employee contributions during the first year. This would create a top heavy situation with a 401(k) (remember, the cutoff is 60 percent), so their best alternatives are a SIMPLE IRA or a Safe Harbor 401(k).

Either plan would permit them to meet their contribution goals, offer an attractive plan that would help to retain their employees, and save administrative time. Manoj and Sarla decide to go with a SIMPLE IRA rather than the Safe Harbor 401(k) to avoid the cost of setting up and running a 401(k).

To start the plan, all they do is complete a couple of forms supplied by the financial organization they selected and have each employee complete an IRA application.

Manoj and Sarla decide on a dollar-for-dollar employer matching contribution limited to the first 3 percent of pay.

Table 12-3 shows how Manoj and Sarla's plan works.

Table 12-3		Sample SIMPLE Plan		
Employee	Employee Annual Income	Employee Contribution	Employer Contribution	Total Contribution
Manoj	$100,000	$7,000	$3,000	$10,000
Sarla	$100,000	$7,000	$3,000	$10,000
Lela	$28,000	$1,960	$840	$2,800
Alicia	$27,500	$1,375	$825	$2,200
Monica	$26,500	$1,060	$795	$1,855

Manoj and Sarla's employees, Lela, Alicia, and Monica, can select any of the funds offered by the financial organization that are appropriate for an IRA. The employers simply need to send the money to be invested at the end of each month. Employees receive detailed statements directly from the investment company.

Adopting the standard 401(k) for a growing business

Margaret left her employer six months ago to start her own business producing training programs for the medical community. Her clients are drug companies that want effective educational materials that inform the medical community on how to best use specific drugs. Margaret and an outside investor own the business.

Because her training programs are highly technical, Margaret had to recruit seasoned personnel. During the interview process, she promised candidates that she would set up a 401(k).

Because her business can't handle the additional expense, Margaret isn't willing to make an employer contribution. She's the only participating owner. Three non-owner employees are eligible to participate in the 401(k) plan, and this number is expected to grow. One of the employees earns $65,000 and wants to contribute the maximum amount. Another employee earns $26,000 and wants to contribute 8 percent of pay. The third employee isn't interested in participating.

Margaret's contributions are expected to be well below 60 percent of the total employee contributions, so a possible top heavy status isn't a concern. The amount the other employees want to contribute to the plan would permit Margaret to contribute the $11,000 maximum amount. As a result, she decides to go ahead with a 401(k).

Table 12-4 summarizes the plan's first-year contributions and shows how employee contributions impact owner contributions.

Table 12-4	How Employee 401(k) Contributions Affect Owner Contributions		
Employee	*Employee Annual Income*	*Dollar Amount Contributed*	*Percent of Pay Contributed*
Margaret	$110,000	$11,000	10 percent
Alan	$65,000	$11,000	16.9 percent
Pen-Li	$28,000	$0	0 percent
Cheryl	$26,000	$2,080	8 percent

The three non-owner employees contribute an average of 8.3 percent of pay (24.9 percent divided by 3). This unusually high average enables Margaret to contribute the $11,000 maximum and pass the 401(k) nondiscrimination test, because her 10 percent contribution isn't more than 2 percentage points higher than the contributions of the non-HCEs. If Alan contributed a more typical 6 percent instead of 16.9 percent, the average for the three non-owners would have dropped to 4.67 percent. Margaret could then have contributed only 6.67 percent (4.67 percent + 2), or $7,337. It helps to have an Alan in your plan.

Attracting employees with a Safe Harbor 401(k)

Rocco and Wes own and run an engineering consulting firm that employs nine other people. The owners are in their fifties and earn $85,000 each. They want to contribute the $11,000 maximum amount to a 401(k). Rocco and Wes are willing to contribute 3 percent of each eligible employee's pay to help attract and retain good employees in a highly competitive area.

The decision to go with a Safe Harbor 401(k) is based on the amount that the two owners are able to contribute. They expect their employees to contribute an average of about 5 percent of pay. As a result of nondiscrimination rules, Rocco and Wes would be able to contribute only about 7 percent of pay — or $5,950 — each to a regular 401(k). The Safe Harbor 401(k) allows them to contribute the $11,000 maximum, regardless of how much the other employees contribute. They and all other eligible employees will also receive the 3 percent automatic employer contribution.

Table 12-5 lists the first-year contributions and shows how the combined employee/employer contributions actually work. Note that employees who don't contribute still get the 3 percent contribution.

Table 12-5	Safe Harbor 401(k) Contributions			
Employee	Employee Annual Income	Employee Contribution	Employer Contribution	Total Contribution
Rocco	$85,000	$11,000	$2,550	$13,550
Wes	$85,000	$11,000	$2,550	$13,550
Chitra	$60,000	$6,000	$1,800	$7,800
Willard	$55,000	$3,300	$1,650	$4,950
Denise	$54,000	$3,780	$1,620	$5,400
Laxman	$47,300	$0	$1,419	$1,419
Russell	$43,450	$2,607	$1,303	$3,910
Irene	$36,930	$4,432	$1,108	$5,540
Darren	$32,110	$963	$963	$1,926
Sandi	$28,725	$0	$862	$862
Indu	$25,850	$1,034	$776	$1,810

Chapter 13

Walking in an Employer's Shoes

● ●

In This Chapter

▶ Weighing what investments to offer in a 401(k) plan

▶ Ensuring that you and your employees don't pay too much in fees

▶ Finding the right company to provide services and investments

▶ Avoiding common mistakes and misperceptions

● ●

*R*unning a 401(k) plan is a significant responsibility for any employer. A company isn't required to offer a 401(k), but if it does, it must comply with the applicable laws and regulations — whether the plan covers only a couple of employees or more than 100,000.

Managing retirement funds is a serious matter that may potentially expose the employer to liability. Employees also have a very strong interest in the plan. After all, their retirement security is at stake!

Meeting the needs of both the company and the employees can be a delicate balancing act. It becomes especially tricky because there are many ways plans can be set up, and lots of financial services companies are vying for 401(k) business. An ancient Chinese proverb advises, "Don't judge a man [okay, a *person*] until you've walked a mile in his shoes." For our purposes, we can say, "Don't judge a 401(k) plan until you've waded through miles of possible 401(k) plan setups."

This chapter is written to help clarify the choices, particularly for those who oversee the 401(k)s at companies with plans that have between $1 million and $100 million in assets. If your company doesn't have a plan, you should also read Chapter 12 for information about starting a plan and alternatives to 401(k) plans for small companies.

Keeping the Essentials in Mind

A 401(k) is a big deal to administer. You need an operational structure that begins with deducting contributions from employees' paychecks and goes on to handle everything up to, and including, benefit distributions for departing employees.

When you set up a 401(k) plan, you'll probably have an eye on the bottom line — how much your company has to pay to run the plan. After all, the cost has to fit into your budget.

However, getting the best deal for your company shouldn't be the major issue when you set up a 401(k) plan. In Chapter 1, we discuss the requirements for a plan fiduciary (generally the employer) under ERISA, the Employment Retirement Income Security Act. One of those requirements is that a company's decisions about plan investments must be made considering solely what's in the *employees'* best interest. You're not running a 401(k) for the benefit of the company; you should always keep this fact in mind. The best financial deal for your company may prove to be very expensive if it results in a lot of employee dissatisfaction and possibly a lawsuit.

Many employers have the misperception that selecting an organization or organizations to run the 401(k) plan gets them off the hook with legal requirements and potential liability. Folks, this just ain't so. The employer can't get out of this responsibility by hiring someone else. (It's like paying someone to prepare your tax return. If that person makes a mistake, you're still the one held responsible by the IRS.) As a result, be sure that you choose your plan provider carefully. (See the section, "Selecting a plan provider," later in the chapter, for some tips.)

You must also monitor the performance of investments offered by your 401(k) plan and make changes when appropriate. Changing plan providers can be a big deal, so you really should only do it if you have a good reason. (For example, your provider may leave the business or be sold, you may outgrow the relationship, the funds may perform badly or be too expensive, or service may be bad.) Employers commonly make bad decisions when they pick their first provider, but they get smart after changing one or two times. Employers who are with the top providers tend to change less frequently.

Choosing Investments to Offer in the Plan

The quality of the investments offered in your 401(k) is the most important consideration when running your 401(k). Unfortunately, many other issues commonly overshadow the quality of investments when companies decide how to run their 401(k)s. We recommend putting investing at the top of the list.

Selecting investments to offer in your 401(k) plan isn't easy. Three essential points to look at are: keeping fees low, choosing a financial services company or companies to run the plan, and deciding what specific funds to offer in the plan.

Keeping fees at a reasonable level

Your plan should give participants at least as good a deal as they can get investing on their own outside the plan. As an employer, you need to carefully consider all the fees charged to the plan.

For example, an investor — call him Joe — can buy essentially any mutual fund through an IRA with a mutual fund company and pay only the regular management fee charged by the mutual fund company. Joe can do research and find funds that cover different investment categories (large-cap stocks, short-term bonds, and so on) and are among the top performers. It doesn't matter if they're from different *fund families,* because Joe can invest with different fund companies or go to a fund supermarket such as Schwab's OneSource. In short, Joe has a lot of investment freedom in his IRA. Joe should be able to get at least as good a financial result through his 401(k) — a broad range of quality funds with total fees that are equal to or less than what he would pay investing in his own IRA.

 A *fund family* is the group of mutual funds offered by the same company, such as Fidelity, Janus, T. Rowe Price, and so on. If you invest only at Janus, for example, you'll be limited to funds in the Janus family. This choice may be fine with you, or you may prefer to own funds from other companies, as well.

Your 401(k) plan should make a wide range of funds available to participants so that they can properly diversify among the various classes of investments. Fees for these investments shouldn't be more than what the fund company would charge an investor outside a 401(k). The funds your 401(k) offers in all investment categories (asset classes) should have track records placing them in the top half among their peers.

401(k) products can be packaged in many different ways, making it difficult to evaluate the various alternatives. Financial institutions that are *plan providers* put together the packages. Consider using only plan providers that openly and willingly explain the fees that the employer and participants pay.

Some organizations' representatives may tell you that you don't pay any fees. Don't fall for this line. (You'd be surprised how many intelligent businesspeople actually fall for it!) There are substantial costs associated with running a 401(k), and companies don't provide these services for free. The question isn't *whether* a specific plan provider gets paid, but *how* and *how much* it gets paid.

Fees can be paid in two ways:

- ✔ Billed directly
- ✔ Deducted from assets in the plan

Direct-billed fees are easy to track, because the provider issues an invoice that must be paid. However, asset-based fees may be hidden, because they're paid as automatic deductions from the return investors receive on their mutual funds or other investments. The participant has a lower return, because these fees are taken out.

These fees are buried, so sales representatives can tell companies that they don't pay any fees. This statement is true in the sense that you don't write a check to the particular financial organization. Fund management fees must be disclosed in the prospectus for *retail mutual funds* (those available to all investors) but not for other types of investments that may be offered to 401(k) participants.

The provider may also deduct additional fees directly from the plan, and it isn't normally required to disclose them. Not surprisingly, higher-cost providers are usually reluctant to disclose their fees, while lower-cost providers are happy to disclose them.

If a provider won't fully disclose its fees to you, they're likely high. This type of provider is like a shop that doesn't display prices on the goods it sells. You should take your business elsewhere.

Most employers try to comply with the Department of Labor *Section 404(c) regulations,* which can provide some relief from fiduciary liability for participant-directed investments. These regulations require employers to provide participants with sufficient information to make informed investment decisions. It's obviously difficult to make informed investment decisions without knowing what fees are paid. As an employer, you should realize that if your employees aren't fully aware of the fees charged to them, it can result in failure to comply with Section 404(c).

Fees are expressed in *basis points*, with one basis point equal to .01 percent, and 100 basis points equal to 1 percent. Here's an example of how higher fees can affect participants' accounts. Say your plan has 100 participants and $2 million worth of assets. If it's run with fees of 75 *basis points* (0.75 percent) or less, including all investment and administrative services, the fees total $15,000 or less. (A *third-party administrator* can achieve this level of fees, as we explain in the "Administrative alternatives" section a little later in the chapter.) However, if a provider charges fees of 200 basis points (2 percent), annual costs will total $40,000 (2 percent of $2 million). The $25,000 difference goes to the plan provider rather than to the 401(k) participants' accounts (that's $250 less, on average, for each participant), and this shortfall will get bigger along with account balances each year.

IBM and Kodak run their plans with total investment and administrative costs of less than 15 basis points (0.15 percent). You can't match this result if your plan has only a few million dollars of assets, but you don't have to accept a 401(k) product that charges 200 or more basis points (2 percent or more) in fees, regardless of your plan's size.

Unfortunately, some employers are only concerned about the fees *the company* pays. These employers fail to realize that they must also effectively manage the fees that *participants* pay. A good financial deal for the company doesn't have to result in a bad deal for employees.

Selecting a plan provider

Looking for investments with low fees to include in your plan is only the beginning. In fact, the biggest challenge facing most employers today is finding a way to include the investments they want in their 401(k) plan.

The funds that are offered may all be *proprietary* funds of the financial organization. For example, a mutual fund company may offer only its own funds. However, this is less than ideal, because a single fund family won't have top performers across all investment categories. The plan would do better to offer top-performing funds from several companies.

On the other hand, the provider may offer *non-proprietary* funds (funds run by another financial institution). Typically, a provider selects only funds that are willing to pay a portion of their management fees to the provider, meaning that the management fees are likely high.

The rest of this section is for employers who want to run their plans by focusing on getting the investments they want rather than being limited to what financial organizations offer as *bundled* (packaged) 401(k) products.

Considering how many investment choices to include

The first step you should take in selecting a plan provider is to determine the number and type of investment choices you want your plan to offer. You should either hire a professional asset consultant or use other research tools to help you. The funds you choose should depend largely on the needs of your participants, including factors such as how many participants you have and their level of investment knowledge.

For example, if most of your participants aren't very interested in or knowledgeable about investments, you should probably offer fewer than ten funds so that they won't be overwhelmed. However, this limited menu won't satisfy the investment-savvy folks who are used to sorting through thousands of funds when they invest outside the plan. The easiest answer is to give the investment-savvy participants an unlimited fund menu by offering a mutual fund *brokerage window* (see Chapter 6).

Figuring out what types of funds to offer

In Chapter 6, we discuss the different asset classes in detail. Participants should have the opportunity to invest in large-cap, mid-cap, and small-cap stocks. They need a bond or stable value fund. A money market fund isn't a good long-term option, but it is a good place to park money during uncertain times. An international stock fund is another alternative many participants like. You should also provide a mix of managed and index stock funds, and value and growth funds.

It's important to give participants the opportunity to diversify their investments. By this we don't just mean that you should offer both stocks and bonds (or other fixed investments), although this is certainly true. We mean that you should offer different types of investments within the stock and bond categories.

After you decide what type of funds to offer, you're ready to consider the specific funds to use. You should use an *independent* investment consultant or research to help you through this process, because you can't always rely on the descriptions that come from the fund company.

A good way to find reliable independent consultants or other sources of information is by asking human resources officials at other companies for references. We can also suggest a couple of good independent sources of information:

✔ Morningstar (www.morningstar.com) can provide hands-on support to help you build the investment selections for your plan and to monitor performance, or you can use the company's material to help you do it on your own.

✔ The Institute of Management and Administration (www.ioma.com) publishes three items that can help you pick your funds and manage your plan:

 • *Report On Managing 401(k) Plans,* a 16-page monthly newsletter. $269 per year at the time of this writing.

 • *Managing 401(k) Plans Yearbook,* a comprehensive and authoritative 220-page annual book on the latest 401(k) plan strategies and approaches being used by sponsors. $229.

 • "Managing 401(k) Operations & Costs," an exclusive research study on the best ways to manage 401(k) plan costs. $119.

Opting for administrative alternatives

If you like the idea of picking investments for your plan, rather than just accepting what one company offers, you may wonder how to find someone to provide the record-keeping and other administrative support functions you need to run your plan.

Enlisting a third-party's help

Selecting a *third-party administrator* (TPA) to provide the non-investment services is one way to handle administration of the plan. TPAs are organizations that design and administer retirement plans, but don't actually manage funds.

TPAs specialize in this business, so they're usually good at it, but you still need to be as discerning as you would with any other supplier of a product or service. For example, a TPA may have strong ties to a major financial organization. In this case, it will probably encourage you to use 401(k) funds offered by this financial organization. You should make it clear early on that you want investment flexibility. If a particular TPA can't give you the investment flexibility you need, consider another one.

Third-party administrators that manage plans with limited invest-ment restrictions, or no restrictions at all, must have a record-keeping system that supports the investment flexibility you're looking for. One specific way to find a TPA is by contacting a firm that sells record-keeping software and asking about TPAs in your area. Two possibilities are:

- ✔ **SunGard Corbel.** This company's Quantech record-keeping system is popular with TPAs. Call 1-800-326-7235, or go to www.corbel.com.

- ✔ **Cascade Technologies, Inc.** This company sells PC-based record-keeping software. Call 732-906-2020, or go to www.cascadetechnologies.com.

Handling the job internally

You may also handle the record-keeping function for your plan internally. Doing so will give you a lot of investment flexibility and tighter control of the plan. For example, you can acquire a license to use the Quantech system (mentioned in the previous section). At the time of this book's writing, the initial cost (including hardware) was approximately $10,000, and the annual fee for technical support, updates to the software to reflect changes in the law, and so on, was in the $3,000 to $4,000 range. You'll need a staff member with basic computer and accounting or math skills to maintain the participant accounts.

You'll need to factor in the cost of this staff member if you use an internal record-keeping system. However, keep in mind that significant staff time is also required when you use an outside firm. As a result, the additional time required to operate the plan internally is likely to be much less than you expect. You can also use plan assets to pay the expense related to running the plan internally.

An additional advantage of running the plan internally is that you eliminate the costly and time-consuming process of looking for a new provider every three years or so.

Complying with the rules and regulations

The tough part in running your 401(k) is complying with all the laws and regulations, including the *nondiscrimination testing* (see Chapter 3). Most TPAs have retirement consultants who can help with the tougher compliance issues. If you don't use a TPA, you'll need outside technical support from a professional who specializes in this area of the law. You can retain a local retirement plan consultant to help you. Or, you can use the Technical Answer Group (TAG), an online firm that provides answers to retirement professionals and employers who administer 401(k)s and other retirement plans. You can reach them at www.tagdata.com or 770-565-8445.

Looking at the Packaging of 401(k) Plans

Some providers offer to run 401(k)s without charging employers any fees. Not surprisingly, these providers win most of the business. You may wonder how they can survive without charging you a fee. The answer is that your plan does pay fees, indirectly. In this section, we help you understand the most common ways 401(k) products are packaged.

Major mutual fund companies such as Fidelity, Putnam, T. Rowe Price, and Vanguard control a large segment of the 401(k) business. These fund companies offer full-service (*bundled*) 401(k) products that provide everything you need. If your plan is large enough and has high average account balances, Fidelity, Putnam, and T. Rowe Price will run the plan without charging any fees other than the normal fund management fees. (Fund management fees are deducted by the fund company, reducing participants' returns.) Vanguard actually *reduces* its fund management fees for larger investors. As a result, it may charge fees for non-investment 401(k) services such as record keeping and compliance testing. (All fee information was correct at the time of writing, but it may, of course, change.)

For example, the funds you select with Fidelity, Putnam, and T. Rowe Price may charge investment fees averaging around 90 basis points (0.90 percent). If your plan has $30 million of assets, the fees will be $270,000 per year. The fund mix you select with Vanguard may average 30 basis points (0.30 percent), or only $90,000. This is why Vanguard may have to charge additional fees for non-investment services.

The fees for non-investment services can be paid from plan assets — in other words, they can be paid from participants' accounts rather than by the employer. Assume that Vanguard charges $15,000 in addition to its $90,000 in investment management fees. That's a total of $105,000. If this money is deducted from plan assets, the total cost to the participant rises to 35 basis points (0.35 percent) — still much lower than what the other three fund companies charge. The point here is that you don't have to select higher-priced funds for your participants in order to give yourself (the employer) a break from paying fees. If you select funds with lower investment management fees, any additional administrative fees may be paid by the plan rather than the employer. This can substantially reduce the cost to participants without changing the employer's cost. This is an example of a win-win strategy for both participants and employers.

Of course, fees aren't the only reason for selecting a particular investment. The ultimate goal is to get the best investment return for your participants, which means that you must consider the actual net return after expenses.

The previous example is just that — an example. The situation for your particular company may be different. Be sure to do thorough research before selecting the firm or firms to provide 401(k) services for your company.

Most of you run plans that are a lot smaller than $30 million. Your plan may be so small that none of the fund companies we mention earlier in this section want to handle it. For example, assume that your plan is in the $1 million to $5 million range. The people calling you get paid for selling 401(k) plans. They usually represent a group of providers offering a product that carries additional *asset-based fees* (fees charged as a percentage of the assets in the plan) to cover the compensation paid to the broker, and other costs of the provider. These additional charges are usually around 100 to 150 basis points (1 to 1.5 percent). When these fees are added on top of the fund management fees, the total fees are typically in the range of 200 to 250 basis points (2 to 2.5 percent).

If your plan has $5 million of assets, 200 basis points is $100,000 per year — a substantial sum. These fees come directly from plan participants. It's amazing that business-savvy senior executives, who are paying the largest share of these high fees, are willing to accept this result.

One alternative for avoiding these high fees is to hire a third-party administrator (TPA) to run your plan. (See the section, "Enlisting a third-party's help," earlier in this chapter for more info.) Typically, a TPA will charge about $15,000 annually for all non-investment services for a plan with $5 million of assets and 200 participants. Say your current provider is charging 200 basis points (2 percent), or $100,000, in fees for the bundled plan. Further assume that the investment management fees total $50,000 (100 basis points), and the provider charges an additional $50,000 (100 basis points) for non-investment services. You can replace the provider with a TPA that lets you keep the same funds in your plan and lower the total cost of the plan from $100,000 to $65,000 ($50,000 plus $15,000). The additional $35,000 would go directly to your participants.

You may be able to find other ways to lower the plan's costs even further, such as working with the TPA to select lower-cost and better-quality funds.

By the way, although most plans let employees choose how to invest their contributions, some plans don't. Ted knows of a $40 million plan that doesn't let the employees choose how to invest their contributions. This doesn't mean that the CEO and Chief Financial Officer are picking the stocks that the plan invests in. (This is to be discouraged!) The employer hired a name-brand mutual fund company to manage a portfolio of individual stocks. The investment management fees are approximately one-fourth of what this company charges for its mutual funds with comparable investments. A bank handles all the record keeping and administration. The total cost for running this plan is approximately 40 basis points.

A 401(k) Is a Terrible Thing to Waste: Educating Employees

If you run your plan on your own, an area where you'll need help is investment education for your employees. One of the many *Section 404(c)* requirements is to provide adequate information for employees to make informed investment decisions. The TPA that you select may be able to run investment education meetings, but many don't offer them. If yours doesn't, you'll have to look elsewhere.

Two organizations that provide education on investment and financial matters are The EDSA Group and Successful Money Management Seminars:

✔ The EDSA Group (which stands for Educational Solutions and Awareness) offers a workshop to help employees maximize the benefits of their 401(k)s, as well as other programs dealing with more general money management issues and retirement planning. The cost typically ranges between $30 and $70 per employee. The EDSA Group Web site is www.theedsagroup.com, and its phone number is 1-800-942-2777.

✔ Successful Money Management Seminars (SMMS, Inc.) licenses generic financial education courses to financial professionals. These professionals offer the SMMS courses throughout the United States and Canada. You can find out about courses available in your area at www.smms.com.

Getting Up Close and Personal — Why You Shouldn't

The most common mistake employers make is to let a personal relationship, rather than economics, influence the selection of a 401(k) plan provider. We have both heard stories from participants about bad plans that were run by a friend, nephew, uncle, and so on of the boss. Participants are often afraid to complain because they can lose their jobs.

Smaller employers often rely on personal relationships when selecting a provider. A personal friend who is a broker, financial advisor or 401(k) consultant can add value to the selection process and to your participants, but you need to know what you're buying and have solid reasons for your decision. All costs should be revealed so you and your participants can evaluate costs versus the services the friend provides. Unfortunately, higher-cost 401(k) products are usually sold through personal relationships. Blindly buying a 401(k) product from a friend without comparing it to others isn't a good way to handle the ERISA fiduciary requirement of picking investments that are solely in the best interest of your participants. Thoroughly checking the quality of the investments and all direct and indirect costs is in the best interest of all parties involved — including you.

Part VI
The Part of Tens

The 5th Wave   By Rich Tennant

Defining your investment risk with the:
TOAST RETRIEVING RISK TOLERANCE TEST

| LOW RISK | Waits for toast to pop up even though it's burning. |

| MODERATE RISK | Goes after toast with wooden toast prongs. |

| HIGH RISK | Goes after toast with all metal butter knife. |

| ULTRA HIGH RISK | Goes after toast with metal butter knife wearing a wet swim suit and a stainless steel colander on head. |

In this part . . .

You can find out a lot from other people's questions — and from their mistakes. This part answers real-life questions from employers and 401(k) participants, boosts your confidence by warning you about common mistakes people make with their retirement plans, and shoots down any excuses you may be tempted to make for not saving in a retirement account.

Chapter 14

Ten Questions Participants Frequently Ask

• •

In This Chapter

▶ Resolving tricky contribution situations

▶ Keeping track of your 401(k) if your company is acquired or goes bankrupt

▶ Questions about loans and rollovers

▶ Figuring out where to get help

▶ Dividing a 401(k) in a divorce

▶ Finding something good about company stock

• •

*Q*uestions about 401(k) plans seem to be as numerous as the 42 million people who use them. So, we chose a few real-life questions to answer in this chapter. Even though this section of the book is called the Part of Tens, we convinced the publisher to let us include a few more than ten (but less than 42 million).

Contributions

I left my employer and then came back six months later. I participated in the 401(k) plan before I left. Do I have to wait one year before I can contribute to the 401(k) again?

Your employer can't require you to satisfy the plan's eligibility requirements a second time if your break in service is less than one year — even though you left and came back to the company.

I can't afford to contribute to my plan now. If I don't join my plan as soon as I'm eligible, do I lose my right to contribute later?

If contributions are out of the question now, you can join the plan later, whenever your plan's rules permit new enrollments. You may be able to enroll at any pay period, or on specific entry dates. However, unless contributing is totally impossible, you should try to do it — even if you start with only 1 percent of your pay. You can increase your contribution a little bit each time that you get a raise.

I changed jobs last year and contributed to two 401(k)s. When I got my W-2s, I saw that I contributed $900 more than the maximum allowed. What do I do?

You can leave the extra money in the plans, but you'll be taxed on it twice — once in the year you contributed it, and once in the year you withdraw it. You'll be taxed on it only once if you notify your employers and withdraw the excess money by April 15 of the year after the year in which you contributed too much.

First decide which plan to withdraw the money from. In general, you can take it all from either plan, or you can split the withdrawal between the two plans. However, some plans won't make *corrective distributions* (distributions to correct this type of error), so find out whether both plans do. If they do, figure out which plan to withdraw the excess from to achieve the best financial result. Look at the employer matching contribution that you received in both plans. Any matching contributions on the excess amount will be taken away when your excess is returned. So, your first preference should be to withdraw from the plan that didn't match your contributions or matched them at a lower rate. Also, look at the vesting schedule of both plans. If the employer matching contributions to your prior plan are fully vested (yours to keep), consider whether you're likely to be with your current employer long enough for that match to vest. (You can read more about vesting in Chapter 2.)

When and how often may I change the amount I contribute?

Your employer sets these rules. It can permit a lot of flexibility or be very restrictive. The most flexible approach is to permit changes each pay period. The most restrictive is to permit changes only at the beginning of the plan year, so that whatever contribution level you choose applies for the entire year.

I recently changed jobs, and my new employer doesn't offer a retirement plan. Can I continue to make contributions to my old 401(k)?

You can't make additional contributions to your old 401(k) account, because you're no longer an employee of your former company. However, you can make contributions to an IRA. The contribution limit is lower than for a 401(k), but it's better than nothing. Whether your IRA contributions are tax-deductible depends on your income level and the kind of IRA you choose. (See Chapter 8 for more on IRAs.)

Should I stop contributing after I contribute enough to get the full employer match?

Your goal is to have enough money when you retire. This may require contributing more than the amount that your employer matches. Keep in mind that you continue to get the full tax breaks for the amount you contribute above the match level.

My company isn't doing well, and it just announced that it's stopping the 401(k) matching contribution. Is this legal?

Your employer can change the match at any time, unless it has a contractual obligation, such as a collective bargaining agreement that requires a specific matching contribution. The plan document may permit your employer to change the match without notice. Most companies will tell you in advance if they're going to make a change in your matching contributions.

My employer just started a new 401(k) plan, but participants aren't able to choose their investments. Is this legal and fair? I was able to pick from 16 different funds in my old plan.

Surprising as it may seem, employers aren't required to let you choose your own investments. The employer is permitted to determine, with the plan trustees, how the money will be invested. It's unusual for employers to choose how to invest employees' money, but it's legal.

Employers sometimes choose investments for their employees because it makes the plan easier and less expensive to administer and eliminates the need to educate employees about different types of investments. Also, your employer may think most of your co-workers aren't capable of making informed choices.

However, most plans give employees the opportunity to split their contributions among a number of different funds. This allows each participant to structure an appropriate investment allocation among stocks and bonds, based on their time horizon and risk tolerance. (We discuss these concepts in more detail in Chapters 5 and 6.)

Mergers and Bankruptcy

My employer was recently sold. The new company told us our money will be transferred into its plan. I don't like the investments for the new plan. Why can't I leave my money in the old plan or transfer it to an IRA?

This situation is common when a company is sold. The buyer typically wants all employees in the same plan with the same investments. This is usually accomplished by forcing the participants of the acquired company to move their money into the new company's plan and investments.

The terms of the purchase agreement between the two companies is a key factor in governing what happens to the old 401(k). The purchase agreement will frequently provide for an automatic transfer of the 401(k) money from the old plan to the new plan. Depending upon the circumstances, your employer may not be able to give you the opportunity to take your money from the plan as a result of the sale of the company. Also, a single transfer to the new plan is much easier for your old employer than having to process a lot of individual benefit payments or IRA transfers. Your old and/or new employer may also want to avoid making these funds available, out of fear that employees will have the opportunity to blow their retirement savings.

The company I work for appears to be in serious financial trouble. I'm concerned about what will happen to my money if it shuts down.

Your employer is legally required to put your contributions into the plan no later than 15 business days after the end of the month in which the money was deducted from your pay. Unfortunately, some employers who are in serious financial trouble abuse this area of the law.

Your money should be safe from the company's creditors when it's deposited into the plan. In this case, the money is considered to be a plan asset, but it can take you a while to get it.

For this reason, and especially if your employer is having financial troubles, you should keep a close watch on when the contributions are deposited into your plan account. Your ability to do so depends on the administrative structure of your plan. For example, it will be easy to tell when money is added if you have daily Web or voice response access to the current value of your account.

Consider stopping your contributions if the administrative structure of your plan doesn't let you track when money is being added to your account, and you think that there's a strong likelihood your company will go out of business.

My employer went out of business six months ago, and I'm still waiting to get my money out of the plan. The former plan administrators are no longer around. The service provider tells me that they can't pay my money to me. What can I do?

Your experience is rather common when a company goes out of business. It is usually a difficult time for everyone, including the former owners. Many creditors and others probably want to find them. The good news is that if your money has actually been deposited into the plan, it should all be safe from the company's creditors. Your payment is probably delayed because, legally, the service provider can distribute benefits only with instructions from a plan representative. This authorization can't be provided if the plan representatives have all disappeared.

The courts should appoint someone to liquidate the business, including shutting down the 401(k). You'll get your money, but it may take a while. Ask the Department of Labor for help through its local office, which you can find listed on its Web site at www.dol.gov. The offices of your senators or congresspeople are other potential sources of help.

Loans and Rollovers

My husband and I both contribute to a 401(k). We plan to borrow 401(k) money to buy our first home. Does it matter from which plan we borrow?

Two primary issues come to mind with this question. The first is the potential that either of you will change jobs during the repayment period. If this happens, you'll have to repay the outstanding balance in a lump sum in order to avoid paying taxes. To resolve this issue, borrow from the plan of whoever plans to stay longest at his or her job.

The other issue involves your ability to handle the loan repayment, the mortgage payments, and continued plan contributions. If you have to reduce your contributions so much that you'll lose out on the employer matching contribution, consider which plan has the larger match. Make sure that contributions to that plan continue up to the full amount that's matched. The other spouse should then contribute whatever additional amount you can afford to his or her plan.

I have more than $70,000 in my 401(k) account. Can I transfer this much money to an IRA even though it exceeds the IRA limit?

The various limits that apply to personal IRA contributions don't apply to rollovers from employer plans. The amount you can roll over from an employer plan into an IRA isn't limited. You can roll over the entire $70,000.

I'm about to retire and roll my 401(k) into my IRA. My 401(k) account includes both pre-tax and after-tax contributions. What can I roll over?

You can roll over the entire amount, including your after-tax contributions. This wasn't possible before the law changed, effective in 2002.

Getting Help at Retirement

I'd like someone to help me decide what to do financially when I retire next year. How can I find a good adviser?

You face a mind-boggling combination of tax, estate planning, and investment decisions. Getting help from someone who is well versed in these issues is advisable, but finding the right person can be challenging. Two good resources for finding an adviser are the National Association of Personal Financial Advisors (www.napfa.org) 1-800-366-2732, and the Financial Planners' Association (www.fpa-net.org) 1-800-647-6340. Another is Dalbar's Advisor Finder (http://moneycentral. msn.com/investor/dalbar/main.asp). You can also ask friends and co-workers for recommendations in your area.

Early on, establish how the adviser will be paid. Choose an adviser who's paid a flat fee rather than a commission. An adviser paid solely by commissions has to sell you products, some of which may not be in your best interest, to get paid.

Although consulting an adviser is often a good idea, totally placing your future in someone else's hands *isn't*. You should have enough knowledge to know whether the advice you're getting makes sense. Reading this book and consulting some of the resources we recommend is a good start.

Divorce

I'm getting a divorce, and my spouse has a 401(k). How can I make sure that I get my fair share? Will I have to pay tax on it?

The 401(k) should be split through a valid qualified domestic relations order (QDRO). A *QDRO* is a court order that allows a portion of your spouse's 401(k) money to go to you. If it's drafted correctly, neither you nor your spouse pays a 10 percent early withdrawal penalty on your portion, even if you're both younger than 59½. (See Chapter 2 for more about this penalty.) Your options for what to do with the money may include leaving it in the 401(k) in a separate account managed by you, or rolling it into an IRA or your own employer-sponsored retirement plan. Either option would keep the money tax-deferred until you withdraw it. You may also be able to withdraw the money right away, but you have to pay income tax on the amount. Your plans for the money must be spelled out in the QDRO; contact your spouse's employer or 401(k) plan administrator to find out what your options are. QDROs are tricky to draft, so hire a divorce attorney who has experience in this field. Some people also hire a certified divorce planner — a financial planner trained to analyze long-term implications of financial decisions made during a divorce.

I haven't seen my spouse for more than two years. I have no idea where he is. When I tried to change my 401(k) beneficiary to my children, I was told that I needed his approval. Why can't I name whomever I want as my beneficiary?

The law requires consent from your spouse in order for you to name someone else as your primary beneficiary. This provision was added to the law years ago to protect the rights of women, but it works both ways. The provision creates a serious problem in situations like yours (until you're able to get a divorce or find your spouse to get his consent). If you change your beneficiary to your children without your spouse's approval, and your employer pays the benefit to your children upon your death, your spouse could, in theory, sue your employer. That's probably why you were told that you needed your spouse's approval. However, not all employers are that strict. If your employer lets you name your children without your spouse's approval, you should do it, because you have nothing to lose.

My husband and I are getting a divorce. He wants half my 401(k) account. This is bad enough, but I don't want his girlfriend to get the money if he dies. Can this money go to my children instead?

Your spouse has a legal right to claim a portion of your 401(k) account; however, the exact details should be resolved during the divorce proceedings and become part of the final agreement. If he is willing, the agreement could give you the right to control who will get this money in the event of his death. However, this right may be workable only while the money remains in the 401(k), because it will be virtually impossible to track after he withdraws money from the plan and mixes it with other money.

I was recently given half my ex-spouse's 401(k) money. When can I get it? Who pays tax on it?

The divorce agreement should specify when you can take the money out of the plan. The agreement may not permit you to take your benefit until your ex-spouse takes his or her benefit. If this point isn't covered by the divorce agreement, you can take the benefit on the earliest retirement date provided under your ex-spouse's plan. You'll have to get this date from the employer. You'll be responsible for paying tax on the money that you receive unless you roll it over.

Company Stock Advantage

I own company stock in my 401(k). Because I'm about to retire and request a distribution, I'd like to know more about the special tax breaks I've heard about that apply to company stock.

Company stock is taxed differently when it's distributed to you from the plan. Any other amount you receive is fully taxable as additional income. With company stock, you pay taxes on the value of the stock at the time that you acquired it through the plan — not the value at the time that it's distributed to you. (This only works if you *do not* roll over the shares into an IRA.)

Assume that you have $50,000 of company stock that originally cost $20,000 when you invested in it. At the time of your distribution, you'll receive $50,000 worth of stock, but you'll pay tax on only $20,000. Later, when you sell the stock, your investment gain will be taxed as a capital gain, which is a lower rate than the regular income tax.

Chapter 15

Ten Questions Employers Frequently Ask

*E*ven employers who know 401(k) rules like the backs of their hands may be confused when it comes to applying them. This chapter provides answers to some tricky real-life questions from employers. We promise ten questions, but you'll notice that we throw in a few more for good measure.

Contributions

I run the 401(k) at my company. Can you explain how I should calculate matching contributions?

Don't feel bad if you're confused, because employers frequently mess up matching contributions. You can either match contributions only during pay periods when employees contribute, or match them based on employees' contributions for the whole year.

For example, assume that you match 50 percent of the first 5 percent of pay contributed. This means that the maximum you'll contribute is 2.5 percent of pay. The question is whether you match 2.5 percent of annual pay or 2.5 percent of the amount paid each pay period.

If you compute the match for each pay period, the employer contribution should be equal to 50 percent of the employee's contribution, if the employee contributes less than 5 percent of pay. If the employee contributes 5 percent of pay or more, the employer contribution should be equal to 2.5 percent of the employee's pay for that period.

If you determine the match on an annual basis, you compute the amount based on the employee's year-to-date pay. Say an employee contributes nothing for six months and then contributes 20 percent of pay during the last six months. Or, say an employee contributes his year-end bonus to the plan in December. In these instances, the entire amount contributed should be matched, as long as the year-to-date match doesn't exceed 2.5 percent of year-to-date pay. This is the case even though the match for the current pay period will exceed 2.5 percent of current pay.

The method you select must be applied uniformly for all participants and should be consistent with the provisions of your plan document.

What's the difference between a variable matching contribution and a profit-sharing contribution?

Profit-sharing contributions are determined at the end of the year, based on the company's financial results. Typically, all eligible employees get a portion of a profit-sharing contribution without having to contribute to the plan. A profit-sharing contribution is usually divided among eligible employees in proportion to total earnings.

Variable matching contributions may be based on the company's financial results, as well, but they only go to employees who contribute to the 401(k).

How can you decide which type of contribution to offer? Consider this story about two workers, Phil and Dave. Phil is married, with three children. He's a great worker, but he can't afford to contribute to the 401(k). Dave is single and a marginal employee, but he contributes 8 percent of his pay to the plan. Both employees will receive a profit-sharing contribution, but only Dave will get a share of the variable matching contribution. This may cause a morale problem for Phil if he sees his less committed co-worker receiving more financial benefits. You need to decide which employees you want to receive any additional contributions as an incentive.

Investment Choices

We're considering offering a mutual fund window in our 401(k) plan that will enable participants to choose from thousands of funds. How will this impact our liability?

Opinions vary on this subject. Some argue that a mutual fund window increases liability, because participants who invest badly and lose money may then sue the employer for not preventing the calamity. Another concern is that employers, in order to get the limited fiduciary protection under *404(c) regulations,* must provide sufficient information for employees to make informed investment decisions. (We discuss 404(c) in Chapter 1, and brokerage windows in Chapter 6.)

You may be able to reduce your risk by requiring the participant to sign a waiver. The waiver should require participants to

- Acknowledge that they consider themselves to be knowledgeable investors

- Waive their right to sue if the investment results are bad

- Acknowledge that they're assuming the full responsibility to secure whatever information is needed to make investment decisions

We're thinking about offering investment advice to our participants, because many are having trouble deciding how to invest. What's the best way to provide advice without increasing our liability?

Opinions vary on this question, too. We believe that investment advice will reduce your liability if it's done right, because providing this additional level of help for your participants is better than letting them decide how to invest on their own. Education is often not enough — all the educational materials in the world haven't turned amateurs into professional investors. Adding investment advice to your plan should bring better results.

We believe that the best way to offer advice is to hire an investment advisor who doesn't have a financial stake in how your participants invest their money. The advisor should be paid a flat amount per participant. Use the same care when you select the investment advisor that you use when you select other service providers for your plan.

Nondiscrimination Tests

When determining which employees are highly compensated (HCEs), should I look at rate of pay or actual pay?

You look at the actual pay. This may give HCEs who are hired during the year a break. For example, an employee hired on Sept. 12, 2003, at a $200,000 salary will earn approximately $60,000 for the year 2003. This employee won't be considered an HCE in 2003, because his actual earnings are less than the $90,000 limit. He won't be considered an HCE in 2004, either, because the determination is based on the previous year's salary at the company. However, regardless of salary, the employee is an HCE if he owns more than 5 percent of the company in either year.

Which employees must be included in the nondiscrimination tests for our plan?

You include all employees who were eligible for any portion of the year that's being tested. An employee who doesn't contribute to the plan may still be eligible.

Take your total number of employees and subtract those who weren't eligible to contribute at any time of the year. The remaining employees are those who should be included in the nondiscrimination tests for your plan.

My company is having trouble passing the nondiscrimination tests. We have to give money back to some of the HCEs every year. How can we better manage this process?

When you do the nondiscrimination test for the current year, you're allowed to use the average percentage the non-HCEs contributed during the *prior* year if you have selected prior-year testing in your plan document. With prior-year testing, you shouldn't fail the test, because you know before the year begins exactly how much the HCEs can contribute.

If you must use *current year* non-HCE results, you should regularly monitor contributions made by both groups — and take action to limit HCE contributions as necessary — to avoid a failure.

Distributions and Loans

How are distributions reported to the IRS, and who's responsible for reporting them?

Distributions from a 401(k) plan must be reported to the IRS on Form 1099-R. The employer is responsible for reporting distributions, but most employers have a service provider handle it. Codes need to be entered on the Form 1099-R to show what type of distribution it is (hardship withdrawal, excess contribution refund, and so on). Make sure that the correct code is entered, otherwise it creates a hassle for you and the participant receiving the distribution.

We're considering adding a loan feature to our 401(k). What do we need to know?

You should consider a number of things. The most significant are the legal requirements for loans and the administrative procedures that are needed for operations.

You'll also need a lot of help from the organization that manages your plan. Ask for a checklist of decisions you need to make when you set up loans, and another checklist of the operating requirements. One of the most important operating issues you'll have to consider is how many loans a participant may have at one time. It's easy to say that you will only permit one at a time, but this can present problems for participants who want to use this money to help with educational expenses. An alternative to multiple loans is to restructure a new loan into one larger combined loan — but there are serious compliance issues associated with this solution. We discuss loans in Chapter 7.

We're considering terminating our 401(k) plan. Are there any special requirements?

Yes. You probably need to formally amend the plan to bring it into compliance with all changes in the law prior to its termination. Also, all contributions become fully vested when a plan is terminated, regardless of years of service and other vesting requirements. The plan trustee(s) and the plan administrator must continue to operate the plan with the frozen assets in accordance with the plan documents and solely for the benefit of participants and their beneficiaries, until all assets are distributed. Typically, benefits are paid to the participants shortly after the plan is terminated or the assets are transferred to another plan. You should contact your advisor to find out any other considerations for your plan.

Assorted Legal Questions

I'm helping my wife start a business. Can I use my 401(k) as collateral for a business loan to help her get started?

You can include your 401(k) balance as an asset when you submit your financial statement to the bank, but you're legally prohibited from assigning the account as collateral. This protects your 401(k) and other retirement benefits from the claims of creditors.

The lender may still be willing to give some consideration to your 401(k) when making its decision on the loan. The lender can't get at your retirement money if you default, but it may bet that you will access your retirement money rather than default on the loan.

What reports must be filed with the government for our 401(k) plan, and who is responsible for filing them?

In addition to reporting distributions using Form 1099-R, the employer must file an annual financial report, Form 5500, with the IRS each year. The filing deadline is seven months after the end of the plan year, unless the employer gets a filing extension. Employers usually have a service provider fill out the form, but the employer signs it and files it.

A couple of participants in our plan may be getting divorced. I've heard that handling those situations can be tough. Where can I get help?

Properly handling a *qualified domestic relations order (QDRO)*, which governs how the 401(k) assets are split, is difficult. You should probably establish policies and procedures for your plan in advance. Divorce attorneys usually aren't familiar with retirement plans. As a result, they often draft QDROs that contain some specific terms that are impossible for employers to comply with. Some employers have a QDRO kit that they give to both parties in the divorce to help them deal with this issue.

You should get professional help from an ERISA attorney who has experience with QDROs. Your service provider should also be able to help. One firm that specializes in this field is QDRO Consultants Company. (Its phone number is 1-800-527-8481.)

I've read that our company can be sued if we pay a benefit to a beneficiary other than a spouse, even if the beneficiary is named by the participant. With constant marital changes, how can we be expected to keep track?

Keeping track of employees' personal lives is difficult. For this reason, you should remind employees to keep their beneficiary designations up to date.

Your company can indeed be sued if it pays benefits to someone other than the employee's spouse without the spouse's consent.

The following are some things you can do to reduce your risk:

- Require a notary (rather than a company employee) to witness the spousal waiver.

- Watch for changes in marital status that may show up elsewhere, such as medical coverage and group life insurance beneficiary changes.

- Inform all participants about the spousal waiver requirements and remind them to keep their named beneficiaries current at least annually.

- Take reasonable steps to make certain that a deceased employee didn't have a spouse before you pay benefits from the 401(k) or other retirement plan to another beneficiary.

Chapter 16

Ten (or So) 401(k) Mistakes to Avoid

• •

In This Chapter

▶ Avoiding participation pitfalls

▶ Countering contribution calamities

▶ Investing appropriately for you

▶ Filling out paperwork

▶ Curbing company stock

• •

Some things are impossible to avoid, such as bad airplane coffee or a nosy next-door neighbor. But other things *are* avoidable and worth keeping away from. The following 401(k) mistakes are common, but we hope that after reading this chapter, you'll know enough not to make them.

Not Participating

If you don't participate in your 401(k) plan, you're cheating yourself. First, you lose out on the tax break that you'd get if you did contribute. Every dollar you put into a 401(k) as a pre-tax contribution reduces your taxes for that year. Also, the money in the account grows tax-free until you withdraw it. That's a great deal.

But perhaps even more important is that you're cheating yourself out of choices in the future. The more money you save for retirement, the more flexibility you'll have when you get there.

After all, where will your income come from when you no longer have a paycheck? Social Security will provide some, but it won't be (and isn't meant to be) enough. A traditional pension from your employer will also help, if you have one. But after that, it's up to you.

Chapter 17 looks at bad reasons people give for not participating and also examines why these reasons are bad. Read Chapter 17 if you still don't think it's worth saving for retirement.

Not Contributing Enough to Get the Full Employer Match

If your employer offers a matching contribution, make sure that you contribute enough to get the maximum amount possible. Would you walk past a 50 dollar bill lying on the sidewalk? We hope not! You shouldn't walk away from your employer's contribution, either.

For example, say you earn $50,000 and your employer matches 50¢ for every dollar you contribute, up to 6 percent of your salary. Six percent of $50,000 is $3,000. If you contribute $3,000 or more to your 401(k), your employer will deposit a matching contribution of $1,500 (50¢ on the dollar). If you contribute less, say $2,000, your employer will only put in $1,000. You leave $500 on that proverbial sidewalk.

Check out Chapter 3 for information on getting the largest possible matching contribution.

Taking a Loan or Hardship Withdrawal Unnecessarily

Removing money from your retirement accounts before you retire is not something to do lightly. Taking money out of your retirement account for another purpose can set you back in taxes, penalties, and lost compounding. It can be difficult — if not impossible — to make up the money.

Explore other alternatives first. If you need the money for a child's education, consider a less expensive school or have your student find part-time work to help pay the bills. If you want to buy a home, consider one that's less expensive or give yourself another year or two to save for the down payment. In other words, plan ahead or scale down your goals so that you can live within your means and keep your retirement savings intact.

Of course, we recognize that you may find yourself in an emergency situation where your 401(k) is your last resort. In that case, use our analysis in Chapter 7 to decide between a loan or hardship withdrawal.

Defaulting on a Loan

If you take a loan on your 401(k), don't default on it. You generally have five years to pay back a loan, with payments deducted from your paycheck. In most plans, if you leave your job (voluntarily or not), you can't continue paying back the loan, so the entire unpaid balance comes due. If you don't pay the entire loan back, the amount counts as an early distribution, and you owe income tax, as well as a 10 percent early withdrawal penalty if you're under 55 when you leave your job.

Contributing Too Much

The federal maximum contribution limits for 401(k)s apply to all contributions you make to all 401(k)s in one year. You don't start over at zero each time you have a new employer. Also, if you work for two employers at the same time, and both offer 401(k)s, the limits apply to both plans combined. See Table 2-1 in Chapter 2 for the limits.

If you go over the limit, you need to withdraw the excess contributions by April 15 of the year following the year you contributed too much. If you don't, you'll have to pay tax twice on those contributions — once for the year you made them, and again when you withdraw money from the plan.

Investing Too Conservatively or Too Aggressively

This issue is tricky, because "too conservative" for one person may be "too aggressive" for another. As we explain in Chapters 5 and 6, how you invest depends on factors that are unique to you — namely, investment goals, length of time until you need your money, and personal risk preferences.

If you invest in a way that's too conservative for you, your money may not grow enough to offset inflation. Even though you earn some return, prices may rise even faster (inflation), leaving you with less spending power in your retirement years.

Investing too aggressively can give you sleepless nights and sweaty palms. The ups and downs may be too much for you to stand, and you may be tempted to sell your investments when they're down (which is exactly the wrong time to sell them).

Failing to Rebalance

When you invest 401(k) money, you first decide on an *asset allocation*, that is, how to divide your money among different types of investments (asset classes), such as stocks, bonds, and cash equivalents. To take a simple example, your asset allocation may be 80 percent stocks and 20 percent bonds. (You can break these into smaller categories, but we want to keep things simple.)

Say bonds do really well for a year, and your stock investments slump. You could end up with a portfolio that's 70 percent stocks and 30 percent bonds. But that's not what you want — you decided that an 80/20 split was a better allocation for you. What do you do? Leaving more money in bonds is tempting, because they're doing well, but that's not the right move. You want to sell the extra 10 percent you have in bonds, now, while the price is high, and use the money to buy stocks, which are low. In so doing, you *rebalance* your account. We recommend looking at your account every year and rebalancing it if necessary.

Day Trading

Day trading may have gone the way of the dodo in the slumping stock market of the early 2000s, but it bears mentioning. *Day trading* means buying and selling stocks daily in an attempt to make large gains. Your long-term retirement accounts are no place for attempts at short-term gains.

 Take it from us — the least stressful and most successful way to invest for retirement is by choosing a solid portfolio of diversified investments, putting your money into those investments, rebalancing annually, and getting on with your life.

Failing to Name a Beneficiary

401(k)s are *beneficiary-designated assets,* which means that your will can't direct where the money goes if you die. You have to fill out a 401(k) beneficiary form with your employer.

If you don't fill out a form, federal law provides that the money goes to your spouse if you die. If you don't have a spouse, the beneficiary default provisions of your plan, which establish a beneficiary priority, will apply. The 401(k) may go to your estate, and whoever inherits your estate will get the money. However, having the money pass through your estate is not as good a deal for the heir as inheriting the 401(k) directly. More may be taken out in taxes and legal fees if it goes through the estate. Worse yet, it may go to someone you don't even like.

Read more about beneficiaries in Chapter 3.

Cashing Out Instead of Rolling Over

When you change jobs, you have a choice of rolling your money over into a new tax-deferred retirement account, which keeps your retirement savings intact, or withdrawing the money and paying income tax (and a 10 percent early withdrawal penalty if you're under 55). You may also choose to leave the money in your former employer's plan. A lot of people make the mistake of cashing out, particularly young workers with low 401(k) balances. They figure it won't matter if they withdraw the money, because it's such a small amount.

They're wrong. A small amount — say $5,000 — can grow to $157,047 over 40 years or $102,070 over 35 years, assuming a 9 percent interest rate. That's quite a chunk of change. Is it really worth giving that up for whatever it is you think you need now?

Loading Up on Company Stock

Some participants end up with a lot of company stock in their 401(k), inadvertently or not, a la Enron. This situation can happen if the employer makes matching contributions in the form of company stock and also lets employees invest their own contributions in company stock.

Loading up on company stock is a bad idea, as we explain in Chapters 5 and 6. Tying your retirement account to the fortunes of one company — no matter how great you think the company is — is dangerous.

If your employer matches your contributions with company stock, take all that your employer gives you. But don't invest your own 401(k) contributions in company stock. Diversify your account as much as you can.

Chapter 17

Ten Bad Excuses People Give for Not Participating (And Why They're Bad)

* *

In This Chapter

▶ Soothing stock market and corporate bankruptcy worries

▶ Determining saving priorities if you're a single parent

▶ Convincing yourself that it's not too soon, or too late, to save

▶ Answering other fears and concerns

* *

Some people have an excuse for everything. They rear-end another car and then blame the other driver for stopping. Or, they can't fit into their favorite jeans after too many late-night pizzas, so they blame the dryer for shrinking them.

Making excuses is sometimes okay if it makes you feel better (even though it can be annoying to the rest of us), but one area where you shouldn't make excuses is your retirement savings. Most people have absolutely no reason not to save for retirement — especially if their employer makes it easy by offering a 401(k) or similar plan.

This chapter takes a closer look at bad excuses people give for not saving in a 401(k), and why those excuses are bad. To paraphrase a familiar big-screen character: Save or save not. There is no try.

I'm Afraid of the Stock Market

Many of the investors burned by the stock market tumble of the early 2000s may be reluctant to put their hard-earned dollars into stocks. Although a reluctance to invest in stocks is understandable, it's not a good reason to ignore your 401(k). Even if your 401(k) investments don't produce spectacular results, you'll still be a lot better off in your retirement years if you save in a 401(k) than if you spend all the money now.

 401(k)s often offer some investments that aren't stocks. If you're really stock-shy, you may have this alternative available to you. However, remember that historically (on average), stocks have provided the highest return of the different types of investments and have done the best job of beating inflation, so you should consider including them in your investment portfolio.

The first step to conquering fear is finding out more about what you're afraid of. Part 3 of this book is a good place to start educating yourself about investment basics.

I'm Afraid I'll Lose My Money if My Employer Goes Bankrupt

The money you contribute to a 401(k) is placed in a trust. The assets of the trust don't belong to the company, so they shouldn't be at risk in a bankruptcy. If your employer goes bankrupt, you should eventually get your 401(k) money — although it may take a while. Of course, if you hold company stock in your 401(k), it will be worthless if the company goes out of business.

You could lose contributions that have been deducted from your paycheck but not yet deposited into the 401(k) by your employer. Employers are supposed to deposit contributions into the plan fairly quickly, but some employers violate this requirement. One month's worth of contributions is the most you'd be likely to lose if your employer is making deposits on time.

I Can't Afford It

Oh yes you can. Most people can find $10 a week if they really try — that's about $500 a year. Invest $500 a year for 40 years, at a 9 percent annual return, and you end up with $169,000. That's certainly better than nothing — and you'll probably be able to afford to save a larger amount sooner than you think.

Don't make the common mistake of expecting it to get easier to save after you start making more money. It never gets easier, so start now. Most people can find ways to reduce expenses without feeling any pain. See Chapter 4 for some of our suggestions. Also, an extra tax deduction is available to retirement plan participants with low and moderate incomes. Details are in Chapter 3.

I'm a Single Parent, and I Have to Save for My Child's Education

This excuse often comes from women, and it is a tough one to refute. Your child's college bills are probably going to be due before you retire, so it may seem logical to save for college first and retirement later. What's more, surveys indicate that women tend to put everyone else's needs ahead of their own.

Note, too, that women, on average, live longer than men, so they need more money to see them through retirement. Statistics show that women end up impoverished in retirement more often than men.

Rather than ignore your retirement savings, put some of the money you'd normally save toward education into a tax-deferred retirement account. Investigate less expensive colleges, encourage your child to get a part-time job, apply for financial aid, and ask other relatives for help paying college costs. After all, what's the point of putting Junior through an expensive college if he's going to have to support you when he gets out?

I Don't Like My Plan

This concern may be valid if you think something fishy is going on with your plan administration; for example, if your contributions aren't deposited into the 401(k) on time, and your company's treasurer just left for an extended holiday in Hawaii. But be sure that your concern is justified before you use this as an excuse.

If you don't like your plan because you think that the fees are too high or the investment selection is inadequate, don't simply throw in the towel and not participate. One strategy you can try is to contribute only enough to get the full company match. (If your employer contributes 50¢ for every dollar you contribute, that's a 50 percent return on your money right there.) Then contribute the maximum to an IRA, as well, to boost your retirement savings. You may not get a tax deduction for the IRA contribution, depending on your salary, but you may be able to contribute to a Roth IRA, which allows tax-free withdrawals. See Chapter 8 for more details about IRAs. Also, try to convince your employer to improve the plan, as we explain in Chapter 2.

I'll Probably Change Jobs Soon

You may be hesitant to join your 401(k) because you're thinking of changing jobs. Well, unless you have a firm job offer to start next week, we have news for you — things don't always go the way you plan. You may be at your job longer than you think. And when you do change jobs, you can roll over your 401(k) money into your new 401(k) or an IRA. Take advantage of the opportunity to save for retirement at your current employer, even if it's only for a few more months.

I Hate Paperwork

Paperwork ranks up there with Mondays and housework when it comes to things most people hate. To make matters worse, you generally receive 401(k) enrollment forms at the same time that you're trying to get used to a new job. The only reason some employees don't participate in their 401(k) is that they just never get around to completing the paperwork. They keep putting it off — sometimes for years.

The key is to remember that your 401(k) enrollment isn't useless paperwork — it's part of a strategy to help you achieve a goal of retiring at a certain age and having flexibility to do what you want.

It's Too Hard to Get My Money Out

This concern is understandable, but it's not a good reason to ignore your 401(k).

You can't withdraw money from a 401(k) like you can from, say, a bank savings account. But remember that you get special tax breaks for contributing to a 401(k). The reason Uncle Sam allows these tax breaks is that he wants to encourage you to save for retirement; that's why the amount you can take out, and the reasons for taking it out, are restricted. This money is supposed to be for retirement!

Most plans permit "hardship withdrawals" and/or loans from your 401(k) for approved purposes, such as higher education expenses, buying a home, or financial hardship. We explain the rules in detail in Chapter 7.

Consider saving for other purposes in different types of accounts. For example, keep an emergency fund in something easy to access, such as a money market fund. Save for your children's college in a tax-advantaged college savings fund. Then put retirement money into your 401(k).

I Don't Need Anything More than Social Security and My Pension

Social Security benefits received during retirement generally replace about 20 to 40 percent of pre-retirement income for someone who retires at Social Security's "normal retirement age." (The higher your pre-retirement income, the lower the percentage replaced by Social Security.) But financial planners estimate that you'll need 80 to 100 percent of your pre-retirement income to have a comfortable retirement.

If you don't get a pension, you're left with a gap of 60 to 80 percent. A pension benefit, if you have one, may provide an additional 15 to 25 percent, reducing the gap. How do you fill this gap? Unless you have certain wealth from another source, you need to save on your own. The more you save in a 401(k) or other retirement account, the better off you'll be.

I'm Too Young (It's Too Soon)

Unfortunately, most young people — even those in their 20s — don't spend a lot of time thinking about retirement. Why start planning now (and deprive oneself of cash every month) for something that's 30 or 40 years away?

To that we answer, *compounding.* Small amounts of money saved regularly over time can grow to large sums, especially in an account like a 401(k) that lets you save without paying taxes on your investment gain each year. Invest $1,000 a year from age 20 until age 65, with a 9 percent average return, and you end up with $525,000. Start saving five years later, at age 25, and you'll only have about $338,000. See how much better off you are if you start early?

You don't have to start big, either. Just $10 a week adds up to about $500 a year. As you move up in your profession and your salary increases, you can increase your contributions, as well — especially if you're already in the habit of saving.

Chapter 4 gives tips for developing a savings plan, and examples of the benefits of starting young.

I'm Too Old (It's Too Late)

Some people in their 50s and 60s worry that they're starting the retirement savings game too late. If you're just beginning to save at that age, indeed, you have some catching up to do. But guess what? Congress passed laws in 2001 that are aimed at helping you save more. The age-50 catch-up contribution and increasing federal contribution limits that we discuss in Chapter 2 were conceived to help baby boomers who hadn't saved enough for retirement save more.

Don't berate yourself if you're in this situation. The retirement landscape has changed dramatically in the last 10 to 20 years, and many people were caught unawares by the increased need to save for retirement rather than depend on Social Security and a company pension.

It's never too late to save in a 401(k). For as long as you work, even if you're older than 70½, you're allowed to contribute to your employer's 401(k). The important thing is to have a plan. Life goes on whether you're ready or not, so be prepared.

Index

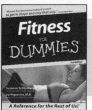

  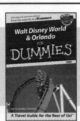

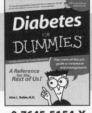  

FOR DUMMIES

Helping you expand your horizons and realize your potential

GRAPHICS & WEB SITE DEVELOPMENT

0-7645-1651-5

0-7645-1643-4

0-7645-0895-4

Also available:

Adobe Acrobat 5 PDF For Dummies (0-7645-1652-3)

ASP.NET For Dummies (0-7645-0866-0)

ColdFusion MX for Dummies (0-7645-1672-8)

Dreamweaver MX For Dummies (0-7645-1630-2)

FrontPage 2002 For Dummies (0-7645-0821-0)

HTML 4 For Dummies (0-7645-0723-0)

Illustrator 10 For Dummies (0-7645-3636-2)

PowerPoint 2002 For Dummies (0-7645-0817-2)

Web Design For Dummies (0-7645-0823-7)

PROGRAMMING & DATABASES

0-7645-0746-X

0-7645-1626-4

0-7645-1657-4

Also available:

Access 2002 For Dummies (0-7645-0818-0)

Beginning Programming For Dummies (0-7645-0835-0)

Crystal Reports 9 For Dummies (0-7645-1641-8)

Java & XML For Dummies (0-7645-1658-2)

Java 2 For Dummies (0-7645-0765-6)

JavaScript For Dummies (0-7645-0633-1

Oracle9i For Dummies (0-7645-0880-6)

Perl For Dummies (0-7645-0776-1)

PHP and MySQL For Dummies (0-7645-1650-7)

SQL For Dummies (0-7645-0737-0)

Visual Basic .NET For Dummies (0-7645-0867-9)

LINUX, NETWORKING & CERTIFICATION

0-7645-1545-4

0-7645-1760-0

0-7645-0772-9

Also available:

A+ Certification For Dummies (0-7645-0812-1)

CCNP All-in-One Certification For Dummies (0-7645-1648-5)

Cisco Networking For Dummies (0-7645-1668-X)

CISSP For Dummies (0-7645-1670-1)

CIW Foundations For Dummies (0-7645-1635-3)

Firewalls For Dummies (0-7645-0884-9)

Home Networking For Dummies (0-7645-0857-1)

Red Hat Linux All-in-One Desk Reference For Dummies (0-7645-2442-9)

UNIX For Dummies (0-7645-0419-3)

Available wherever books are sold.
Go to www.dummies.com or call 1-877-762-2974 to order direct